THE GRANDEUR OF GANDHARA

The Grandeur of Gandhara

The Ancient Buddhist Civilization of the Swat, Peshawar, Kabul and Indus Valleys

Rafi-us Samad

Algora Publishing
New York

Library of Congress Cataloging-in-Publication Data —

Samad, Rafi U.
    The grandeur of Gandhara : The ancient buddhist civilization of the Swat, Peshawar,
Kabul and Indus Valleys/ Rafi-us Samad.
        p. cm.
    Includes bibliographical references and index.
        ISBN 978-0-87586-858-5 (soft cover: alk. paper) — ISBN 978-0-87586-859-2
(hard cover: alk. paper) — ISBN 978-0-87586-860-8 (ebook) 1. Gandhara (Pakistan
and Afghanistan)—Civilization. 2. Gandhara (Pakistan and Afghanistan)—History.
3. Gandhara (Pakistan and Afghanistan)—Intellectual life. 4. Gandhara (Pakistan and
Afghanistan)—Religious life and customs. I. Title.
    DS392.G36S26 2011
    954.91'32—dc22
                            2011014303

Printed in the United States

For Kashfa

TABLE OF CONTENTS

This book aims to introduce readers to the history and achievements of a "lost" civilization in what are now part of northern Pakistan and south-eastern Afghanistan. This civilization and its culture flourished during the first four centuries of the Common Era in the valleys of the Swat, Kabul and Indus Rivers. This region, south of Hindu Kush and Karakoram mountains, was known in ancient times as Gandhara.

Gandhara was suddenly exposed to the outside world between the 6th century BCE and 6th century C.E. through a series of high-profile invasions from mighty conquerors and empire builders. In the 6th and 5th centuries BCE, the Persians under Cyrus and Darius crossed the Khyber Pass to establish two Persian satrapies, one in the Peshawar Valley and the other in the Taxila region. Between 327 and 323 BCE, Alexander the Great battled with the Aspasian, Gourian and Assakan tribes of Bajaur, Dir and Swat, opening this region to subsequent Greek cultural influences through the Bactrian Greeks and the Hellenized Scythians, Parthians and Kushans, who ruled Gandhara from the 2nd century BCE till the 5th century CE.

The Persian, Greek and Central Asian invasions of Gandhara, rather than causing wide scale destruction in the region, promoted the development of a multi-cultural, multi-ethnic society. After a gestation period of about half a millennium, this region blossomed into a unique civilization in the opening years of the Common Era. This is the focus of the current book.

What is known as the Gandhara Civilization reached its pinnacle during the first five centuries CE, when Gandhara became the base of the mighty Kushan Empire. After its golden age under the Central Asian Kushans, the civilization went through a prolonged period of decline, set in motion by the invasion of the Ephthalites in the late 5th century CE.

The Gandhara Civilization ushered in the historic era in the South Asian sub-continent. Original information on the Persian satrapies of Gandhara and Taxila appears in the rock inscriptions of the Persian emperors at the Persian sites of Behishtun, Persepolis and Susa, and in the *Histories* of Herodotus; detailed accounts about Alexander's invasion and the geography and the sociology of Gandhara appear in the records compiled by Alexander's companions; the brief account by Pompeius Trogus on the exploits of the Indus Greek rulers, Menander and Apollodotus, is supplemented by the inscriptions on a large number of coins left by the Indus Greeks, Indo-Scythians, Indo-Parthians and the Hellenized Kushans and by the donative inscriptions on stone and metal found at various sites belonging to the Gandhara Civilization; finally, about half a dozen famous Chinese Buddhist pilgrim-scholars, such as Fa-Hsien and Hsuien Tsang, recorded detailed accounts of their visits to the Gandhara region.

Detailed archaeological excavations were started at sites in northern Pakistan and Afghanistan in the late-19th century. Through these excavations, eminent archaeologists such as Aurel Stein, Alexander Cunningham, John Marshall, J. Barthoux and Professor A.H. Dani recovered hundreds of thousands of beautiful stone sculptures belonging to the Gandhara Civilization.

In the last century or so, much has been written about the artistic quality of these beautiful stone sculptures. But hardly anything has been written about the Civilization itself that gave birth to these extraordinary pieces of art. In this book an effort has been made to present Gandhara in its wider perspective, highlighting the different features of a unique civilization in which many different races contributed and many cultures merged to bring about a major sociological change and establish a distinct cultural identity in this region of the South Asian sub-continent.

This book is based on my analysis of the reports of renowned archaeologists who carried out excavations at various sites and information I gathered during the past decade through extended visits to numerous archaeological sites associated with the lost Gandhara Civilization, including those in the Taxila, Peshawar, Charsadda, Mardan and Swat regions in Pakistan. My study of the large number of artifacts from these sites, which are on display in museums at Taxila, Peshawar and Karachi, also provides substance to my work.

My research reveals a great deal of continuity in the field of socio-cultural development of the region, which is referred to in this book as Greater Gandhara, from the time it became a part of the Achaemenid Empire in the 6th century BCE till the end of Kidara Kushan's rule in the 5th century CE.

Further, it reveals that after the Achaemenids had established the physical and administrative infrastructure in Greater Gandhara, the continuity in socio-cultural development in the region was maintained mainly by the growing Buddhist population.

This book illustrates the spirit of independence and features in the character of the ancient people of the Gandhara region which facilitated the sustained progress towards the emergence of the Gandhara Civilization. Following the invasion of Alexander the Great, his successors had no difficulty in colonizing Bactria (Northern Afghanistan) and Sogdia (Uzbekistan), but they could not do the same in Gandhara. Similarly the Scythians, Parthians and the Kushans ruled over the Central Asian region as colonizers, but not so in Gandhara. Here they ruled not over the people, but with the people. Their administration was highly de-centralized, with the locals playing a major role in the regional administration and having a major say in the social and cultural affairs of the entire population.

Finally, the book highlights the interactive environment which prevailed in Gandhara throughout the transient and mature phases of the Gandhara Civilization: Alexander's companions hobnobbing with the naked fakirs of Taxila; Menander, the great Indus-Greek ruler, finding time to engage in prolonged question-and-answer sessions with Buddhist scholars at the monastery near Sagala (Sialkot); and the greatest of the Kushan conquerors, Kanishka, finding pleasure in the company of local intellectuals and artists such as Asvaghosha and Vasumitra, and presiding over the official launch of Mahayana Buddhism.

Rafi-us Samad

CHAPTER 1: INTRODUCTION

The region along the northern boundaries of the huge, culturally and ethnically diverse, South Asian sub-continent was known in ancient times as Gandhara. It remained isolated until the beginning of 6th century BCE, not only from the other regions in the South Asia but also from the region beyond its northern boundaries.

Around 535 BCE the massive wall formed by the Hindu Kush and Karakoram mountain ranges, which had since times immemorial protected the fertile plains of Gandhara and other regions in the South Asian sub-continent against major incursions from the north, was ultimately breached by the Persian armies under the command of Cyrus the Great. In 438 BCE, Darius the Great extended the Persian possessions in South Asia by conquering the Taxila region east of the Indus. As a result of these conquests a cultural union of Gandhara, west of the Indus, and Taxila, east of the Indus, came into existence, which we refer to in this book as Greater Gandhara.

The invasions of Gandhara by Cyrus and Darius the Great had far reaching consequences for the people of this region. Gandhara was drawn out of its dreary isolated existence, into the highly proactive international orbit, where powerful forces were at work. Alexander invaded the extended Gandhara region in South Asia in 327 BCE. Alexander's rule in Gandhara did not last long but the most important outcome of his invasion of Asia was that a number of Greek colonies were established in the regions to the north and west of Gandhara, which maintained close contacts with Gandhara.

Between 323 BCE and the first century CE, Greater Gandhara came successively under the rule of the Mauryans of Pataliputra, the Bactrian (Indus) Greeks, and the Hellenistic Scythians and the Parthians. Under these regimes two important developments took place. Firstly, the borders of Greater Gandhara were further extended to include Southeastern Afghanistan into this socio-political and cultural union of Gandhara and Taxila. Secondly Buddhism, which had virtually been eliminated in the rest of South Asia, emerged as a powerful force in Greater Gandhara due to the relatively liberal environment provided by these regimes.

While these changes were taking place in Greater Gandhara, important developments were also taking place in the international arena and along the northern borders of Greater Gandhara. The Romans conquered Greece in 146 BCE and almost immediately afterwards the Silk Road operations commenced. These operations involved long distance trade in luxury goods between Roman and Parthian Empires and China, as well as short distance trade among the countries located on the Silk Road or connected to the Silk Road. Greater Gandhara gained access to the Silk Road through Taxila-Kashgar and Pushkalavati (Charsadda)-Bactra links and began to reap rich profits through the Silk Route Trade.

In 60 CE the Kushans conquered Greater Gandhara. Kushan conquests in Central Asia and benefits of trade with countries along the Silk Route provided a tremendous boost to the economy of Greater Gandhara. There was a major surge in socio-economic and cultural activities all over Greater Gandhara. Urbanization began to take place on a large scale and there was marked improvement in the quality of life of the common man.

The distinct political, administrative and cultural identity of Greater Gandhara in South Asia was reinforced by the close cooperation between the Buddhist establishment and the alien, mostly Hellenistic regimes. The Buddhist religious establishment remained neutral on political issues and cooperated with all the alien regimes in the administration of the region. In return for this cooperation, the alien regimes extended patronage to the Buddhist religious institutions.

The partnership between the Buddhist clerical establishment and the alien ruling regimes achieved a perfect balance in the Kushan period, when each party took upon itself what it could do best. The Kushans were great conquerors and empire builders. They carved out a vast empire and used the wealth of the conquered nations to bring prosperity to their adopted land. The Kushans were also adept in external relations and managed to maintain healthy diplomatic and trade relations with the Roman Empire, the Chinese, and the Persians. Meanwhile, the predominant local Buddhist population took charge of moral, cultural and socio-economic issues.

The cooperation between the Kushan conquerors and the Buddhist pac- ifists and intellectuals worked to the good of both. The Kushans came to Gandhara with a reputation of being uncouth, uncivilized nomads who had no appreciation for the finer things in life. In Gandhara they became great patrons of art, and proved to be liberal, tolerant, and benevolent adminis- trators. They adapted much better to the local conditions than any of the previous conquerors who had ruled in Gandhara. Gandhara overwhelmed the conquerors with its natural beauty; it conquered their hearts and minds with the purity of its thought, its pursuit of peace and harmony and its craving for understanding the mysteries of nature. As a result the boorish conquerors, clad only in a thin mantle of Hellenistic culture, began to grow in intellectual stature within the civilizing environment of thousands of dy- namic socio-religious Buddhist institutions, the sangharamas. They took a genuine interest in the works of Buddhist intellectuals and in the evolving art and culture of the region.

Gradually the politically, socially and culturally integrated region of Greater Gandhara evolved into a unique civilization. The civilization was at its peak in the first four centuries of the Common Era. In this period Greater Gandhara had developed into a highly interactive region and the impact of its culture was felt in distant regions of Central Asia and China. Around Jalalabad, the modern Afghan capital of Nangarhar Province, at Chari- kar, Bagram (ancient Kapisa) and Bamiyan, and on either side of the Oxus River, huge Gandhara style monasteries and statues emerged; Khotan at the southern edge of the Taklamakan Desert in the Xinjiang Region of Western China, developed into a major center of Gandhara culture.

EVOLUTION OF GANDHARI & KHAROSHTHI AS UNIVERSAL LANGUAGE AND SCRIPT IN GREATER GANDHARA

In the Dark Period which prevailed in South Asia before the rise of the Gandhara Civilization, a large number of dialects were spoken and there was no single language which could serve as an effective means of commu- nication between various small groups living in semi-isolation. The situation changed rapidly after the Achaemenids conquered Gandhara and the territories around Taxila on the eastern side of the Indus River.

The Achaemenids had carved out a vast empire and had already developed effective tools for the governance of their territories. They employed the same tools to effectively govern the satrapies of Gandhara and Taxila (Sindh). Their first priority was to consolidate the various territories included in the two satrapies and to employ and train local manpower, which would help them in their task of governance and tax collection. For this they required a single spoken language and a script which would be used to communicate effectively with people living in all the regions included in the satrapies.

The Achaemenid administrative organization promoted the use of the Gandhari dialect through frequent interactions with the local population. The progressive increase in the use of Gandhari worked towards greater administrative, social and political integration, which in turn further promoted the use of the Gandhari language. Thus gradually Gandhari emerged as the dominant, and then universally-spoken, language in the satrapies of Gandhara and Taxila. A single spoken language used by such a large population was a new phenomenon in South Asia. The effective use of Gandhari contributed immensely to the political and social integration of the Achaemenid satrapies.

The Achaemenid administrative structure was very much centralized. The real power rested with the Achaemenid emperors based in their capital cities in Persia. The local satraps were initially Persians and most of them came from royal families. The job of the satrap was to build up an administrative organization at the satrapies manned almost exclusively by the locals. The Achaemenids needed a strong administrative and physical infrastructure to optimize agricultural production and collection of taxes.

In the Achaemenid system written communication and written records played a very important part. The Imperial organization sent inspectors periodically to each satrapy to examine the accounts and other records and provide feedback for improving their systems. Absence of any form of local script posed a major problem. The Achaemenids used the Aramaic script in their correspondence with fellow Persians and the bordering regions of Mesopotamia, and they would have considered promoting the use of Aramaic script by local officials to a limited extent in their correspondence in Gandhari language. This was, however, found to be impractical because Aramaic was phonetically inadequate to express the sounds of the Gandhari language. Thus, using Aramaic as the base, Kharoshthi emerged as the first written script in Gandhara, and infact the first written script in the entire South Asian sub-continent.

The efficacy of the Achaemenid organization can be gauged by the fact that around 260 BCE, just sixty-six years after the Achaemenid rule ended in Gandhara, the Gandhari language and Kharoshthi script were being usefully applied by Mauryan emperor Asoka for addressing the Gandharan public at large, through his edicts inscribed on stones in public places.

In 190 BCE the Indus (Bactrians) Greeks conquered Gandhara. Bactrian Greeks, the Seleucids and the Achaemenids had also been ruling in Bactria after 535 BCE, but no indigenous script or language emerged in Bactria during all this period. The Bactrian Greeks issued coins with only Greek legends in Bactria (cursive Greek script was introduced in Bactria sometime later). But immediately after Demetrius captured Gandhara, he issued bilingual coins in which Gandhari-Kharoshthi legends appeared on one side of the coins. This is yet another proof of how far Gandhari-Kharoshthi had advanced as the dominant, even universal, language and script in this region.

During the rule of the succeeding regimes, the scope of Gandhari broadened considerably. It was used in inscriptions on coins and for donative purposes, and was later extensively employed in the compilation of Buddhist religious texts.

Recent discoveries of Buddhist texts and inscriptions in the Gandhari language, and the conclusions reached among linguists and other scholars that the originals of all the early Buddhist Chinese texts were texts compiled in Gandhari language, have led to the recognition of Gandhari as one of the very important languages of the ancient world. Gandhari was extensively employed in the transmission of Buddhism to Central Asia and the Far East and began to be commonly understood and employed by monks of various nationalities as well as by businessmen, traders and administrators in regions which came under the influence of the Gandhara Civilization. It thus acquired an international significance.

Gandhari and Kharoshthi continued to be extensively employed through all phases of the Gandhara Civilization. As mentioned above, in the 3rd century BCE, when Asoka Maurya wished to address the people at large in the Gandhara region through the messages inscribed on rocks (Rock Edicts) at suitable locations in Gandhara, he used the Gandhari language; in 2nd century BCE, during the rule of Menander, when an inscription on a casket (Bajaur Casket Inscription) was required to certify that the contents in the casket were ashes belonging to a Buddhist devotee, Gandhari was employed; during the rule of Menander, when his court clerk recorded Menander's conversations *(Milandapanha)* with the Buddhist monk, Nagasena, Gandhari was employed; when in 1st century BCE, during the rule of Scythian king Maues, Kshema, a resident of Taxila, wished to honor the Scythian satrap of Taxila, while dedicating a stupa in memory of his parents, Gandhari was employed; when in early 1st century CE, a Scythian-Parthian monk compiled the Rhinoceros Sutra on birch bark, Gandhari was employed; when in late 1st century CE, Agesilas, the Greek Superintendent of Works, prepared the dedication statement for Kanishka's Casket at Shahji-ki-Dheri, Gandhari was employed; when during Kanishka's reign, Vasumitra wrote a Treatise on Eighteen Schools of Buddhism, Gandhari-Kharoshthi were employed[1]; when in the first century CE, Asvaghosha wrote "Buddhist Dramas on Palm Leaves" (Prof. Luder's Manuscripts from Turfan), Gandhari was employed; and when in the second century C.E, a Buddhist monk wrote the Dharmapada (Dutreuil de Rhins Manuscript from Khotan), Gandhari was employed.

The development and emergence of Gandhari and Kharoshthi as universal language and script in the Greater Gandhara Region contributed immensely towards the rise and sustenance of the Buddhist civilization in Gandhara.

EVOLUTION OF MAHAYANA BUDDHISM AS UNIVERSAL RELIGION IN GREATER GANDHARA

The evolution of Mahayana Buddhism also took place all through the various phases of the Gandhara Civilization. In the embryonic phase of Gandhara Civilization the Mahasanghika and Sarvastivadin views on Buddhist theology continued to attract steady converts. The Mahasinghakas de-emphasized monastic hegemony over religion and proclaimed that every individual had the power and spiritual capability to pursue the goal of enlightenment. Attracted by promises of achieving Nirvana, growing number lay-Buddhists thronged the stupa sites after third century BCE. The acceptance of the principles advocated by the Mahasinghakas and the Sarvasti-

---

1 S. Beal. *Eighteen Schools of Buddhism*, a translation of Vasumitra's treatise, Indian Antiquary, 1880.

vadins by the people of Greater Gandhara ultimately opened the way for Mahayana to emerge as major sect in Buddhism.

Gradually an all-pervasive moral and spiritual environment began to take shape in Gandhara, in which every individual sought to reorder his daily life to pursue the supreme goal of enlightenment. The path of enlightenment was through service to humanity, which gave rise to heightened concern for the well-being of all the members of the Sangha (community), which in turn led to the development of the image of a compassionate Bodhisattva and that of an Eternal Buddha. Basic Mahayana principles began to gain universal recognition in Gandhara.

The intellectual pursuits among the Buddhist community in Gandhara ultimately gave shape to the doctrine of Trikaya, which explained the three-fold nature of Buddha. The unanimity of views among the Buddhist scholars in Gandhara on the basic doctrine of Trikaya, established the foundations of Mahayana faith.

Mahayana Buddhism received official recognition when Mahayana texts (Sutras) were presented at the 4th Buddhist Council convened by Kanishka around 128 CE.

Buddhism never developed into a major or dominant religion in any region of South Asia except Greater Gandhara. There were two reasons for this.

Firstly, after the death of Buddha in 483 BCE, Buddhism faced a serious threat from within its own establishment. Deep divisions crept in, which led to the emergence of a large number of sects. Strong differences emerged between the different sects, particularly between the traditional and liberal factions, on the interpretation of Buddha's teachings. These divisions posed such a serious threat that a large number devotees belonging to the liberal factions had to migrate to distant Gandhara.

Secondly, Hindu revivalist forces suddenly became more active. Towards the end of second century Hinduism became better organized and reformed. This change in socio-religious environment created stiff competition for competing ideologies, and Buddhism, already weakened through its own internal dissensions, began to face a serious threat to its survival.

In Greater Gandhara, the situation was entirely different from that in the rest of South Asia. The Persian and the Hellenistic regimes, which ruled Gandhara in succession after 535 BCE, had no inclination or desire to impose their religious views on the conquered people and the indigenous people had no desire to meddle in politics or State administration. The harmonious relationship between the rulers and their subjects created a social environment, which allowed Buddhism to sink its feet deep into the soil of this region.

Almost all the Buddhists who migrated to Gandhara belonged to the liberal factions, such as the Mahasanghika and Sarvastivadin sects. On most religious matters they saw eye to eye. Therefore no conflicts arose in their missionary activities and they interacted well with each other. With the passage of time, the various liberal sects in Gandhara began to move ever closer to each other and ultimately, to a large extent through the untiring efforts of Vasumitra, a consensus emerged, which saw the birth of Mahayana Buddhism in Gandhara towards the beginning of second century CE.

Buddhism appealed to the psyche of the people of Greater Gandhara. Politically unobtrusive and spiritually inclined, they found tremendous attraction in the teachings of Buddha. As a result Buddhism made rapid progress in Gandhara even before the consensus on Mahayana philosophy had emerged. Towards the beginning of second century BCE it was already the dominant religion in this region and monks and missionaries had started compiling Buddhist texts in Gandhari-Kharoshthi during the period of rule of the Scythians and the Parthians.

Because of the prominent place of Buddhists in society, every regime patronized the Buddhist establishment and provided funds for the construction and upkeep of new stupa complexes and sangharamas. They interacted with the Buddhist population through Buddhist scholars who were appointed as advisors in the regime. The rapid increase in the density of sangharamas during the Kushan Period brought the people closer and closer to the Buddhist establishments located in their area. The result was that by 128 CE Mahayana Buddhism had virtually become the universal religion in Greater Gandhara and it continued to enjoy this status at least till the end of Kushan rule in Gandhara.

COMPILATION OF BUDDHIST SCRIPTURES IN WRITTEN FORM

Between the period 528 BCE when Buddha achieved enlightenment and 200 BCE all transmissions of Buddhist scriptural traditions took place orally. It was around 150 BCE that manuscripts of Buddhist religious texts began to be compiled in Greater Gandhara using the Gandhari language and Kharoshthi script. A new era had begun because written texts provided authenticity, which was always suspect in oral transmissions.

In the period 150 BCE till 150 CE Greater Gandhara remained the only region anywhere in the world where Buddhist religious texts were produced in written form, and the only language and script in which Buddhist manuscripts were compiled were Gandhari-Kharoshthi. Around 150 CE, translations of Buddhist scriptures from Gandhari to Chinese commenced. Thereafter during the next two centuries Buddhist religious manuscripts were available only in Gandhari and Chinese. Original manuscripts of Buddhist texts in Gandhari-Kharoshthi dating to the period around first century are available in the British Library and in the Schoeyen and Senior collections. Some original translations of early Buddhist texts in Korean, Tibetan and Japanese languages are also available. However no original manuscripts or prints in Sanskrit or Pali language dating to period before the 17th or 18th century are currently available. A number of scholars, who have studied and analyzed the early Buddhist manuscripts written in Chinese, believe that all written Buddhist religious texts were originally compiled in Gandhari-Kharoshthi.[2] From Gandhari language they were first translated into Chinese, and when the Sanskrit scholars adopted the Devnagri script for writing Sanskrit, the texts available in Chinese were translated into Sanskrit and Pali.

URBANIZATION

Early in the 6th century BCE, Gandhara comprised of large number of villages, some large, others small, where extended family groups engaged in farming activities. The activities were so dispersed that the occasion for large settlements did not arise.

In the embryonic phase of Gandhara Civilization, things began to change very rapidly. The Achaemenid satraps of Gandhara and Taxila ruled over large areas and their mandate was to optimize state income through a broad range of commercial and industrial activities. Their focus on a diversified economy required the pooling of skills in centralized locations. To meet the

---

2 John Brough, who published a study on Gandhari Dharmapada in 1962, summarizes the views of many scholars in the following words:

'Sufficient evidence, however, has now accumulated to establish that the originals of these early translations were mostly, if not exclusively, texts written in the North-western (Gandhari) Prakrit.'

challenges of the diversified economy and to provide accommodation for their comprehensive administrative and military organizations, they built the first two urban centers in this region, one at the Bhir Mound site near Taxila (Takshasila-Bhir Mound), and the other in the vicinity of Charsadda (Pushkalavati-Bala Hisar) on the banks of the Kabul River.

As prosperity increased, more and more people belonging to diversified professions began to congregate in areas where their skills were in demand. A complex society began to take shape, which produced a sizeable impact in settlements all over the region. As a result large number of villages began to grow into towns, and towns into cities.

The capital city of each regime, being the symbol of power, occupied a special place among all the cities and towns. The city, which served as the capital of one regime, was not necessarily retained as capital by the succeeding regime. Every succeeding regime wished to have its own stamp on the city, which served as its capital. This was sometimes done by extending an existing city, and at other times leveling the structures of an existing city and constructing a new city over the ruins. Thus we find different occupation layers one on top of the other at the site of an ancient Gandharan city, each occupation layer above the lower one representing new constructions carried out by the new regime.

Very often a powerful regime, which after it came into power, wished to make a complete break from the image of the previous regime. One of the ways this was done was by constructing a new capital city at a different site. Thus we find in the region around Taxila, the remains of at least three cities located at the sites of Bhir Mound, Sirkap and Sirsukh, which served as capitals of different regimes during different periods in the evolving phases of the Gandhara Civilization. Similarly around Charsadda (Pushkalavati), there are remains of cities at the sites of Bala Hisar and Shaikhan Dheri, which served as regional capitals in different periods, before the Kushans developed their own capital city, Purushapura, about 27 kilometers from Charsadda.

Archaeological investigations have revealed a large number of cities belonging to the regimes, which ruled Gandhara during different phases of the Gandhara Civilization. But quite often no physical traces of important cities belonging to the Gandhara Civilization remained, as the entire area where the city was located has been brought under cultivation, or densely populated urban centers have emerged where these ancient cities were located.

MAHAYANA BUDDHISM: MAIN PROPELLING FORCE IN GANDHARA CIVILIZATION

Mahayana Buddhism provided the cultural base and cohesion to all sections of population in Greater Gandhara. It served as the main propelling force of all social and cultural activities and played a crucial role in the evolution and sustenance of the civilization in Gandhara. The progress of the Gandhara Civilization from infancy to maturity corresponds to the corresponding progress made by liberal Buddhist sects in Gandhara, from the point Buddhism arrived in Gandhara till Mahayana Buddhism became the universal religion in Gandhara.

The even spread of a very large number of Buddhist monuments in all regions of Greater Gandhara, leaves no doubt that in the mature phase of the civilization, Mahayana Buddhism was the universal religion in Greater Gandhara and that it was pursued with a great deal of devotion, zeal and enthusiasm.

Mahayana Buddhism brought about major changes in the socio-economic environment of Gandhara. A distinctive cultural pattern emerged, which produced a powerful effect on all aspects of life in Gandhara.

The vehicle for the socio-cultural revolution in Greater Gandhara was provided by the sangharamas. These Buddhist socio-religious and cultural institutions, were constructed in scenic locations, and were decorated with hundreds of thousands of beautifully carved statues of Buddha and Bodhisattvas, and other forms of decorations glorifying Buddhist religion and culture. They served as a source of immense pride and spiritual inspiration for the devotees.

In the mature phase of Gandhara Civilization, from the plains of Purushapura to the mountainous regions of Dir and Bajaur, and from the gentle hills of Takshasila to the fertile plains of Jamalgarhi, every nook and corner resounded with the sounds of Buddhist chants and bells. The gurgling sounds of the mountain streams joined in the celebrations with their own particular brand of background music to go with the chants of the devotees singing hymns in praise of nature. Incense burning in Gandharan homes and temples filled the air with its aroma, and, as the sun began to set behind the wooded hills, millions of flickering oil lamps lighted the night sky.

DYNAMIC BUDDHIST INSTITUTIONS

Due to favorable socio-economic and political environment in Greater Gandhara, the Buddhist institutions in Greater Gandhara developed on quite different lines from those in rest of South Asia.

In other regions of South Asia, Buddhism ultimately survived only in pockets such as Sanchi, Bharhut, Mathura and Ajanta. The stupa complexes at these places served communities comprising of limited number of devotees, who did not relate to the population in the surrounding regions in the way the population of Greater Gandhara interacted closely with the Buddhist establishment based in sangharamas in their region.

There was a qualitative difference too, between the Buddhist institutions in Greater Gandhara and those in other regions of South Asia. Among the more than 3000 Buddhist institutions in Greater Gandhara, a very large percentage had spacious viharas attached to the stupayards. The two together, referred to as sangharamas, became highly dynamic institutions. The viharas, besides serving as residential compounds of Buddhist monks, had provisions for training of missionaries, and conference halls for religious discussions. A fairly large number of sangharamas had Scriptoriums, where huge volumes of Buddhist religious texts were compiled in Gandhari-Kharoshthi for the missionaries operating within Greater Gandhara and in foreign lands such as China and Central Asia.

Another variation in the character of Buddhist institutions in Greater Gandhara and those in other parts of South Asia was the difference in design, style and composition of sculptures used to decorate these institutions. Gandharan sculptures project Mahayana beliefs and show substantial Greek and Persian influences. On the other hand the sculptures and decorations in Buddhist monuments in other parts of South Asia incorporate figures and themes from Hindu Mythology and the compositions show substantial influence of Hinduism.

COSMOPOLITAN NATURE OF POPULATION

A large number of people from half a dozen nations and races, which invaded Greater Gandhara during the embryonic, transient and mature phases of the Gandhara Civilization, remained behind in Gandhara and ultimately settled down in this region.

The invasion of the Achaemenids opened the doors of Gandhara to immigrants, more from the Achaemenid Persianized colonies in Bactria and Sogdiana than from the Achaemenid homeland in Iran and Mesopotamia; Alexander's invasion brought Greek-Macedonians as well as people from the lands conquered by Alexander's armies prior to the invasion of Gandhara; the Indus Greek conquest of Gandhara resulted in flow of large number of immigrants of Greek extraction, who had settled in Asia Minor, Mesopotamia and Bactria; and the invasions of the Scythians, Parthians and the Kushans further enriched the ethnic mix.

The large scale immigration during various phases of the civilization introduced new skills which contributed towards diversification and strengthening of the economy. People with Persian and Hellenistic backgrounds also made valuable contributions to the culture of the region. Their gradual fusion and integration with the local population resulted in cosmopolitan character of Gandhara's civilization.

SPREAD

In the mature phase, the Gandhara Civilization covered a core area of about 200,000 square kilometers. In the north, this area was bounded by the Hindu Kush Mountain Range, in the north-east by the Karakoram Mountains, in the east by Kashmir, in the south by the Jhelum River and in the west by a line joining Kohat with Kalabagh. In terms of present administrative set-up, the regions which became a part of the civilization included the Kabul District of Afghanistan from the source of the Kabul River in the Hindu Kush to the Pakistani border, the administrative Division of Peshawar included the regions around the towns of Peshawar, Charsadda, Nowshera, and Takht-i-Bahi, the Mardan Division included the region around Mardan and Swabi, the Malakand Division from Malakand to Swat Kohistan included the Swat, Buner, Shangla, Swat Kohistan and North and South Dir, Rawalpindi Division included Taxila, Chakwal and Attock; the Hazara Division included Haripur, Abbotabad, Mansehra and Balakot, and Bajaur, Mohmand and Khyber Agencies in the tribal areas bordering Afghanistan.

TOPOGRAPHY & PHYSICAL ENVIRONMENT

The topography of Greater Gandhara, its geography and physical environment, played a major role in the development of the Gandhara Civilization. They promoted interactions between people living in the region and facilitated the growth of a social infrastructure.

Topographically, Greater Gandhara was a diverse region comprising of high mountains, green hills and fertile plains watered by the Kabul and

Swat Rivers and a number of other tributaries of the Indus including the Haro, Soan, Dhamrah Kas and Lundi Kas Rivers.

Peshawar Valley, occupying 7176 square kilometers of territory in Western Gandhara, is endowed with a number of physical features which enabled it to play such an important role in the Gandhara Civilization. It is bounded on the west by Afghanistan, in the north by the Swat Valley, in the north-east by Buner and in the southeast by the Indus River, and in the south by Kohat District. The average elevation is 345 meters above mean sea level, and the total area mostly consists of fertile plains, interspersed with bare knolls. The Valley includes, besides the Peshawar District, the administrative districts of Nowshera, Charsadda, Mardan and Swabi.

The Kabul River crosses the Pak–Afghan border near Warsak about 30 kilometers east of Khyber Pass and flows towards Charsadda, where it is joined by the Swat River. It ultimately joins the Indus River near Attock Khurd.

The plains of the Peshawar Valley watered by these rivers made this region ideally suitable for the rise and sustenance of the Gandhara Civilization. The area was thickly populated and well-cultivated. Traditionally a large variety of fruits are grown in the immediate vicinity of Peshawar, and corn, sugarcane and tobacco have been cultivated on a large scale in the areas around Charsadda, Nowshera, Mardan and Swabi. Everywhere one goes in the Peshawar Valley one finds abundant remains of Buddhist monuments dating to the period of the Gandhara Civilization.

Taxila, one of the most important cities of the Gandhara Civilization, is located east of the Indus River, about 30 kilometers from Pakistan's capital, Islamabad. The city was known in ancient times as Takshasila. The 20-kilometer long valley in which the city of Taxila is located is bounded on the east by Murree Hills, an outcrop of the Himalayas. Spurs of the Murree Hills serve as the northern and southern boundaries of the valley.

Three ancient cities, which served as capitals of different regimes in various phases of the Gandhara Civilization, were located in the Bhir Mound, Sirkap and Sirsukh sectors of Taxila, within a distance of six kilometers from each other.

Taxila owed its importance in the Gandhara Civilization to the fertility of its soil and to its location on important trade routes linking the Gandhara region with Central Asia, Kashmir and eastern regions of South Asia. The Haro River, a tributary of the Indus, along with two tributaries of the Haro

River, the Dhamrah Kas and Lundi Kas, provide enough water for extensive cultivation of crops and to support a large population. Soft stone, which is abundantly available in the Taxila valley, was extensively used in construction of buildings and in production of sculptures and utensils.

The third most important region in Greater Gandhara was the Swat Valley, known in the Gandhara Civilization period as Uddhyana or the Gardens because of its luscious alpine scenery.

The Swat Valley is a mountainous region spread over an area of 10,400 square kilometers. It displays varied topographic features which are quite distinct from those of the Peshawar and Taxila Valleys described above.

The Valley is bounded on the north by mountains of Chitral and Gilgit, on the east by the mountainous Hazara Division and the Indus River, in the south by the Mardan-Swabi region of the Peshawar Valley and on the east by mountains of Dir. In the southern part of the wide valley of the Swat River, there are relatively low mountains and tree-covered hills. Mount Elam is the highest peak in this region. It rises to a height of 2811 meters. In the northern region of Swat, known as Swat Kohistan, the mountains are much higher, Mount Falaksair reaching a height of 5918 meters. In the south low mountain passes provide entry into various regions of Peshawar Valley

The 700-meter long Swat River runs through almost the entire 130 kilometer length of the valley from north to south, before leaving the Swat Valley near Malakand to join the Kabul River near Nowshera. The River receives its water from the Ushu and Utrot Rivers, which have their headwaters near the mountain ranges bordering Chitral and Dir. During their passage through the narrow valleys in the upper mountainous region of Swat Kohistan, the Ushu and Utrot Rivers gather water from numerous mountain streams to provide Swat River a fairly large volume of water at its source.

The fairly large network of rivers and streams in the upper part of Swat Kohistan, along with water brought by the monsoon rain, give rise to lush green forests populated with a large variety of trees and shrubs. Long-needled pines cover the upper slopes of huge mountains, while cedars and different varieties of oaks are found in abundance at the lower end of the slopes and in the plains.

There were few regions in Greater Gandhara where nature presented such luxuriance and diversity as in the valleys of Ushu, Utrot and Gabral

Rivers in Upper Swat Kohistan. These valleys present the beauty of Swat Kohistan in its most quintessential form.

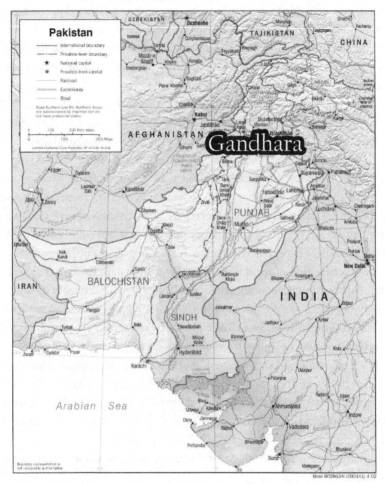

Figure 1.1: Regions interacting with Gandhara Civilization

The elevation around Saidu Sharif, the capital of Swat located in the Lower Swat Valley, is around 990 meters while on the other end of the Swat River, near Utrot in Swat Kohistan it is about 2580 meters. The ascent from Saidu Sharif to Kalam and Utrot is gradual. Also, at the northern end, the Swat River Valley is very narrow. It opens up around Kalam, and then reverts to its narrow width until it reaches the Lower Swat Valley around Saidu Sharif and Mingora, where the river flows through wide open plains.

The most thickly populated and cultivated areas are in the Lower Swat Valley.

On either side of the fertile Swat River plains, glens and narrow wooded dales lead to low mountains or hills covered with trees and pastures. During the period of Gandhara Civilization, Buddhist stupas and monasteries were located not only in the plains, but also in the side valleys, on plateaus and on steep slopes of mountains—anywhere and everywhere, 1400 of them, according to the Chinese pilgrim Hsiuen Tsang. About 100 Buddhist sites have been surveyed or excavated in the Swat Valley to date.

SPHERE OF INFLUENCE BEYOND THE BORDERS OF GREATER GANDHARA

The socio-economic and cultural revolution brought about by Mahayana Buddhism was not confined to borders of Greater Gandhara. From the core area the influence of Gandhara Civilization spread to most countries with which Gandhara maintained trade relations and which were included in the Kushan Empire during Kanishka's reign. The areas which came under tremendous artistic, cultural and religious influence of the Gandhara Civilization included what are now the Tarim Basin of Chinese Turkistan, the Bamiyan and Balkh regions of central and northern Afghanistan, southern Uzbekistan, Tajikistan, south-eastern Kyrgyzstan, and the regions around Merv and Ashkabad in Turkmenistan.

Buddhist missionaries trained in monasteries attached to stupa complexes of Gandhara established their bases in the Xinjiang, Gansu, Henan and Shaanxi regions of China. They played an important role in spreading Mahayana religion and culture to more distant areas such as central and eastern China, Japan and Korea.

BODHISATTVAS IN THE GARB OF MISSIONARIES

Compassion and care for fellow human beings is an important part of the Mahayana doctrine. The concept of Bodhisattva, which is central to the Mahayana philosophy, underlines this feature. Bodhisattvas postpone their entry into the state of Nirvana in order to help the human beings to achieve that path.

The Gandharan missionaries, who embarked on their missions in distant lands in hundreds during the period of the Gandhara Civilization, were also inspired and motivated by the Bodhisattva ideal. They spent their entire lives in difficult conditions in the caves of Xinjiang and Central Asia, motivating people to order their lives according to the Eightfold Path so that they could also achieve Nirvana.

This concern for humanity as a whole was central to the character of Gandhara Civilization. It shows a marked difference in attitudes from that of people belonging to other contemporary cultures.

LITERATURE PRODUCED IN GREATER GANDHARA

The limitations of the oral tradition, which dominated the literary scene in other regions of multi-lingual South Asia centuries before and after the emergence of the Gandhara Civilization, are quite obvious. From the point of view of authentic originality there is always a considerable element of doubt. In this respect Greater Gandhara was fortunate because of the emergence of Gandhari-Kharoshthi in the period around the 4th century BCE. From this time onwards, religious and secular texts could be put into writing and carried over long distances, retaining their authentic form over a long period.

Originals of religious texts produced in Greater Gandhara have been recovered from Afghanistan and from western regions of China.

GREEK AND PERSIAN INFLUENCES IN ART AND ARCHITECTURE

A striking feature of the Buddhist civilization in Gandhara was the special quality of art and architecture which developed during this period.

The predominant means of artistic expression in this period were sculptures in schist and stucco, and rock carvings of Buddha and stupas on the faces of cliffs in mountainous areas. Hellenistic and Persian artists were extensively employed for the decoration of stupas and other religious buildings. Their liberating influence is quite apparent in the art and architecture of Gandhara.

It was because of the liberating influence of the Hellenistic artists that images of Buddha first began to appear in the decorations of Buddhist establishments in Gandhara. The Hellenistic sculptors initially developed the images of Buddha on the pattern of images of Apollo in Classical Greece. Gradually a hybrid image of Buddha emerged, which made use of Greek art forms but incorporated the spiritual characteristics of Buddha through facial expressions, postures (mudras), attitudes, and symbols (nimbus, ush-nisa, urna).

Greek influence in the sculptures of Greater Gandhara is not restricted to the Buddha image. It appears in various forms and compositions of the sculptures—in the dress and form of Buddhas, Bodhisattvas, Devas and monks and Malla Chiefs, in their hairstyles and headdresses, in the motifs and mythical creatures.

Similarly Persian influences are apparent in the use of the solar disc, in the flames emerging from the shoulders and feet of Buddha, and the use of flame pillars in various sculptural compositions.

In the field of architecture also Greek and Persian influences are quite apparent. Cities were constructed on Hippodamian pattern and Greek and Persian architectural elements such as Corinthian, Ionic and Persepolitan columns and pilasters, were incorporated in the design and decorations of stupas and other buildings and monuments located in the sangharamas. The shapes and decorations on the entablatures, the shapes and style of plinths and bases of stupas, the fire altars in front of images of Buddha, all show Greek and Persian influences.

ECONOMIC ENVIRONMENT

After solid foundations for a sound economy were made during the embryonic phase of the Gandhara Civilization through large scale invest-ment in physical infrastructure and improvements in methods of agricul-ture, Greater Gandhara was firmly placed on the path of rapid economic progress.

In the early period of Hellenistic rule, construction activity picked up and production of craft item were on the rise. Thus, starting from the Saka-Parthian period, Gandhara embraced a multi-dimensional economy.

The Kushan period in Gandhara, in particular, was one of great afflu-ence and prosperity. Major extensions of the Kushan Empire during the rule of Kanishka and other Kushan rulers brought increased wealth into Gandhara. Trade and commerce were promoted through the Silk Route and Gandhara, which was once linked to the Silk Route only by feeder channels, became more directly involved in the trade between China and Rome and its colonies in West Asia and North Africa.

As commerce picked up, new features of a diversified economy appeared. A number of business houses and brokerages emerged; overland and river transport systems improved, providing employment to many people in the transport trade and allied professions; the construction industry was organized on professional lines. With so many sangharamas being constructed and the founding of new cities and up-grading of existing towns, stone masons, carpenters and well diggers were in great demand.

Legacy

The Buddhist civilization in Gandhara provided an effective bridge between the classical and the modern age.

After the prolonged period of decline, starting from the end of Kidara Kushan rule in the 5th century CE and culminating in the rule of the Hindu shahis in the 9th and 10th centuries, Gandhara Civilization and its main driving force, Mahayana Buddhism, all but disappeared from the land of their birth.

It was, however, in north-east Asia that the Gandhara Civilization made its greatest impact and China, Japan and Korea still exhibit considerable Gandhara influence in the social, spiritual and cultural fields.

Mahayana Buddhism brought by missionaries from Gandhara got a firm foothold in China. From there it spread to Korea and Japan. Mahayana Buddhism serves as the base for all the schools of Buddhism which exist in China, Japan and Korea today, including Chang (Zen) and the Pure Land Schools.

Nomenclature

The use of the word 'Gandhara' to designate the civilization requires some explanation. The only time that a geographical entity by the name of Gandhara appears in historical records is in the inscriptions of Achaemenid emperors at Behishtun, Persepolis and other sites in Ancient Persia, where a satrapy by the name of Gandhara is mentioned in a list of satrapies belonging to the Achaemenid Empire. Using this as his basis, Herodotus also mentions an Achaemenid satrapy by the name of Gandhara in his *Histories*, written in 5th century BCE. Where was the Gandhara satrapy located, or what were its boundaries, cannot be said with certainty. However, one thing is sure: the Achaemenid emperors Darius and Xerxes did conquer territories in the north-western regions of South Asia, both to the west of the Indus and to the east, and established two satrapies, one with a capital near Pushkalavati (Charsadda) and the other with the capital near Takshasila (Taxila). It is generally believed that the satrapy with its capital at Pushkalavati near Charsadda was the one referred to by the name of Gandhara in ancient Persian inscriptions.

A number of renowned archaeologists and art connoisseurs have coined the phrase 'Gandhara Art' to describe the beautiful Buddhist sculptures retrieved from the Buddhist monuments (commonly referred to as stupa complexes or sangharamas) in the region surrounding the Kabul River Valley. This extended area in the north-western region of South Asia and south-eastern Afghanistan, which was the home of Gandhara Art, is referred to in this book as Greater Gandhara.

Chapter 2: Rise and Growth

> Gandhara was the seat of series of powerful dynasties from the
> 3rd century BCE to 4th century CE. Well known from abundant ar-
> chaeological remains, it was crossroads of cultural influences from
> India, the West, China and East Asia, and a meeting point of Greeks,
> descendents of Scythian invaders from the north and many others.
> —Peter Monaghan[3]

Important events were taking place around Gandhara in the mid-6th
century. Cyrus the Great had united the Medes and the Persians, the two
main tribal factions in the region around Iran, and founded the great Achaemenid Empire. He was on a mission to conquer the world. The Lydians and
the Babylonians had submitted to the might of the great Achaemenid conqueror. The Achaemenids were now heading east to establish their control
over Sogdiana and Bactria. Next in line was Gandhara.

The isolation of Gandhara was about to end. In the next five centuries
Gandhara opened up more and more to the external world and came into
contact with diverse cultures. The Persians, Macedonians, Mauryans and
philhellenic Indus Greeks, Scythians (Sakas), Parthians and Kushans invaded Gandhara one after another, and most of them stayed on and made
Gandhara their home. During the rule of these alien regimes, some features
of their cultures were absorbed into Gandhara's own evolving indigenous
cultural fabric. The geographical location of Gandhara in the South Asian

---

3 Peter Monaghan: 'A Lost Buddhist Tradition is found'. *Chronicle of Higher Education*,
   October 4 2002.

sub-continent also meant it was exposed to varying degrees of cultural influences from the cultures of this region.

Gandhara Civilization		
Phases	Period	Regimes
Embryonic	535–317 BCE	Achaemenid Macedonian-Greek
Transient	317 BCE–60 CE	Mauryan Indus Greek Saka-Parthian
Mature	60–463 CE	Kushan Kushano-Sassanian Kidara Kushan
Decline	463–1025 CE	Ephthalite Sassanian Turk Shahi Hindu Shahi

Figure 2.1: Phases of Gandhara Civilization

Thus Gandhara, while maintaining close links with various South Asian
cultures, developed a distinct identity in the South Asian region—an identity in which strains of foreign cultures were clearly discernable. In the cultural fabric woven through interactions with various cultures, the dominating feature, however, was still that of the region where the Gandhara
Civilization emerged.

Gandhara had entered an exciting phase. Rapid changes were taking
place in the political, social and cultural fields.

Once naked fakirs could be seen performing mental and physical exercises in the countryside, while sheep and cattle roamed around the dusty
roads and squares in towns and villages; a few decades later planned cities
with well laid-out streets and spacious houses began to appear, and mules
and ox-carts laden with a wide variety of agricultural products made their
way from the farming villages to urban centers.

A few centuries later, people of different races and different cultural
backgrounds rubbed shoulders with each other on the city streets. Among
them were famous architects and engineers from distant lands, local and
foreign artists, highly skilled masons, well diggers, metal workers and
carpenters.

Gold and silver ornaments, plates and utensils, decoration pieces and other fancy goods started pouring in from the west and the east; local workshops produced a large variety of goods including religious statuary and other decorative items, jewelry, cloth and furniture.

Beautifully decorated stupas began to appear all over the region; scholars engaged in lengthy debates on religious and spiritual matters; scribes started writing down religious texts on birch bark and palm leaves; sangharamas began to develop into complex religious and social institutions.

Trading activity picked up; Shops, business centers, warehouses and trading houses began to appear in ever increasing numbers; roads and highways were constructed to facilitate overland trade and maritime communication channels were developed to facilitate movement of goods along rivers and over the Arabian Sea.

While these changes were taking place, a vast interacting region was developing around Gandhara, which was to give shape to the expanded cultural union which we call Greater Gandhara.

Gandhara Civilization was on the rise.

The ingredients of the Gandhara Civilization were established over a period of five centuries commencing with the arrival of the first Buddhist missionaries in the Achaemenid satrapy of Gandhara soon after this region was conquered by Cyrus the Great in the 6th century BCE. The process of integration and socio-economic development, which took place all through the Achaemenid period, facilitated the spread of Buddhism in this region. By the time Alexander invaded Gandhara in 327 BCE, the Buddhists were reasonably well established at places such as Taxila. Buddhism continued to gain ground after Gandhara became a province of the Mauryan Empire, and, after Asoka Maurya provided active support, it was well on its way to becoming the most prominent religion in Gandhara.

The process of advancement of Buddhist religion was accompanied by major changes in the socio-economic environment of Gandhara. A distinctive cultural pattern began to emerge which produced a powerful effect on all aspects of life in Gandhara. This process of providing a concrete shape to the Gandharan society was sustained during the subsequent rule of the Indus Greeks, and the Hellenized Sakas, Parthians and Kushans. Through a unique arrangement based on mutual trust and respect between the alien rulers and the local population a new civilization took shape.

The civilization reached its peak between the 1ˢᵗ and 4ᵗʰ centuries CE. Like all great civilizations, the Buddhist civilization in Gandhara developed a distinct character and a strong cultural identity.

Chapter 3: Embryonic Phase

The embryonic phase of the Gandhara Civilization covers two specific periods.

- The first period stretches from 535 BCE to 326 BCE, when Gandhara became a part of the Great Achaemenid Empire.
- The second period starts with the invasion of Gandhara by Alexander the Great in 326 BCE and ends in 317 BCE when last of the Greek-Macedonian satraps fled Gandhara to take part in the battles for succession which were being fought in Persia and Mesopotamia after the death of Alexander.

The Achaemenid Period

> 'Darius says: ----These are the countries, which I seized outside Persia; I ruled over them; they paid tribute to me; what was said to them by me they did; my law-that held them firm: Elam, Parthia ----Gandhara, Sindh, Maka ----'[4]

Gandhara and Taxila became part of the great Achaemenid Empire in the 6th century BCE.

Around 535 BCE, Cyrus the Great crossed the Hindu Kush Mountains to enter the fertile valley of the Kabul River and succeeded in conquering the region up to the banks of the Indus River. At that time this region

---

4 Inscription in the upper register of the Tomb of Darius the Great at Naqsh-i-Rustum, north of Persepolis, Iran.

was inhabited by a large number of small farming communities. The Achaemenids brought the entire region west of the Indus under one satrapy, the Satrapy of Gandhara. Gandhara became a single political unit and was governed by a satrap who enjoyed the full confidence and support of the powerful Achaemenid emperor.

Then in 518 BCE the Achaemenid forces once again crossed the Himalayas to conquer new territories. The forces under Darius the Great crossed the Indus River and conquered the region between the Indus and the Jhelum Rivers. They established the second Achaemenid satrapy in the newly conquered regions, the Satrapy of Sindh (Sindh referring to the Indus River, which was called Sindhu in ancient times, and not to the Province of Sindh in present-day Pakistan). Taxila became the capital of the Satrapy of Sindh and a similar process of consolidation was initiated in the Taxila region.

After the conquest of Gandhara and Taxila by the Achaemenids, we find, for the first time in the history of these regions (and also the first time in South Asia), the appearance of definitive written material, which throws some light on the socio-economic conditions prevailing in Greater Gandhara and on the events which took place in this region from 535 to 326 BCE during the rule of various Achaemenid emperors. This written material comes in the form of inscriptions on walls and columns of the palaces of Darius the Great at Persepolis and Susa, at his tomb at Naqsh-i-Rustam, and on cliffs and stone tablets at Behishtun and Hamadan. Further details appear in the *Histories* written by Herodotus. Although very sketchy, this written material, along with the detailed accounts written later by the companions of Alexander the Great, together with the study of the physical remains of this period unearthed by archaeologists, helps to lift the veil which shrouded Gandhara during the Dark Age preceding the Achaemenid conquest.

Achaemenid Satrapy of Gandhara

The Achaemenid Satrapy of Gandhara was probably spread over the entire Peshawar Valley and covered an area of 7176 square kilometers. It was bounded by the Swat Valley in the north, the Indus River on the southeast, Buner in north east, Afghanistan in the west and Kohat District in the south. Its capital, referred to variously as Pushkalavati, Peuceloitus and Proclais, was located on several mounds near Charsadda.

The archaeological excavations at the mounds of Charsadda were carried out by Sir Mortimer Wheeler 1962, who identified some structures there belonging to the Achaemenid period. The carinated and tulip bowls

(bowls with a particular shape to the side walls) found by Sir Mortimer Wheeler are typical of bowls found from sites in Persia, belonging to the period of rule of the Achaemenids.

Besides the inclusion of the name of the Gandhara satrapy among various inscriptions of Achaemenid emperors at several historic sites in Persia, there is a bas relief at Apadana Palace, Persepolis, showing the members of the Gandhara delegation taking part in the annual Procession of Tribute-Paying Countries. The Gandharan bull is depicted in this bas relief along with members of the Gandhara delegation wearing Gandharan dress.

The Satrapy of Gandhara appears in the list of tribute-paying nations published by Herodotus.[5] Gandhara together with three other satrapies included in the group are said to have paid 170 talents annually as tribute to the Achaemenid treasury.

There is mention in the Achaemenid inscriptions of yaka (teak) wood being supplied by Gandhara for use in the construction of Imperial palaces.

Achaemenid Satrapy of Sindh (Taxila)

The Achaemenid Satrapy of Sindh probably covered an area of about 7000 square kilometers. It was bounded on the north by the Hazara region, on the west by the Indus River, and in the south and on the east by the Jhelum River. At the time of the Achaemenid conquest, a small settlement existed at the village of Bhir Dargahi. The Achaemenids constructed their capital city near to this settlement at Takshasila-Bhir Mound.

The archaeological excavations at Bhir Mound carried out by Sir John Marshall in the period 1913 to 1934, revealed heavy masonry of buildings belonging to the Achaemenid city at the lowest stratum of the archaeological site.[6] There is evidence of soak pits being used in the houses for disposal of sewerage. Water for domestic consumption was probably obtained from wells dug in the nearby plains or from the Dhamrah-Kas River, which flows nearby. Among other finds belonging to the Achaemenid period were ornaments and beads made of shell, green glass and polished crystal. The scaraboid beads found from the site were very similar to those used in Achaemenid Persia and other parts of the Achaemenid Empire. Although no coins belonging to the Achaemenid period were found from the site, some silver coins found nearby indicated Achaemenid influence as they were produced

---

5 Herodotus. *Histories*, Book III. Aubrey de Selingcourt's translation, Penguin Books, 1972.

6 Sir John Marshall. *Illustrated Account of Excavations at Taxila 1913–34*, Cambridge 1951

on the Achaemenid standard and of weights used in the Achaemenid Sigloi and coins of lower denomination.[7]

The Satrapy of Taxila (also referred to as the Satrapy of Sindh or India) was the most heavily populated and richest of all the satrapies in the Achaemenid Empire. Herodotus mentions in *Histories* that this satrapy paid an annual tribute of 360 talents of gold dust, equivalent to 4680 Euboean talents, which was about one third of the tribute paid by all the 20 satrapies in the Achaemenid Empire.[8]

Achaemenid Administrative Skills

The Achaemenid skills in administration have been recognized by most Western scholars. They made substantial investments in all their satrapies on administrative and physical infrastructure and communications. They constructed irrigation canals to boost agricultural production and constructed a vast network of roads to facilitate the movement of agricultural commodities and other goods.

The tribute which the Achaemenids levied was based on their assessment of wealth of each satrapy. Under Darius the Great, all lands were re-surveyed, estimates of yields were made on averages over several years, and tributes were fixed based on these assessments.

The Achaemenids used all their administrative skills to create a nation out of various heterogeneous groupings. They achieved consolidation of Gandhara and Taxila through a series of administrative and socio-economic reforms:

- The Achaemenids delegated vast powers of governance to the satraps of the two satrapies. These satraps exercised administrative control over the region through three or four local chieftains called rajas or deputy satraps.

- To establish effective political control over a vast potentially rich but socio-economically underdeveloped region, the Achaemenids established an effective communications network spread over the entire region. They built roads and caravanserais (rest houses). During the rule of Darius the Great, a royal highway was constructed, which linked the capitals of all the 23 satrapies in Darius' Achaemenid Empire. Provision was made on the royal highway for horse-mounted relays which carried messages to the remotest corner of the Achaemenid Empire in less than

---

7 Sir John Marshall. *A Guide to Taxila*, Cambridge University Press, 1960
8 Herodotus. *The Histories*, Book III, Aubrey de Selincourt's translation, 1972.

15 days. Obviously a network of roads existed in each satrapy, which could be used to link up with the royal highway.

• For the first time in the history of this region, official correspondence was carried out in written form. Aramaic, the language extensively used in the Great Achaemenid Empire, was initially used in these communications. Subsequently a local derivative of Aramaic, the Kharoshthi script, emerged, which made it possible to employ the Gandhari dialect in written communications. Thus Gandhari was gradually elevated to the status of *lingua franca* in the region and Kharoshthi became the universal script.

• There are indications that to facilitate trade transactions and enforce a produce-unit based revenue collection system in the country, the Achaemenids introduced a standard system of weights and measures and a currency system based on the gold and silver standard of the Achaemenid currency, the Darics and the Sigloi.

Tolerance of Local Religions

It was during the Achaemenid rule that the tradition of maintaining peaceful relations with local religious groups was established.

The neutral attitude of the Achaemenids towards religious affairs and their belief in Ahura Mazda as the benevolent, wise creator and symbol of purity and morality found common ground with the teachings of Buddha. This, together with the fast improving socio-economic environment in Gandhara during Achaemenid rule, attracted Buddhists to Gandhara from their distant homeland around Pataliputra at quite an early stage.

While the Buddhist missionaries were winning converts under the Achaemenid regime, the Zoroastrian population in Gandhara remained negligible. We find, however, some of the Zoroastrian religious practices such as veneration of the flame being incorporated into the beliefs of the Buddhists and other religious groups.

Exploration of Maritime Routes

During the reign of Darius the Great, Skylax, a Greek mercenary of Caryanda, was commissioned to explore the maritime route connecting the Achaemenids' easternmost satrapies with the western region of the Empire. Skylax sailed down the Indus and then, via the Arabian Sea and Indian Ocean, reached the Red Sea. The exploratory trip undertaken by Skylax led to the establishment of a maritime route via the Indus for active trade during the rule of the Hellenistic regimes in Greater Gandhara.

Military Engagements

Throughout the tenancy of their empire, the Achaemenids were extensively engaged in fighting wars. If they were not engaged in conquering new territories, they were quelling rebellions in different parts of their vast empire. To fight these wars they maintained a well-trained and well-equipped army which included personnel from all the satrapies.

As in other Achaemenid satrapies, Persian military commanders were posted in Gandhara and Taxila, who recruited and trained local manpower for fighting wars in distant lands. One of the satraps of Gandhara, who was actively engaged in recruiting and training army recruits from Gandhara, was Megabazus son of Megabates, who is mentioned in the inscribed stone tablets that were found in Persepolis. Megabazus later became one of the fleet commanders in the Achaemenid campaigns against Greece—campaigns in which, according to the contemporary Greek historian, Herodotus, complete cavalry and infantry regiments from Gandhara took part.

Cultural Union of Gandhara & Taxila

The two Achaemenid satrapies of Gandhara and Taxila were politically independent and were governed by separate satraps. Therefore the consolidation process set in motion by the Achaemenids was carried out in the two satrapies separately. However, during the 200 years of Achaemenid rule, the two diverse regions, one west of Indus and the other east of the Indus, assumed a singular cultural identity. A sort of social and cultural union emerged, which ultimately led to the establishment of Greater Gandhara, the core area of the Gandhara Civilization.

Collapse of Achaemenid Administration before Alexander's Invasion

Political and administrative conditions in the Achaemenid satrapies deteriorated sharply after the death of the last great Achaemenid emperor, Antaxerxes II, in 358 BCE. During the rule of Antaxerxes II, from 358 BCE till 328 BCE, the loyalties of some eastern satrapies remained suspect. Darius III succeeded Antaxerxes II in 358. In 331 BCE, Alexander defeated Darius III at Gaugemala in 331 BCE; Darius III fled to Ectabana and sent urgent messages to the satraps of the eastern satrapies to preserve their loyalty. However Bessus, the satrap of Bactria, revolted, killed Darius III in Ectabana, and fled to Bactria, where he declared himself emperor and assumed the title of

Antaxerxes V. The Achaemenid satrap of Gandhara, Astes, and of Taxila, Ambhi, recognized Antaxerxes-V as emperor and declared their loyalty to him. But after Alexander defeated Antaxerxes-V in 330 BCE, Astes and Ambhi became independent rulers of Gandhara and Taxila and Achaemenid rule in this region finally came to an end.

Progress during Achaemenid Rule Towards Emergence of Gandhara Civilization

In the context of the evolving Gandhara Civilization, progress was made in the following areas during two centuries of Achaemenid rule:

• Political, administrative and physical infrastructure was developed in the satrapies of Gandhara and Sindh (Taxila)

• Gandhari emerged as the common language in Gandhara and Taxila

• Kharoshthi developed as the first indigenous script in South Asia

• A cultural union of Gandhara and Taxila was established

• The first two cities in the region were constructed at the site of Bhir Mound in Taxila and Pushkalavati, near Bala Hisar, Charsadda

ALEXANDER'S INVASION

Among the many features which make Alexander's invasion of Greater Gandhara so very different from all others is the fact that it provided to the world such a wealth of information not only about battles fought but also about the country, its people and their peculiar customs and lifestyles. Alexander was accompanied on this mission by historians, scientists and littérateurs. The information which they were able to provide, therefore, bears not only a certain degree of stamp of authority but also scientific accuracy.

The accounts written about Alexander's invasion by his generals, particularly Ptolemy, Aristoboulos, Nearchus and Onesikritos, suddenly lift the curtain on a society which had remained unreported and obscure for over a millennium. We are given a view of how far the Gandharan society had evolved towards a phase with which we are more familiar and which is more within our grasp. This is no longer an early social group learning to extract enough yield from the land to make ends meet. Nor are we talking of primitive crafts or of people obsessed with charms and amulets. We are now in the realm of thinking men trying to unfold the mysteries of nature. We are talking of organized societies, of natural leaders making their mark—some selfish and tyrannical, others benevolent and responsive to the needs of people with whom they share their every day lives.

The dusty and overcrowded marketplace in the summer heat of Taxila of 326 BCE already bears some resemblance to the Mandi (market) towns of the 18th century. The ancient Greek accounts of crudely crafted stalls (kho-kas) of vendors in these ancient parts of Gandhara, as well as the goods offered for sale—fruits, vegetables, ceramic vessels, and woven straw baskets and floor matting—sound quite familiar to a person living in the 20th or even 21st century in this part of the world. There were parrots for sale, 'parrots that could speak like humans'[9] and monkeys trained to beg for alms. And the people roaming around these ancient bazaars look familiar too—some dressed in cotton lungis (loin-cloth wrapping) and chadars (loose cloth covering upper part of body) and wearing 'white leather shoes with thick soles to make them look taller,'[10] others bare-footed with just a strip of loin cloth to cover their private parts. There were Sadhus too, with henna-dyed hair, and monks with begging bowls—some helping themselves to whatever was available in the stalls, others voluntarily served by the shopkeepers.

We hear about ascetics like Kalanos, lying stark naked in the scorching heat of the sun. They felt the urge to distance themselves from the materialist urban society and free themselves of the artificiality of clothing and shelter in order to remain spiritually pure to converse with nature.

West of the Indus, particularly in the mountainous regions, the influence of Persian religions, dress and food was more apparent due to greater interactions with groups living across the mountains, and migrations, nomadic or permanent, from Bactria and other regions of Central Asia.

Generally, ancient Greek writers like Strabo and Curtius, who based their accounts on information provided by Nearchus and other Greek generals accompanying Alexander on his mission, found plenty of wealth in this region, and the cities great and flourishing.

We also get a picture of the feelings of the people accompanying Alexander on this mission—their fatigue and their frustrations. One can empathize with Alexander's elderly general, Koinos, when he makes that passionate appeal to Alexander to return to Greece. Koinos talks about the large number of Greeks and Macedonians who had lost their lives, about

---

9 Arrian's *Indike*' chapter 15 based on information supplied by Nearchus, one of Alexander's generals.
10 Ibid, Chapter 16.

the pain and depression of the troops who were still alive, and about their yearning to see their parents and wives and children from whom they had been separated for so long.[11]

But Alexander is unmoved. He was made of a different stuff to that of most other human beings. He himself lays claim to divinity. Divine he was not, but certainly a man possessed with the extraordinary ambition of becoming master of the world.

Conquests

Prior to invading Greater Gandhara Region of South Asia, Alexander divided his army into two divisions. One division was put under his trusted General, Hephaistion, and he himself took control of the other division.[12] The two divisions were to meet at Hund and then the combined army would enter the Taxila region of Eastern Gandhara by crossing the Indus River on boats.

The division under Hephaistion entered the Peshawar Valley near the Khyber Pass and proceeded towards the Pushkalavati (Charsadda), the capital of Western Gandhara. The division under Hephaistion was engaged in battle at Pushkalavati by the ruler of Western Gandhara, Astes[13]. Astes was defeated and killed in the battle and Hephaistion appointed Sanjaya as the Greek-Macedonian satrap at Pushkalavati. After building a cantonment near Pushkalavati, Hephaistion's Division moved to Hund, as pre-arranged with Alexander.

The division led by Alexander crossed from the Kunar Valley in Afghanistan into the Bajaur area of Greater Gandhara. Alexander's forces captured Arigaon without a battle as the local Asvaka tribes fled to the mountains when Alexander's armies approached this town. Most scholars believe that

---

11 Arrian. Anabasis Chapter XXVII (J.W. M'Crindle's translation.)

12 J.W. M'Crindle. *The Invasion of India by Alexander the Great*, Indus Publications Karachi in 1992.

13 Astes, the Achaemenid satrap at Pushkalavati, and Ambhi (Taxiles), the Achaemenid satrap at Taxila had become independent rulers of their respective satrapies after Alexander defeated and killed the last Achaemenid emperor, Bessus (Antaxerxes V), at Bactra (Balkh). However according to Arrian's Anabasis, before invading Gandhara, Alexander called Astes and Ambhi for a meeting at Nikaia (Begram) and asked them to accept him (Alexander) as the successor of the Achaemenids and place their respective satrapies under Greek-Macedonian rule. At this meeting both Astes and Ambhi accepted Alexander's demand, but later Astes went back on his promise.

Arigaon of the Greek writers was located in the vicinity of the present day town of Nawagai, the capital of Bajaur Agency.

After crossing the Guraios (Panjkora) River, Alexander's forces captured Massaga (Chakdara), the capital of the Assakans in Southern Dir, without too much trouble, and then laid siege to two heavily fortified fortresses of Bazira and Ora in the Lower Swat Region. Bazira and Ora surrendered to Alexander's forces after their food supplies were cut off. Preliminary surveys indicate that Bazira and Ora were located in the Swat Valley in the vicinity of modern towns of Barikot (Birkot Hill) and Udegram respectively.[14]

Alexander's forces faced their toughest opposition in this region at the Rock of Aornos. Here the usual tactic adopted by the tribal people in the mountainous regions of taking refuge in the mountains when attacked by the enemy, was succeeding to a very large extent. From the safety of the hill-top of Aornos, they were able to keep Alexander's at bay and even inflict heavy losses on them. Alexander's forces faced a desperate situation until they were helped by some deserters, who showed Alexander a secluded path, which could take his forces to the top of the hill without facing the barrage of arrows from forces defending Aornos.

Preliminary investigations and surveys carried out by General Abbot, Col. Wauhope and Sir Aurel Stein[15] indicate that the Rock of Aornos of the Greek writers is Pirsar Hill, located near the town of Besham Qila on the west bank of the Indus.

After these victories the regions of Bajaur, Dir and Swat were added to the Satrapy of Taxila.

After completing their conquests in the Swat Valley, Alexander arrived with his army in Hund, where most of the arrangements for crossing the Indus River by boats had already been completed by Alexander's general, Hephaistion. Ambhi, the former Achaemenid satrap at Taxila, who had already assured Alexander of his loyalty, was also present at Hund to receive Alexander and escort the Macedonian Greeks to Taxila.

At Taxila Alexander and his men took part in festivities to celebrate their victory and Alexander sacrifices animals to honor the Greek gods. After resting in Taxila for about two weeks, Alexander's army together with men provided by Ambhi left for Jhelum, which lies at the eastern border of Greater Gandhara, for battle with the local chief, Porus. The battle between

---

14   Aurel Stein. *On Alexander's Track to the Indus*, Indus Publications, Karachi, 1995.
15   Ibid.

Alexander's forces and the forces of Porus resulted in a compromise. After this compromise Alexander's forces sailed down the Indus and engaged in further conquests. Alexander left behind his own satraps to govern the satrapies of Gandhara and Taxila.

Administrative Organization

As in the Achaemenid Period, the Greek-Macedonian Satrapy of Gandhara covered the entire Peshawar Valley and its capital was Pushkalavati. A local chief, Sanjaya initially assumed charge after the death of Astes. Later Alexander appointed Philip son of Machatas as satrap of the both satrapies of Gandhara and Taxila, with his seat of Government at Pushkalavati. Around 325 BCE, Philips was murdered and the administration reverted to separate satraps for each satrapy. Nikanor became the satrap of Gandhara, while Sanjaya served as his deputy.

The Greek-Macedonian Satrapy of Taxila included besides the area in the Achaemenid Satrapy of Taxila, the newly conquered territories of Bajaur, Dir and Swat. Eudemos was appointed the Greek-Macedonian satrap and was based in Taxila. Ambhi served under him as deputy satrap, but due to his familiarity with the area enjoyed the lion's share of the powers in this satrapy.

After Alexander's death in 323 BCE, the Greek-Macedonian satraps posted by him at Pushklavati and Takshasila, could not maintain control of their satrapies and ultimately fled to Persia in 317 BCE. Thus Macedonian-Greek colonial presence in Gandhara was restricted to less than a decade.

Greek-Macedonian Cities

The Greek-Macedonians constructed their cities on top of the cities constructed by the Achaemenids at Pushkalavati-Bala Hisar and Takshasila-Bhir Mound.

The archaeological excavation carried out by Sir Mortimer Wheeler at Pushkalavati in 1956 revealed the ditch and rampart constructed by Hephaistion after he laid siege to the city.

At Takshasila-Bhir Mound the archaeological excavations carried out by Sir John Marshall in the period 1913-34 revealed the remains of the city constructed by Alexander's satraps over the remains of the Achaemenid city. Among the antiquities recovered by Sir John Marshall from the stratum of the Greek-Macedonian city were two silver didrachms of Alexander and one of Philip Aridaeus, and some typically Greek ceramics.[16]

Alexander also laid the foundations of a number of regular Greek cities (Alexandrias) in various parts of Greater Gandhara on the pattern of cities established in Asia Minor. These cities were heavily fortified. Initially these cities were to serve as cantonments for Greek-Macedonian troops left behind by Alexander. After he had settled himself comfortably in Babylon, and established Babylon as one, if not the only, capital of his vast Empire (as some sources indicate), he would have perhaps attempted to populate these cantonments with Greeks from the mainland Greece or from the Greek settlements in Asia Minor. Whether he would have succeeded is anybody's guess.

The question arises that if the Greeks could retain control of other regions, which they conquered in Asia, why could they not do the same in Gandhara. The answer to that is that Gandhara was different from most regions conquered by the Greeks. The status of Gandhara vis-à-vis the other Asiatic nations conquered by Alexander has been beautifully explained by J.W. M'Crindle:

> The Asiatic nations in general submissively acquiesced in the new order of things, and after a time found no reason to regret the old order it had superceded. Under their Hellenic masters they enjoyed a greater measure of freedom then they had ever before known; commerce was promoted wealth increased, the administration of justice improved, and altogether reached a higher level of culture both intellectual and moral, than they could possibly have attained under a continuance of Persian supremacy.

> India (read Greater Gandhara) did not participate to any great extent in these advantages. Her people were too proud and warlike to brook any long burden and reproach of foreign thralldom, and within a few years of the Conquerors death they completely freed themselves from the yoke he imposed....[17]

After Alexander's death, the dream of the cities he proposed to establish in Gandhara went with him. Not a clue survived of the cities-in-embryo, which Alexander had hoped to develope into regular Greek cities.

---

16   *A Guide to Taxila*, by Sir John Marshall, Cambridge University Press, 1960.

17 J.W. M'Crindle. *The Invasion of India by Alexander the Great*: Introduction. Indus Publications, Karachi, 1992.

PHYSICAL ENVIRONMENT & ECONOMY

The Greek writers accompanying Alexander in Gandhara portray Greater Gandhara as a prosperous region. It was socio-economically more advanced than the northern lands of Bactria and Sogdiana which Alexander captured earlier. During the rule of the Achaemenids, the Peshawar Valley and the region around Taxila had emerged as well-settled areas with sound agricultural economy. In the river valleys around Swat also, life around the mud and stone fortresses which dotted the region was well organized. All along the perennial rivers agriculture sustained a sizeable population. Alexander was particularly impressed with the cattle found in this region.

The physical infrastructure constructed by the Achaemenids was intact when Alexander invaded Gandhara. It permitted rapid movement of heavy battle equipment as well as boats and army personnel along the Kabul and Swat Rivers.

After two centuries of Achaemenid rule, Gandhara had passed the nascent phase of a potentially great cultural revolution. A delicate stage had now been reached when a change in regime could undo all that had been achieved in the previous two centuries, or it could carry the development process a step forward in the direction it had taken.

The likelihood of the development process being reversed or at least stalled was very much there when Alexander the Great, after his final victory over the Achaemenids at Ectabana and Bactria, decided to invade Gandhara. The policies of the Macedonian Greeks towards their conquered subjects were quite different from those of the Achaemenids. The Macedonian Greeks looked down upon other cultures, had little tolerance of other religions, and were least inclined to enter into any sort of partnerships with the conquered people. Therefore the likelihood was that, had Alexander's invasion led to full colonization of Gandhara by the Macedonian Greeks, this would have reversed the cultural evolution of a Buddhist civilization in Gandhara. But due to Alexander's death, the actual colonization of Gandhara never took place.

After almost two centuries of Achaemenid rule in Gandhara, the rule of Alexander's Greek-Macedonians barely covered six years. Alexander's army crossed the Hindu Kush and the Karakoram mountains in May 327 BCE to enter regions of Greater Gandhara at two points. A year later, in June 326

BCE, the combined forces of Alexander exited from Gandhara by crossing the River Jhelum near the modern town of Jhelum to enter Central Punjab.

The Greek Macedonian satraps left by Alexander to govern the western and eastern regions of Greater Gandhara barely remained in the region for three years. One of them was murdered, while two of his successors abandoned their posts and left for Persia between 323 BCE and 317 BCE for the battles for succession, which followed Alexander's death.

Progress Towards Emergence of the Gandhara Civilization

Three positive developments took place during the short rule of Macedonian Greeks:

Bajaur, North and South Dir and the districts of Swat, Buner, Shangla and Kohistan were added to the Satrapy of Taxila. These territories were placed under a resident governor who was administratively under the Satrap of Taxila. These newly integrated territories north of Malakand Hills came to be known as Uddhyana. In due course, Uddhyana became one of the core areas of the Gandhara Civilization and served as a conduit for trade and transmission of Mahayana Buddhism to Xinjiang and other areas in Western China.

Alexander's invasion opened up of avenues for fruitful cultural interaction between Gandhara and the Macedonian-Greeks who were settled in Babylonia and Bactria. As a result, Gandhara acquired special technical skills in the fields of sculpture and architecture.

The maritime link between the Indus Valley and West Asia was reinforced through the journey of Alexander's naval troops under Nearchus, first down the Indus, and then from the Indus Delta to Persian ports.

Chapter 4: Transient Phase

In the transient phase of the Gandhara Civilization, which begins around 317 BCE, the regimes which came to power, taking full advantage of the developed infrastructure, focused on other key issues.

Major developments in this period included regional consolidation (i.e., strengthening of political and cultural ties with the regions which recently became a part of Greater Gandhara—Swat, Dir, Bajaur, Buner and Shangla), strengthening of socio-economic infrastructure, and establishing of a new cultural identity based on fusion of cultures of the east and the west.

Buddhism moved from its status of a prominent religion in Gandhara towards becoming the universal religion in Greater Gandhara. Hellenistic influences in the art and architecture of Gandhara increased and a vastly improved system of currency was introduced.

Inside the region, socio-economic activity increased considerably. Strategically important and economically resourceful regions had now become a part of Greater Gandhara. Swat, Dir, Bajaur and Hazara Regions were now linked administratively and politically with Taxila region, east of the Indus, and with the Kabul River Valley west of the Indus. The pooling of material and human resources made this vast region strong, economically and militarily. The extension of its borders had opened up new opportunities for trade and cultural exchanges.

Outside the borders of Greater Gandhara the political, cultural and economic environment changed considerably. Alexander was no longer there, but one of his generals, Seleucus Nikator, was in the process of carving a vast empire out of the territories conquered by Alexander. The Seleucids were well established along the western and northern borders of Gandhara. Arachosia, covering an area from Kandahar and Quetta to the western bank of the Indus, shared its northern boundary with Gandhara. Bactria and Sogdiana were in Seleucid control. The Seleucids, as successors of Alexander, had claims on Greater Gandhara also. The situation was fluid, and was resolved in due course through a military engagement between Seleucus Nikator and Chandragupta Maurya in 305 BCE, when Chandragupta Maurya finally defeated Seleucus.

The Mauryan Period

Around 321 BCE Chandragupta Maurya established the Mauryan Kingdom in Magadha and immediately embarked on a mission of expanding his empire.

Chandragupta is said to have met Alexander prior to Alexander's battle with Porus in 326 BCE.[18] What exactly was the nature of this meeting has not been explained but it is likely that Chandragupta Maurya may have provided manpower support to Alexander in the battle against Porus. A number of scholars believe that Chandragupta received his inspiration for establishing an empire from Alexander.[19] Chandragupta remained in the Taxila-Jhelum region for some time and in the period 326 BCE to 322 BCE managed to raise a sizeable army there, which he used to overthrow the Nanda kings of Magadha. Once established in Magadha, he kept a close watch on the developments taking place in the Taxila Valley.

After Alexander's departure from Taxila, the satrap posted by Alexander to govern Greater Gandhara, Philip son of Machatas, was murdered and Eudemos, who was appointed satrap of Taxila in place of Philip, was unable to control the situation. Taking advantage of the deteriorating political situation in Taxila after Alexander's death, Chandragupta Maurya launched his attack on Taxila in 317 BCE. He drove out the last Greek-Macedonian satrap of Taxila, Eudemos, and established his control over the Taxila satrapy. Subsequently his armies crossed the Indus River and extended his conquests to Afghanistan. The entire Kabul River Valley from the source of

---

18   Plutarch 62-3
19   "But for Alexander's example it is most unlikely that Chandragupta would ever have built the Maurya Empire ..." W.W. Tarn: *Alexander the Great*, I page 143.

Kabul River in the Hindu Kush till its meeting place with the Indus River in Hund was added to Chandragupta Maurya's Empire.

After conquering the Kabul River Valley, Chandragupta and his Minister, Kautilya, both of whom were familiar with the newly conquered regions, because of their past associations with Taxila,[20] set about the consolidation of the conquered territories in the north-western part of his Empire. A Mauryan province was established with twin capitals in Taxila and Pushkalavati. Thus the borders of Greater Gandhara were further reinforced and the Kabul River Valley in Southeastern Afghanistan became a part of Greater Gandhara. Greater Gandhara remained a province of the Maurya Empire till 195 BCE.

During the rule of Chandragupta, his son Bindusara was appointed the first governor of Gandhara Province. Because of the distance of more than 1500 kilometers between Pataliputra, the seat of government of the Mauryan emperors in Magadha (Bihar), and Taxila, the provincial capital of Gandhara, Gandhara was only loosely controlled from Pataliputra. Bindusara enjoyed wide powers and virtually ruled over Gandhara as king. To reinforce the governor's position in Gandhara, the number of troops under his control was increased, and the local administrative organization was strengthened.

While these developments were taking place in Greater Gandhara, the turmoil created by the battle of succession in Persia and Mesopotamia finally subsided and one of Alexander's generals, Seleucus-I, established an independent Greek-Macedonian kingdom there. During his rule, Seleucus-I encouraged migrations from Greece and Macedonia to Mesopotamia to strengthen his position. In the last decade of the 4th century BCE, Seleucid-I felt secure and powerful enough to make an attempt to reassert Greek-Macedonian authority in Bactria, Parthia, Sogdiana and Gandhara. He was successful in conquering all these territories and establishing Seleucid control in all these regions except Gandhara. In 305 BCE, Seleucus-I came face to face with the powerful army of Chandragupta Maurya in Gandhara, and the Seleucids suffered a heavy defeat. A treaty was signed after the battle, on the basis of which the Kabul River Valley as well as the Greek-Macedonian (Seleucid) Satrapy of Arachosia officially became a part of the Mauryan Empire.

---

20   Some scholars believe Chandragupta Maurya was born somewhere in this region. Kautilya is said to have received his education in Taxila.

In 298 BCE, Chandragupta Maurya abdicated in favor of his son, Bindusara, and Bindusara's son Asoka Maurya became governor of Gandhara.

In the period when Asoka was governor, the political unity of Gandhara was fully re-established and Kabul Valley became an integral part of the province of Greater Gandhara. The institutions created by the Achaemenids were revived and the economy further strengthened.

Asoka succeeded Bindusara as emperor in 270 BCE, while his son, Kunala, became the governor of Gandhara. After he became emperor of the Mauryan dynasty, Asoka's close ties with Gandhara continued. Asoka embraced Buddhism in 261 BCE and from then on until his death in 232 BCE he took keen interest in the spread of Buddhism. He sent a number of missionaries to Gandhara and Central Asia.

Figure 4.1: Dharmarajika Stupa, Taxila (Photo: Paramount Archives, Karachi)

Asoka died in 232 BCE. In the period between 232 BCE and 195 BCE, the Mauryan hold on Gandhara and Kabul Valley continued to diminish. The last significant Mauryan king, who ruled the Kabul Valley and Gandhara, was Sophagasenus. In 206 BCE, Sophagasenus thwarted the attempt by the Seleucid emperor Antiochus III to regain the territories ceded by Seleucus Nikator (Seleucus-I) to Chandragupta Maurya. Around 195 BCE, the invasion of Kabul Valley and Gandhara by the Bactrian Greeks formally put an end to Mauryan rule in Gandhara.

Stupa Culture takes Root in Gandhara

After Buddha's death in the 6th century BCE, his ashes were placed in eight caskets and buried under eight mounds, probably located in the vicinity of Bihar. These mounds came to be referred to as stupas and they soon became an object of veneration of the Buddhists.

After converting to Buddhism, Asoka had the stupas opened, took out Buddha's ashes and distributed them to large number of regions in his vast empire. Among the recipients of Buddha's ashes were the three principal regions in Greater Gandhara, Taxila Valley, Peshawar Valley and Swat Valley. The first three stupas in Greater Gandhara were constructed around 270 BCE at the sites of Chir Tope near Takshasila Bhir Mound, Jamalgarhi near Mardan in the Peshawar Valley, and Butkara near Mingora in Swat (Uddhyana), where the ashes of Buddha donated by Asoka, were interred. During Asoka's period these stupas were simply mounds of earth without any decorations. Subsequently they went through major extensions and were lavishly decorated and stupa complexes emerged with statues of Buddha and Bodhisattvas and other decorations carved in stone.

The stupa constructed in the Asoka period near Takshasila-Bhir Mound came to be called Dharmarajika ('The Lord of the Dharma') stupa, a title given to Asoka by the Buddhists fraternity for Asoka's service to Buddhism.

The seeds of Buddhism sown by Asoka continued to blossom after Asoka's death. Stupas constructed in Greater Gandhara during Asoka's reign began to attract a large number of devotees. The stupa culture introduced by Asoka and his active involvement in missionary activities related to this faith, went a long way in strengthening the base of the Buddhism in Greater Gandhara.

Asoka's Edicts

It was during the reign of Asoka that the earliest Buddhist inscriptions appeared at least at two strategic locations in Gandhara. These inscriptions of the 14 Edicts of Asoka were carved on rocks at Shahbaz Garhi near Mardan and at Mansehra in the Hazara Region. Both these sites were located on important trade routes, one linking the heartland of Gandhara to Swat and the other to Xinjiang.

The inscriptions both at Shahbaz Garhi and Mansehra are in the Kharoshthi script, which is an indication of the fact that Kharoshthi script was universally employed in all regions of Gandhara. The inscriptions refer to Asoka as Priyadarshi or the "beloved of the gods," and describe the efforts made by him for spreading Buddhism. The edicts generally focus on social and moral precepts aimed at promoting the welfare of the people.

Asoka's Edicts carved on rocks are said to be inspired by Achaemenid inscriptions at Behishtun and other places in Persia. The influence of the Achaemenids is also visible in Mauryan architecture.[21]

Trade and Cultural Exchanges

Gandhara's trade and strategic links with countries in the east and west were considerably strengthened after Chandragupta Maurya constructed the royal highway linking the Mauryan capital city of Pataliputra with Takshasila, the provincial capital of Gandhara. The Achaemenids had previously constructed a highway, which connected the capital of their eastern satrapy, Takshasila, with West Asia and the Mediterranean Region.

Asoka was a contemporary of the Seleucid rulers Antiochus-I and Antiochus-II, as well as Bactrian Greek rulers Diodotus-I and Diodotus-II. He established contacts with these rulers for the purpose of spreading Buddhism. Similar contacts were established by Asoka with the emperor of Rome and Ptolemy of Egypt.

The contacts established by Asoka with these distant regions opened up avenues for trade and cultural exchanges of Greater Gandhara. Gandhara reaped substantial benefits from the diplomatic and trade relations established between the Mauryan regime and the Macedonia-Greek regimes in West and Central Asia and Egypt towards the end of Chandragupta's reign. Active trade with these countries is indicated by ornaments of gold and silver of Greek design found among the ruins of the Mauryan city. Ivory items also found their way into Mauryan Gandhara from Siberia through Bactria.

Mauryan City in Taxila

The Mauryans constructed their city on the ruins of the Achaemenid and Greek-Macedonian city at Takshasila-Bhir Mound. The Mauryan city was spread over an area of three acres. The layout was somewhat irregular. Except for the seven-meter wide main street, which runs in a straight line from north to south, the other streets are narrow and follow a winding path. The arrangements for street and house drainage and sewage disposal were not as elaborate as in the Greek cities constructed later, but adequate. Surface drains inside the houses were constructed with limestone and sewage disposal in each house was through soak pits.[22]

---

21 *Journal of Royal Asiatic Society of Great Britain and Ireland*, 1915.
22 Sir John Marshall. *An illustrated account of Archaeological Excavations* at Taxila Cambridge University Press, 1951.

There were separate quarters reserved for affluent and the not-so-affluent residents. The sector for the elite had relatively large houses, with a floor area of around 325 square meters and one or two spacious courtyards paved with pebble stones. Most of these houses were double storied and their walls were plastered with mud and white-washed in certain places.

The excavations carried out by Sir John Marshall revealed residential buildings constructed on a plan commonly adopted in this part of the world. The rooms were located on one or more sides of an open courtyard. Bathrooms and washing places were paved with cobble stone.

A fairly large number of items for decoration, personal adornment and vessels for domestic use were found from the ruins of the Mauryan city. Artifacts such as iron vessels, utensils and weapons indicate predominant use of this metal in Mauryan Gandhara. Taxila has long tradition of producing various items used in kitchen and ornaments out of hard stone. This is confirmed by stone cups, bowls and saucers recovered from the Mauryan city.

Progress Towards Emergence of Gandhara Civilization

The 120-year rule of the Mauryans was the only period in the history of the Gandhara Civilization when formal political and cultural links existed between Greater Gandhara and other regions of South Asia. This relationship was mutually beneficial. During the period of Mauryan rule following positive developments took place:

• Stupa culture was introduced in Greater Gandhara and some degree of official patronage became available to Buddhist institutions in Gandhara.

• The issue of Greek-Macedonian claims on Gandhara was settled once and for all and the entire Kabul River Valley officially became a part of Greater Gandhara.

• Trade, diplomatic and cultural relations with Hellenized countries in West and Central Asia were promoted.

HELLENISTIC GANDHARA

During their rule in Gandhara, the Mauryans had been engaged in prolonged battles with the Bactrian Greeks in the Hindu Kush area and in this early period for control of the upper Kabul River Valley the Mauryans came out victorious. But after Asoka's reign, the tide began to turn against the Mauryans. Gradually the Bactrian Greeks regained full control over the areas north of the Khyber Pass and around 200 BCE, the Bactrian Greek army under Demetrius crossed into Gandhara and established themselves in this region. With the defeat of the Mauryans at the hands of the Bactrian Greeks, a new era began in Gandhara. Invaders from Bactria and other parts of Central Asia forced themselves one after the other during the next two centuries into the fertile plains watered by the Kabul and Indus Rivers. Gandhara was now entering a more interactive and culturally rich phase in its history.

Unlike previous conquerors, these new invaders came here to stay, but they continued to maintain links with Bactria and other regions in Central Asia, the regions from where they came, the region they had begun to consider their own 'hereditary' lands due to their prolonged stay there as masters of the land. They were either driven out from the lands they previously occupied or they were attracted to this region by its wealth, its culture and its natural environment. Some of the customs, beliefs and practices of the land of their forefathers continued be embedded in the memories and lifestyle of the new rulers of Gandhara, but that did not prevent them from adjusting to the local cultural environment of Gandhara and interacting well with the local population.

The Indus Greeks had become familiar with the Buddhist culture to a certain extent before they entered Gandhara. They had become familiar with the socio-political environment of Gandhara. It did not take them long to realize that that they would not be able to rule Gandhara as traditional colonizers. Gandhara was politically as well as socially much better organized than Bactria. The Buddhist establishment could not be pushed around at the will and mercy of the conquerors. At the same time the Buddhist population did not pose any serious threat to the occupation of Gandhara by the foreign invaders. The Bactrian Greeks realized that with the doors of Bactria closed to them, their best option was to learn to co-exist with the locals and for that they needed to interact more effectively with the local population by breaking down cultural barriers. The Indus Greeks set the pattern for maintaining a healthy working relationship with the locals. The Scythians, Parthians and the Kushans just stepped into their shoes.

Buddhism had received a boost provided during the rule of Asoka Maurya. After that it continued to grow from strength to strength in Gandhara, and it was playing a dominant role in shaping the lives of the common man when the Indus Greeks conquered Gandhara. The Hellenistic Indus Greek,

Saka and Parthian regimes fully cooperated with the pacifistic Buddhist establishment in Gandhara. They realized that that was essential to counter
the threats to their power from within their own ranks and from outside.

The real threat to the security and to the rule of all the Hellenistic regimes
came from their kinsmen and from other tribes, which had taken their place
in Bactria. With so many ethnically and culturally diverse groups vying for
power and ruling the region in successive periods, one would expect this
to be a very turbulent period for the people of Gandhara also. Turbulent it
was—but mainly for the ruling regimes. The growing Buddhist population
in Greater Gandhara remained politically neutral and avoided confronta-
tion with the foreign tribes vying for power in the region and in Gandhara.

Thus, while the aliens continued to engage in military warfare amongst
themselves and in the neighboring territories, the overall socio-economic
conditions in Gandhara remained relatively undisturbed. Each succeeding
regime welcomed the neutrality of the Buddhist establishment and appreciated the need to establish close working relationships through the Buddhist
establishment with the dominant local Buddhist population. Each regime
appointed as their advisors Buddhist scholars who enjoyed the confidence
of the Buddhist population, and the advisors saw to it that the needs of the
Buddhist community were fully met and their growing aspirations realized
to the maximum extent.

This arrangement worked splendidly. The Indus Greeks as well as the
Scythians and Parthians were a quarrelsome lot. They were divided into
various factions, and the different factions were always fighting among
themselves. The Buddhist population was left to manage its own affairs,
to work for the welfare of their community and to strengthen the Buddhist
institutions.

With their own religious leaders occupying a position of substantial influence as advisors to the ruling regime, the Buddhist community was well
taken care of. The advisors, while channeling funds for the welfare of the
Buddhist community, ensured that the funds were properly utilized. They
exercised administrative control and also provided spiritual guidance for
the proper functioning and development of the Buddhist institutions. The
system ensured that proper care was taken of the spiritual as well as the
social, economic and cultural needs of the Buddhist community.

With the administration and control of the Buddhist institutions exclusively in the hands of the Buddhist establishment in Gandhara, the role of

the alien regimes in the governance of the State over which they ruled was considerably curtailed. The Buddhist establishment functioned as a regime within a regime. It played the dominant role in the socio-economic, cultural as well as spiritual affairs of almost the entire population of the country.

The rulers did not merge their identity with the local population. There were also pockets of Greeks and other alien populations who showed no inclination to adopt local ways and continued with their lifestyle based on drinking and dancing and pagan practices. Also the foreigners who took part in the military activities quite understandably continued to follow the customs and beliefs of the rulers. But by and large the rest of the foreigners, especially those belonging to the second generation, gradually adopted local customs, beliefs and ways of life and became a part of the population under the overall control of the Buddhist establishment.

The assimilation of the foreigners with the locals broadened the cultural base of the country. It also accelerated the process of transfer of special skills, which the foreigners brought with them. Some ethnic divisions may have existed in the society due to migrations of such large number of peoples from different regions, but after the new-comers converted to Buddhism and intermarried with the locals, ethnic divisions in the society also became less pronounced and less consequential. Whatever little element of ethnicity remained in the Gandharan society came in handy in foreign trading operations and missionary work in the regions with the regions from where they had come.

There is substantial material evidence belonging to the Hellenistic period in Gandhara. Tangible information on the cultural and socio-economic conditions prevailing in Gandhara are provided by the thousands of beautifully carved coins with bilingual legends, the remains of new cities and monuments, and a large number of artifacts recovered from the sites belonging to this period. Several Greek and Roman writers, such as Trogus, also provide useful information pertaining to Hellenistic rule in Gandhara. Details are given in the descriptions below of the rule of individual Hellenistic regimes.

The Indus Greeks

The Indus Greeks were descendents of the Greeks who had settled in Bactria after Alexander invaded that area in the 4th century BCE, and of other Greeks and Macedonians who migrated from mainland Greece to the newly conquered Greek territories during the period of rule of the Seleucid Dynasty.

Around 312 BCE Seleucus Nikator emerged as the successor of Alexander in the Middle East and Central Asia, and Bactria. Seleucus cut off political links with mainland Greece and established the Seleucid Empire, in which Bactria was one of the satrapies. After severing political links with mainland Greece, Seleucus continued to maintain close trade and cultural relations with them and with other Hellenistic regimes in Asia Minor and Egypt. Thus a great deal of culture of mainland Greece was retained by the satrapies of the Seleucid Empire.

In 255 BCE, Diodotus, the Seleucid satrap of Bactria, declared independence from Seleucid rule and an independent Bactrian Greek Kingdom came into existence. After their kingdom seceded from the Seleucid Empire, the Bactrian Greeks became more isolated from mainland Greece and its culture. Some trade and cultural contacts with the Hellenistic regimes in Asian Minor and Egypt continued, because of which their Greek identity was maintained. However, the Bactrian Greeks also began to adopt a lot of the customs of the non-Greek population of Bactria. The indigenous Bactrians had come under some influence of the ancient Persians, Parthians and Mesopotamians, and they probably worshipped a number of their deities. But the worship of local deities is not reflected in the coins issued by the Indus Greeks, in which only gods and goddesses from the Greek Pantheon are portrayed.

After secession from the Seleucid Empire, the Bactrians broke into several factions, who were often at war with each other. Because of this continuous infighting among different Bactrian Greek factions, the Bactrian Greek regime remained continuously unstable.

In the period 230 to 200 BCE Euthydemos was the King of the Bactrian Greeks. Euthydemos died in 200 BCE, and was succeeded by his two sons; Antimachos ruled in Bactria, while his brother Demetrius became the ruler of the Kabul Valley. In 195 BCE, Demetrius invaded Gandhara. His conquests in this region lasted for about five years and Demetrius succeeded in adding Western and Eastern Gandhara to his Kingdom. Thereafter till 180 BCE, Demetrius ruled Gandhara from Kapisa in the Kabul Valley through Pantaleon, who was posted as Governor (Sub-King) of Eastern and Western Gandhara with his headquarters at Takshasila-Bhir Mound.

The invasion of Demetrius came at a time when Buddhism was on the rise in Gandhara. After conquering Gandhara, Demetrius established a close working relationship with the Buddhist community. The Buddhist-friendly policies of Demetrius earned him the title of 'Dharmamita' or 'Friend of the Dharma'. These policies were continued by subsequent Indus Greek rulers and this was the single most important factor in perpetuation of Indus Greek rule in Gandhara.

Pantaleon continued to rule Greater Gandhara as sub-king till 180 BCE, when Demetrius was murdered by one of his rivals (Eucratides). After 180 BCE, Pantaleon became the first full-fledged ruler of Eastern and Western Gandhara and these regions began to be ruled directly from Takshasila-Bhir Mound. The Bactrian Greeks, who ruled in Eastern and Western Gandhara, came to be referred to as Indus Greeks.

Pantaleon was succeeded in 170 BCE as the Indus Greek king of Greater Gandhara by his brother Agathocles. In 165 BCE, Menander succeeded Agathocles.

The 30-year rule of Menander was the high point of Indus Greek rule in Gandhara. Menander established the cultural and administrative parameters for Indus Greek rule in this region. Menander's policies mark a major shift from the traditional Greek colonial attitudes and the policies of keeping at a distance the local population. The close rapport he established with the people he ruled is reflected in a number of revolutionary steps taken during his rule.

Menander combined within himself the qualities of a great conqueror, an intellectual with a broad range of interests, and a statesman of the highest order. This extraordinary combination enabled Menander to play an important role in putting Greater Gandhara on the path of a great civilization.

During Menander's rule Kharoshthi became the principal language in which administrative matters were handled. From now on Greek was used only for official communications with Hellenistic states.[23] Greek and Kharoshthi legends were both inscribed on the coins of Menander, which were minted in Taxila.

As a conqueror, Menander had already distinguished himself during the rule of his uncle, Demetrius.[24] In this early period of his career Menander was given the command of the Bactrian Greek forces in various regions south of

23   Sir John Marshall. *A Guide to Taxila*, Cambridge University Press, 1960
24   W.W. Tarn. *The Greeks in Bactria and India*, Cambridge 1951.

the Hindu Kush. He was highly successful in bringing southern Afghanistan within Bactrian Greek control. After he became king of Greater Gandhara in 165 BCE, Menander's spectacular run of successes on the battlefronts continued. Through these conquests Menander established his control over a vast region, which included the valleys of the Kabul and Swat Rivers, Taxila Region, parts of Punjab east of the Jhelum, Kashmir and the Hindu Kush region around Kabul and Kapisa.[25] His achievements on the battlefield also found recognition in the writings of Apollodorus of Artemita, a Greek historian who was a contemporary of Menander[26].

For the governance of such a vast region, Menander maintained his administrative base in more than one city. This seems to have been a common practice in that period. The politics and logistic situation in this period required that the king spend extended period of time—months or years at a stretch—in different regions of his empire. According to *Milandapanha* the capital of Menander's kingdom was Sagala, at the time when Menander's meeting with the Buddhist monk Nagasena took place. (Some scholars identify ancient Sagala with the modern city of Sialkot, near the border of Punjab with Jammu, but A.K. Narain thinks it was located in Uddhyana[27].) Archaeological investigations indicate that Takshasila-Sirkap, the city founded by Menander[28], may have also served as the capital of his kingdom.

Menander's intellectual credentials are established on the basis of his discussions with the Buddhist monk Nagasena on religion and philosophy. The Buddhist religious text "Questions of Milanda" describes Menander as "learned, eloquent, wise and able, and a faithful observer. He possessed knowledge of the holy tradition and secular law, systems of philosophy, arithmetic, medicine, astronomy and poetry.... As a disputant he was hard to equal, harder still to overcome; the acknowledged superior of all the various schools of thought."[29]

---

25   The extent of Menander's kingdom is indicated by the large number of Menander's coins found from all these sites. The coin-finds are recorded in number of essays contributed by Sir Alexander Cunningham in the period 1868 to 1892 to the Numismatic Chronicle, and by Schlumberger, Martin and others in various journals.

26   Pompeius Trogus. *Historiae Philippicae*, preserved by Justin. Translation by Roger Pearce, 2003. (The only existing sources for writings of Apollodorus are Trogus and Strabo.)

27   A.K. Narain. *The Indo-Greeks, Appendix III*, Oxford, at the Clarendon Press.

28   Dr. Saifur Rahman Dar. *Taxila & the Western World*, Lahore 1998.

29   T.W. Rhys Davids. *The Questions of King Milanda. The Sacred Books of the East*, Oxford, 1890.

With regard to Menander's more worldly attributes, this is what Mila-ndapanha has to say:

> "As in wisdom, so in strength of body, swiftness, and valor, there was none equal to Milanda in all India. He was rich too, mighty in wealth and prosperity..."[30]

As a statesman par excellence Menander gave up traditional Greek atti-tudes of looking down upon the conquered people. He took bold initiatives to establish a sound working relationship with the Buddhist establish-ments and through these establishments established a close rapport with the people of Greater Gandhara. As a result of these wise policies Menander was able to maintain relative peace and stability in the region throughout his 30-year rule.

The cultural and administrative parameters of rule in Gandhara estab-lished by Menander became a tradition which was strictly followed by the Hellenistic Saka, Parthian and Kushan regimes during the next six centu-ries. This pattern of governance was the single most important factor in the emergence of the Gandhara Civilization.

Menander is said to have adopted the Buddhist faith. The discussions of Menander with the Buddhist monk Nagasena had a profound influence on him. A translation of *Questions of King Milanda* by T.W. Rhys David indi-cates that after these discussions, Menander decided to give up his worldly life and became a Buddhist monk.[31] (Menander abdicated in favor of his son Strato-I. Menander's wife Agathoklea served as regent until Strato became old enough to shoulder the responsibilities of the Indus Greek kingdom.)

For his services to Buddhism, Menander is regarded at par with two other great rulers of Gandhara—Asoka and Kanishka.

Menander's reign was an exceptional period during the rule of the Indus Greeks. Except for the period when Menander was king, the political con-ditions remained unstable in Gandhara. Maintaining unity among their ranks was not in the character of the Bactrian/Indus Greeks. One reason for this was that they never quite got over their ethnic affiliations. There always remained a wide gulf between the Macedonians and the Greeks; but there were also many other ethnic divisions. A Bactrian Greek originally from one Hellenistic state in Asia Minor, for example Lydia, would hesitate to give full cooperation to a leader from another state in the same region. For this

---

30 Ibid.
31 Ibid.

reason the Bactrian/Indus Greeks never quite achieved the discipline, cohesiveness and political maturity necessary to maintain continuity in their rule. They were always a power hungry and divided lot, as the events after the demise of Menander indicate.

Menander did not leave behind a successor who could automatically step into his shoes. When Menander died (abdicated?—see quotation from T.W. Rhys Davids, above) in 130 BCE, his son Strato was too young to shoulder the responsibilities of the state. Menander's wife Agathokleia was appointed regent. But her regency did not turn out to be a great success. Strato-I was driven out of Taxila by Antialcidas, who belonged to a rival faction of the Bactrian Greeks, The House of Eucratides. Kings belonging to the Eucratides faction continued to rule Taxila till 90 BCE, when the invading Scythian (Saka) tribes under Maues put an end to Indus Greek rule in the region. After driving out Strato-I from Taxila in 125 BCE, the rulers belonging to the Eucratides faction ruled only the territory between the Indus and the Jhelum with Taxila as the capital. The Western regions were split up into a number of petty kingdoms; kings belonging to the Euthydemus faction of Indus Greeks ruled Swat, Dir and Bajaur till 60 BCE, when the Indus Greek finally came to an end in the entire Greater Gandhara Region.[32]

The Indus Greek rule in Greater Gandhara or parts thereof lasted for 135 years from 195 BCE till 60 BCE.[33] During this period they formally introduced Greek culture in this region. Hellenistic architects, engineers, artists and skilled craftsmen, who migrated to Gandhara after establishment of Indus Greek rule in this region, brought about qualitative improvement in the art, sculpture and architecture of Gandhara.

The Indus Greeks constructed at least two new cities on the Hippodamian pattern, one at Sirkap site of Taxila and the other at Shaikhan Dheri near Charsadda. Some other monuments like the Jandial Temple were also constructed in the vastly superior Greek style. Greek language began to be used extensively in official correspondence in which expatriate population was involved, and in trade and international communications, while Gandhari-Kharoshthi remained the language-script of the indigenous population. The vastly superior Greek type of coinage was introduced. Buddhism grew from strength to strength and was looked upon with respect by the Indus

---

32   A.H. Dani. *Bactrian and Indus Greeks—a Romantic Story from their Coins*, Lahore 1991.
33   A.H. Dani. *Bactrian and Indus Greeks—a romantic story from their coins*, Lahore 1991.

Greeks all the Indus Greek rulers. During the reign of Menander, the Buddhist religious establishment also received some degree of State patronage.

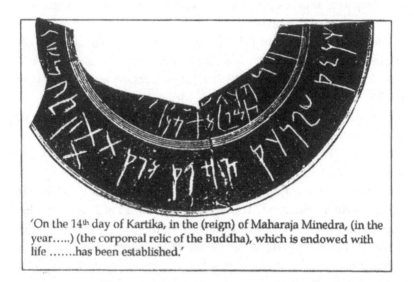

'On the 14th day of Kartika, in the (reign) of Maharaja Minedra, (in the year…..) (the corporeal relic of the Buddha), which is endowed with life …….has been established.'

Figure 4.2: Bajaur Casket Inscription pertaining to Menander's reign

Figure 4.3: The Greek temple in Jandial sector of Taxila (Photo of Jandial Temple from Paramount Archives Karachi)

Politically the conditions remained unstable during most of the period of Indus Greek rule in Gandhara. Except for the period when Menander was King, there were several Indus Greek rulers in different parts of Gandhara. As a result, the economy of Gandhara remained very much subdued.

Indus Greek Cities & Monuments in Greater Gandhara

After conquering Greater Gandhara, the Indus Greeks initially established their presence in the cities constructed by their predecessors, the Mauryans. Shortly afterwards they constructed their own cities at Takshasila-Sirkap and at Pushkalavati-Shaikhan Dheri, a new site in the Charsadda area. Both the Indus Greek cities were planned on the chessboard pattern, with the whole city divided into blocks by streets and lanes intersecting each other at right angles.

Sir John Marshall, who carried out the archaeological excavations at Takshasila-Sirkap, believes that Hellenistic town planners, architects and engineers were involved in the selection of the site for the city and in the city's construction.[34] In the selection of a site for their new city, the Indus Greeks took into consideration the availability of natural defenses for the city in the forms of hills on the northern boundary and the Dhamrah-kas River which flows along the western boundary. They then fortified the entire city by constructing six-meter thick and nine-meter high stone walls with bastions all along the perimeter.

The archaeological excavations carried out by Sir John Marshall identified seven strata which represent the constructions made at the site by the Indus Greeks, the Saka-Parthians and the Kushans. At the time of the excavations very little remained of the construction belonging to the Indus-Greek city as it was destroyed by the construction of the Saka-Parthians over it. However, the basic layout planned by the Indus Greeks was retained by the Saka-Parthians and the Kushans, when they carried out construction over it.

About 650 meters from the site of the Indus Greek city at Takshasila-Sirkap, Menander ordered a temple to be built[35]. The site where the temple was constructed is known as Jandial and the temple is known as Jandial temple. Enough remains of the temple built by the Indus Greeks to enable the archaeologists to reconstruct the plan and design of the original temple.

---

34   Sir John Marshall. *A Guide to Taxila.* Cambridge 1960.

35   Dr. Saifur Rahman Dar. *Taxila & the Western World,* Lahore 1998

The Jandial temple was constructed in the mid-second century BCE. The temple, which is constructed on the pattern of temples of classical Greece, was probably designed by a Hellenistic architect from Asia Minor.[36]

As in all temples of classical Greece on mainland Greece and in Asia Minor, the Jandial temple was surrounded on all sides by a peristyle of columns. The approach to the main portion of the temple was through the front porch, which was preceded by an antechamber.

Both at the outer and the inner ends of the antechamber, two Ionic columns were provided in the center and two Ionic pilasters on the flanks. The columns and pilasters on the outer end of the antechamber supported the architrave, which itself supported a pediment decorated with friezes.

Sir John Marshall, who carried out the archaeological excavations at the site, believes that instead of the statue of a Greek deity, which is normally provided at the center of the Naos, a Ziggurat-like tower was provided. The tower is normally used by Zoroastrians, who believe in fire-worship. The presence of this tower indicates that in the period when the ancestors of the Indus Greeks were settled in Bactria, they had absorbed some elements of Zoroastrian religion.

Menander constructed the Indus Greek capital city in Western Gandhara at the site of Shaikhan Dheri in the Charsadda area of Peshawar Valley. The archaeological excavations at the site were carried out by Professor A.H. Dani in 1963–64. Like Takshasila-Sirkap, this city was constructed on the Hippodamian concept. A large hoard of coins of Menander and other Indus Greek rulers was found from the site of Shaikhan Dheri.

Indus Greek Coinage

An important contribution made by the Indus Greeks was in the field of standardization of currency. The high artistic quality of the coins issued by them reflects the dignity, prestige and the power of the rulers. Their currency system was comprised of several denominations of gold stators, silver drachms and copper chalkoi, and each denomination was produced to a specific standard of weight and purity of metal. Highly skilled artists, sculptors and die engravers were employed in their production. The sculptors produced lively portraits of the rulers and the Greek deities, which were faithfully reproduced by the die-engravers.

---

36   Sir John Marshall. *A Guide to Taxila*, Cambridge 1960.

In all, 31 Indus Greek rulers issued coins in Gandhara. All the coins were bilingual. All except Pantaleon and Agathocles used Greek and Kharoshthi legends on the obverse and reverse faces. The Kharoshthi legends indicate the exclusive use of Gandhari-Kharoshthi in Gandhara even in this early period of the Gandhara Civilization

Almost identical legends comprising of the names and titles of the rulers were employed in the two languages. Along with the title 'Great King (Maharaja)' or 'King' and the name of the ruler, another title was used by the Indus Greek ruler. The most popular additional titles used in Indus Greek coins are 'Savior (Soter, Tratara)' and 'Righteous (Dikaios, Dharamika)', which indicate what they considered as their most important attribute.

The vast majority of the Indus Greek coins carry the portrait of the ruler on one side and that of a Greek deity on the reverse. In all, portraits of 14 Greek deities appear on Indus Greek coins, among which Nike (Victory) and Zeus (Jupiter), Athena (Pallas, Minerva) were the most popular. A typical drachm of Menander carries his helmeted bust with the legend 'King Savior Menander' (Vasileos Soteros Menandrou) on one side and a portrait of Athena (Pallas) hurling a thunderbolt along with the Kharoshthi legend, 'Great King Savior Menander' (Maharajasa tratarasa Menadrasa), on the other.

A large number of coins of Indus Greek rulers have been found in different regions of Greater Gandhara. Two large hoards of Indus Greek coins were found from Bajaur[37] in extension of Uddhyana; another large hoard was found in Shaikhan Dheri.[38] Other large finds are recorded from Swat[39], Taxila,[40] Hazurjat[41] and Kabul[42]. A great deal of reliance is placed on these coins to build up the history of the Indus-Greeks in Gandhara, because literary and epigraphic information pertaining to their period of rule is scarce.

Contribution Towards Gandhara Civilization

• During the period of Indus Greek rule, the tempo was building towards the maturing of the Gandhara Civilization. A number of features

---

37   Martin. *Numismatic supplement, Journal of Asiatic Society of Bengal*, 1926–27.
38   *Numismatic Chronicle*, 1940.
39   Ibid., 1923
40   Sir John Marshall. *Taxila—an Illustrated Account of Archaeological Excavations during 1913–34*, Cambridge 1951. Here, 519 coins of Indus Greeks from various sites in Taxila are recorded.
41   *Journal of Asiatic Society of Bengal*.
42   Sir Alexander Cunningham.

of the Gandhara Civilization introduced earlier were retained and further promoted, and a number of new features introduced.

• Buddhism began to play an increasing role in the lives of the common population. It had become the dominant religion in the region and
the Buddhist community held the key to political power in the region.
Menander became the first ruler after Asoka to bolster the interactions
with the Buddhist monks. Patronization of the Buddhist institutions,
which began in the Mauryan period, was continued.

• Extensive use of beautifully produced coins became an important
feature of the Gandhara Civilization. The Indus Greeks introduced refined design of coins with bilingual inscriptions, and for the first time in
the history of Gandhara Civilization coins began to be employed extensively in trade and other commercial transactions. Acceleration in trade
and commerce is indicated by the large number of Indus Greek coins
found from a vast region.

• The Indus Greeks were the first to introduce the concept of
planned cities in Greater Gandhara. They were also the first to introduce monumental architecture in Gandhara.

• The Indus Greeks laid the foundations for future production of
beautiful images of Buddha and Bodhisattvas in Gandhara. An environment was created in which the skills of Greek artists and sculptors
could be extensively employed.

• The Indus Greeks promoted the use of Gandhari-Kharoshthi
through inscriptions on coins.

Indo-Scythian Rule

The Indo-Scythians, who invaded Gandhara in 95 BCE under their
Chief, Maues, belonged to the Sai tribes (Sakas) who were driven westwards from their homeland, Wusun (Tarim Basin), by the Ta-Yueh-chih in
the second century BCE.

Chinese sources[43] mention:

> [The country of the Wu-sun] was originally occupied by the Sai.
> The Ta-Yueh-chih, moving westward, defeated the Sai-wang [King
> of the Sai], who was forced to flee. The king of the Sai went to the
> south and passed the Hsien-tu. The Ta-Yueh-chih settled them-
> selves in the country [of the Sai]. Afterwards Kun-mo [title of the
> King of Wu-sun] attacked and defeated the Ta-Yueh-chih. The
> Ta-Yueh-chih settled migrated westwards, and subjugated Ta-
> hsia [Bactria]. The Kun-mo of Wu-Sun settled himself there [in the
> country of the Ta-Yueh-chih]. Therefore it is said that there are ele-

---

43   *Ch'ien Han Shu*, Book 94b.

ments of Sai population and that of Ta-Yueh-chih among the subjects of the Wu-sun.

The same source[44] further states:

> The Chi-pin kingdom [Gandhara]...In the northwest it borders Ta-
> Yueh-chih, and in the southwest it borders Wu-i-san-li. Anciently
> the Hsiung-nu beat the Ta-Yueh-chih, the Ta-Yueh-chih moved
> westward as far as Ta-hsia [Bactria], which they ruled as kings, and
> the king [or royal family] of Sai moved southward, as far as Chi-pin,
> which he controlled as their Chief.

In other words the Sakas were driven from their homeland in Tarim
Basin by the Yueh-chih. The Sakas fled westwards to Bactria around 125
BCE. Around 95 BCE, one faction of the Sakas, under their Chief, Maues,
invaded Eastern Gandhara and established himself at Taxila.

The Chinese sources indicate that the route taken by the Sai to enter
Chi-pin (Gandhara) was through Hien-tu, the Hanging Pass (Khunjerab
Pass). This was also the route taken in 403 CE by Fa-Hsien, but Fa-Hsien
after reaching Gilgit went along the Gilgit River to Swat, while the Sai Chief
(Maues) proceeded from Gilgit along the Indus River and entered Taxila via
Mansehra and Abbotabad in the Hazara region.

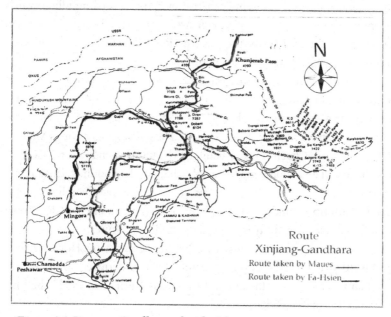

Figure 4.4: Route to Gandhara taken by Maues

---

44 *Ch'ien Han Shu*, Book 96a

On his way to Takshasila, Maues engaged in tough battles all along the route, establishing his control in one region after another over a period of ten years, before finally establishing himself in Takshasila-Sirkap. The invasion of Maues came at a time when the Indo-Greek Kingdom was in tatters. It was badly fragmented, and different regions were being controlled by different Indo-Greek princes. Antialcidas, who ruled in the Taxila region, was no longer fully in control over Hazara in the bordering regions of his kingdom. Thus, in a way the invasion of Maues saved Gandhara from further fragmentation and brought a degree of stability in the eastern region of Gandhara.

A number of inscriptions in Kharoshthi script belonging to Maues are available, which indicate his route to Takshasila-Sirkap. Three of these inscriptions belong to the period when he was battling his way against stiff opposition before he reached Takshasila-Sirkap. The Shahdaur inscription of Maues indicates that Maues established control over this region of Hazara in 90 BCE and appointed Dandida as his satrap before moving towards Mansehra from the Khunjerab Pass. His next inscription at Mansehra dates to 87 BCE, indicating that in the intervening period of 3 years, Maues had not advanced beyond Mansehra. Thereafter he proceeded rapidly towards Fatehjung, which is located between Attock and Taxila. The inscription found at Fatehjung dates to the same period, 87 BCE. The inscription at Tofkian (Sirsukh) belongs to the period after Maues had fully established himself in Taxila. It provides useful information on the political and socio-cultural environment in Eastern Gandhara during Maues' reign. This inscription on a copper plate is dated 77 BCE. It is inscribed in the Kharoshthi script and mentions the names of Maues ('The Great King of Kings Maues') and his satrap in Chach (Liaka Kusulka). The inscription is a sort of a commemorative plate announcing the establishment of a Buddhist sangharama by Kusulka's son, Patika, along with a stupa containing the relics of Buddha. The inscription indicates that by that time (i.e., around 77 BCE), Taxila as well as Maues were fully immersed in Buddhist culture.

Maues founded the Indo-Scythian Dynasty in Gandhara. However, during his 30-year rule Maues only controlled the eastern region of Greater Gandhara, between the Jhelum and the Indus Rivers. He established his capital at Takshasila-Sirkap.

Maues' 30-year rule fostered further continuity in emergence of the Greater Gandhara Civilization. He adopted the Indus Greek system of administration, and issued coins on the same pattern as those of the Indus Greek rulers.

R.B. Whitehead provides detailed description of 31 coins belonging to Maues, which are in the Punjab Museum, Lahore. All the coins, silver and copper, are bilingual. They carry a Greek legend on one side and Kharoshthi legend on the opposite side. They are designed on the pattern of the coins introduced by the Indus Greeks in Gandhara. A large number of the coins carry portraits of Greek deities. Zeus, Nike, Artemis appear commonly on one side. Some coins have portrait of King seated on horseback on one side, while on the opposite side is a portrait of Nike or some eastern deity.[45]

After the death of Maues in 60 BCE, his successor Vonones (60–40 BCE)[46] completed the mission of Maues by defeating the Indus-Greek King Hippostratus, who ruled in the western regions of Greater Gandhara, and establishing Indo-Scythian control over the entire region of Greater Gandhara.

After the death of Vonones the important Scythian rulers, who ruled Gandhara, were Azes-I (38 BCE–10 BCE) and Azilis (10 BCE–5 CE). During their rule Buddhism established its dominant position in Greater Gandhara, and embellishment of existing stupas and construction of new stupas gained momentum. Most of the Buddhist and Jain temples that one sees at Takshasila-Sirkap were probably constructed during the reign of Azes-I. Also the Ionic Temple at Maliaran about 1.5 kilometers outside Takshasila-Sirkap belongs to the same period.

Another lasting legacy of Azes-I is the foundation of the Azes Era. Azes era begins in 58 BCE and many inscriptions in Greater Gandhara are related to the founding of this era e.g. 'in the year 136 of Azes, on the 15th day of the month of Ashadka, on this day relics of the Holy One [Buddha] were enshrined by Ursaka....' (This inscription was found from a chapel at Dharmarajika Stupa, which belongs to the Kushan Period.)

Indo-Parthian Rule

The Chinese sources quoted above in the section on Indo-Scythians indicate that one faction of the Sakas, after being driven westwards by the

---

45 *Catalogue of coins in the Punjab Museum, Lahore,* R.B. Whitehead, Oxford University Press 1914.

46 Sir John Marshall, in his book *A Guide to Taxila,* indicates that Vonones belonged to the Scythian-Parthian faction, which was settled in Seistan Province of Eastern Iran.

Ta-Yueh-chih, settled in Bactria. When the Parthian Empire began to disintegrate due to Roman pressure, the Parthians were forced to move westwards, where they intermixed with the Sakas of Bactria. Another faction under Mithradates-II moved south and moved to Seistan in Eastern Iran, where a number of Sakas had settled. Thus another mixing of the Sakas and Parthians took place in Seistan.

One of Parthian Chiefs, who made his mark in Parthian Seistan, was Gondophares. Gondophares established himself in the western borders of Baluchistan, declared independence from the Parthian emperor, and became emperor in his own right. In 20 CE, Gondophares crossed the Indus, defeated the Scythian King of Gandhara, Azes-II, and made Gandhara a part of his Kingdom.

Gondophares was the greatest of the Indo-Parthian rulers who ruled in Gandhara and was in fact the only significant ruler of this dynasty. Gondophares died in 50 CE and was succeeded in Gandhara by Pakores. Pakores succumbed to the onslaught of the Kushans in 60 CE and this brought an end to the Indo-Parthian rule in Gandhara.

The Parthians were more deeply immersed in the Hellenistic culture than the Indo-Scythians because a large number of Asiatic Greeks had settled in the areas which were a part of the Parthian Empire. The conquest of Greater Gandhara by Gondophares created a more conducive environment for the Hellenistic artists and skilled craftsmen from West Asia and Egypt, who migrated in large numbers into Gandhara. Coming from a culturally rich Hellenistic-Parthian environment, Gondophares made effective use of the skills of these Hellenistic artists and craftsmen to inject a heavy dose of Hellenistic culture in this region.

Gondophares produced a deep impact on the socio-economic environment of Greater Gandhara. During his reign, an atmosphere of affluence prevailed in the capital, Takshasila-Sirkap. A large number of foreigners were among the rich people who lived in Takshasila-Sirkap in this period. They had relatively sophisticated tastes and sought luxury items from abroad to maintain an affluent lifestyle. Thus we find among the artifacts recovered from the Parthian layers of Takshasila-Sirkap a large number of imported items of gold and silver jewelry, silver goblets, flasks, bowls and copper ware, and items of decoration such as the bronze statue of the Egyptian god Harpocrates and a silver head of Dionysus in repoussé.

There is no evidence to suggest deep involvement on the part of Gondophares in the affairs of the pre-dominant Buddhist community in Gandhara. However, the Buddhist establishment continued to receive favorable treatment, and funds were always available from the government treasury for the maintenance and extensions of existing stupas. There is also evidence of acceleration in missionary activities carried out by Buddhist monks from Gandhara in various regions along the Silk Route. One monk, whose Chinese name is given as An Stigao, carried a large number of Buddhist texts to China during the Parthian period, where they were translated into the local language.

An inscription pertaining to Gondophares dated 46 CE is reported to have been found from Takht-i-Bahi, 95 kilometers northeast of Peshawar.[47] There is evidence also of substantial additions to the Takht-i-Bahi, Butkara and other stupa complexes in Greater Gandhara during the reign of Gondophares. Large scale reconstruction of Takshasila-Sirkap city was also carried out after the damages to buildings and other structures caused by the earthquake in 30 CE and the Buddhist and Jain temples in the city were renovated and provided fresh decorations. Among the artifacts recovered from the Apsidal Temple in the Sirkap city, are a large number stucco heads of Bodhisattvas and Greek deities belonging to the period when the city was being ruled by Gondophares.

Gondophares rule is linked with the visit of two important personalities from the West.

Apollonius of Tyana visited Takshasila in 44 BCE along with his companion Damis. On the basis of diary maintained by Damis, Philostratus wrote the biography of Apollonius of Tyana in which he describes the visit of Apollonius to the city of Takshasila-Sirkap and the Jandial temple, which was located near to this city.[48]

The apostle St. Thomas is said to have visited Takshasila and other parts of Gandhara in 40 BCE. The name of St. Thomas appears in early traditions of Christianity, and he is said to have been sold in Syria to an envoy of Gondophares, who was on a mission to recruit carpenters and other skilled ar-

---

47   R.B. Whitehead. *Catalogue of Coins in the Punjab Museum*, Oxford 1914. Also in *A Guide to Takht-i-Bahi* written by Dr, Abdur Rehman, ex-Consultant, Directorate of Archaeology & Museums Khyber Pukhtunkhwa.

48   Philostratus Bk II 17.42 provides detailed description of the temple visited by Apollonius at Taxila. On the basis of this description Sir John Marshall has identified that temple to be the Jandial Temple (*An illustrated account of the archaeological excavations carried out at Taxila* by Sir John Marshall, Volume I published by Cambridge University Press, 1951).

tisans for the construction of a grand palace for Gondophares. St. Thomas in the garb of a carpenter is said to have distributed the advance money received from Gondophares as alms to the poor, saying that this act of charity would ensure a grand palace for Gondophares in heaven.[49]

A fairly large number of coins of Gondophares have been found from all regions of Gandhara. They throw some light in the extent of his kingdom. His coins bear Greek and Kharoshthi legends. Most of them depict Gondophares sitting on horseback. On the reverse side of the coin a Greek deity, Zeus, Nike or Athena, is mostly portrayed.

Gandhara was firmly under the control of the Indo-Parthians as long as Gondophares ruled this region through local Governors. However, after his death sometime around 50 CE the situation began to deteriorate. This situation in Gandhara coincided with the emergence of Kujula Kadphises as the dominating figure among the Yueh-chih tribes settled in Bactria. For the rejuvenated and united Kushans of Bactria the situation was ideal for launching an attack on Gandhara. This they did in 60 CE, and the days of the Indo-Parthians in Gandhara came to an end.

Religious Environment in Indo-Scythian-Parthian Period

The Scythian and Parthian rulers maintained healthy relationship with the Buddhist clergy, on the pattern which emerged during the rule of the Indus Greeks. Some Parthian rulers, such as Azes-I and Azilis-I, were fully committed to the Buddhist cause. During the rule of these rulers Buddhism virtually became the state religion, and Buddhist institutions received substantial patronage from the ruling regime.

Unencumbered with the task of administering his region or engaging in political and military ventures, the Buddhist population developed its own set of values and its own culture, and was reasonably well off when it came to satisfying their worldly desires. Buddhist institutions matured; Buddhist religion flourished. This was the period when Sarvastivadins and the Dharmaguptika sects were dominating the religious scene in Gandhara. Their ideas were to give birth to the Mahayana School of Buddhism about a century later.

A large number of inscriptions belonging to this period have been discovered from Taxila, Takht-i-Bahi and other sites all over Gandhara. These inscriptions are mainly of donative nature—inscribed on metal plates or

---

49 *Cambridge History of India*, I, pp 578-79. Also *Acts of Thomas* A.F.J. Klijin, Leiden 1962.

vases or stones alongside stupas donated by Buddhist devotees. They are almost exclusively written in Kharoshthi script and Gandhari language and point to the fact that in this period the literacy level in Gandhara was already quite high and fairly large number of Buddhists in Gandhara were actively engaged in various socio-religious activities.

In the Saka-Parthian period the construction of Buddhist monuments gained momentum. Substantial additions were made to the stupa complex *cum* vihara of Dharmarajika in Taxila and a number of Buddhist stupas emerged in the Saka-Parthian city of Sirkap. A number of stupas in other parts of Gandhara as far as Takht-i-Bahi and Dir were also initially constructed in this period.

Linkages with Silk Route

The Saka-Parthian period is noted for heightened activity in the fields of trade and commerce. This was mainly because in this period linkages were established between Gandhara and the states along the early Silk Route. The acceleration in commercial activity is indicated by the large number of Saka-Parthian coins found from all regions of Greater Gandhara. Also a large number of imported luxury and decoration items, and sophisticated Saka-Parthian gold and silver jewelry and silver vessels, jars, dishes and plates, have been recovered from the ruins belonging to this period at Taxila and elsewhere in Gandhara.

Saka-Parthian City at Takshasila-Sirkap

Maues undertook the construction of a new city over the ruins of the Indus Greek City at Takshasila-Sirkap. It was almost as if all the structures belonging to the Indus Greek city were systematically brought down and new buildings constructed over their ruins. At Takshasila-Sirkap one hardly sees any structures belonging to the Indus-Greek period. All that remains of the Indus Greek city is the city's Hippodamian plan and perhaps portions of the city walls, which were retained by the Indo-Scythians and the Indo-Parthians, who succeeded them.

The Saka-Parthians rebuilt on a grander scale the city established by the Indus Greeks at Sirkap. Most of the Buddhist and Jain temples and other constructions which one sees among the ruins of the ancient city of Sirkap belong to the Saka-Parthian period.

The Hippodamian layout of the Indus Greek preserved by the Saka-Parthians left the position of the main and other streets and lanes undisturbed, and the new buildings were constructed on the existing foundations of the buildings in the Indus Greek city. As per standard arrangement of Greek cities, the Saka-Parthian city included a lower city in the north and the Acropolis on high ground at the southern end.

The entrance to the lower city from the north is through an impressive gateway. Inside the Gateway one is confronted by the 32-meter wide main street, which runs all through the center of the lower city from north to south dividing the city into parts.

Figure 4.5: Foundations of Royal Palace at Takshasila-Sirkap (Photo: Paramount Archives Karachi)

Along its length from north to south, the main street is crossed at right angles at regular intervals by 14 side streets, which divide the entire lower city into 28 blocks, 14 on the eastern side of the main street and 14 on the western side. The front rows of each block facing the main street were lined with shops constructed on a slightly raised level to that of the main street. Thus almost along the entire length of the street on either side there were shops, single storied and comprised of one or two rooms.

Figure 4.6: Jain Temple, Takshasila-Sirkap (Photo: Paramount Archives, Karachi).

The rectangular blocks formed by the main and the side streets were occupied by houses, public squares and stupas or temples. There was at least one stupa in each block on the eastern part of the city. The houses of the more affluent people were located at the southern end of the lower city. The expanded blocks on the southern part of the lower city were occupied by the royal residence or palace.

Beyond the southern end of the lower city, on elevated land was the Acropolis. As expected the Mahal or Palace of the Parthian rulers was the most impressive building on the Acropolis. It was not monumental but spacious. It occupied a core area of about 1000 square meters and may have served as an alternate residence where the royals relaxed in the shadow of the hills.

The royal palace, at the southern end of the lower city is a sprawling complex of buildings, which includes the royal chamber, the private and public audience halls, the courts of the royal guards, state guest houses and the women's quarters. A private chapel (stupa) was provided at one end of the women's quarters surrounded by pools with aquatic animals. [50]

Figure 4.7: Plinth decoration Shrine of the Double-headed eagle.

Figure 4.8: Shrine of the Double-headed Eagle.

50 Sir John Marshall. *A Guide to Taxila*, Cambridge University Press, 1960.

A striking feature of Takshasila-Sirkap city is the large number of religious buildings located in different parts of the lower city. The more important among them were the Griha stupa or the Great Apsidal Temple and the Shrine of the Double-Headed Eagle.

The Griha-Stupa, which was destroyed by an earthquake in the Scythian period, was rebuilt by the Parthians. It is located inside a courtyard measuring 70 meters by 41 meters located in Block D, the fifth block to the east, from the northern gateway. At the entrance of the courtyard, on either side, two small stupas were constructed on raised platforms. The main temple is constructed on a raised plinth at the center of the courtyard. There is a porch in the front, which provides entrance to the Pradakshina or the ambulatory passage.

Another important stupa is located in Block A, the second block to the east from the northern gateway. The stupa court at this stupa is amongst the most spacious of the stupa courts in the city. At the center of the stupa court was the stupa, surrounded by residential rooms on all four sides for the monks. A beautiful crystal casket containing the ashes of Buddha was enshrined inside the relic chamber in the stupa.

The Shrine of the Double-headed Eagle is another important Buddhist stupa in Takshasila Sirkap. It is so named because of the decorations on the plinth of the stupa, which include the carving of an eagle with two heads. The shrine is located in the central part of the lower city in its eastern flank. The decorations on the façade of the plinth have Greek as well as Scythian elements. The eagles are generally associated with Scythian traditions but the frame formed by Corinthian pilasters is of Greek design. Also Greek style pediments appear inside the two inner frames on either side of the stairs leading to the stupa.

The stupa dome was surmounted by three chattras or umbrellas. The decorations on the stupa dome, as well as the plinth were made in stucco and red paint was applied over it.

Artifacts from a Saka-Parthian City

A large number of beautiful pieces of gold and silver jewelry, silver and bronze jugs, bowl and other types of vessels, decoration pieces of Greco-Roman origin and design, hordes of coins and other luxury items have been recovered from various locations inside Saka-Parthian city of Takshasila-Sirkap. The artifacts found from various sites in Takshasila-Sirkap 'constitute the richest and the most varied collection of personal ornaments, household utensils, implements and arms that has yet been found in the Sub-continent.'[51]

Figure 4.9: Parthian jewelry from Taxila Sirkap

Among the decoration pieces of foreign origin found from Takshasila-Sirkap from the ruins belonging to the Parthian period is a beautiful bronze statuette of Harpocrates, the Egyptian child god, which probably came from Egypt, and a silver mirror with head of Dionysus in repousse. Among the earliest pieces of Gandhara sculpture were stucco heads found from the premises of the Griha-stupa.

Progress during Saka-Parthian Rule

During the rule of the Scythians and the Parthians in Gandhara the Hellenistic cultural foundations were considerably strengthened. The pattern for socio-economic and cultural development, which emerged during the Indus Greek rule, gained increased momentum after the Saka-Parthians seized control in Gandhara.

A large number of Hellenistic artists made their way into Gandhara during the Saka-Parthian Period and the production of stone sculptures and construction of stupa complex increased considerably. The Hellenistic artists possessed outstanding skills in producing stone sculptures. In the initial period of rule of Gondophares, they produced a large number of stone

---

51   Sir John Marshall. *A Guide to Taxila*, Ch.2 p. 31, Cambridge University Press 1960.

sculptures, which were alien to the culture of Greater Gandhara. These sculptures portray bawdy Bacchanalian scenes and drinking parties, and also statues of Greek gods and goddesses such as Athena and Caryatids. In due course production of these purely Hellenistic sculptures gave way to sculptures connected with the Buddhist faith, and stucco heads of Bodhisattvas and scenes from the life of Gautama Buddha began to appear in different regions of Greater Gandhara.

Figure 4.10: Carving on pedestal: Parthian Period (Courtesy Archaeological Department, Pakistan)

Buddhist texts began to be produced in the stupa complexes and sangharamas and missionaries traveled to countries along the Silk Route.

Trade and commerce picked up as more links were established with the Silk Route.

CHAPTER 5: KUSHAN EMPIRE

Figure 5.1: Kushan Empire

ORIGINS

The Yueh-chih, as the ancestors of the Kushans were known, were settled in the Tarim Basin in the 3rd century BCE. This was the time when the Central Asian nomadic hordes, known as Hsiung-nu (Xiong-nu) became organized into a Confederation and started raiding China. All through the period of the Chin and Han Dynasties in China the Hsiung-nu caused im-

mense problems to the Chinese. In second century they advanced westwards and drove the Yueh-chih out of the Tarim Basin. After being driven
out of the Tarim Basin the Yueh-chih settled on either side of the Amu
Darya, in a region called collectively in ancient times as Bactria. *Hou Han Shu*
provides detailed information on the migration of the Yueh-chih to Bactria
and their initial history in this region:

> When the Yueh-chih were destroyed by the Hsiung-nu, they mi-
> grated to Ta-hsia [Bactria] and divided the country into five *Hsi-*
> *hou* [Chiefdoms],that is to say, Hsiu-mi, Shuang-mi, Kuei-shuang
> Kuei-shuang-tun and Tumi.' Then 100 years later 'Ch'iu-chiu-ch'ueh
> [Kujula Kadphises] *hsi-hou* [Chief] of Kuei-shuang having attacked
> and destroyed [the other] four *hsi-hou* became independent and set
> himself on the throne. His kingdom was called Kuei-Shuang-wang.
> He invaded *An-hsi* [Parthia] and took the district of Kao-fu. He also
> destroyed P'u-ta [Paktiya] and Chi-pin, both of which were com-
> pletely subjugated to him. Ch'iu-chiu-chu'eh [Kujula Kadphises]
> died at the age more than eighty. Yen kao-chen became the king in
> succession.

The events described by the paragraph above cover more than a century.
The Yueh-chih first arrived in Bactria around 125 BCE. The five hsi-hou or
regions where the five tribes established their presence were located on either side of the Amu Darya—approximately the territory included in modern Bactria, Southern Tajikistan, and Southern Uzbekistan (Sogdiana). The
Kabul region (Kao-fu) and Parthia were initially not occupied by any of the
Yueh-chih tribes.

Early in second century BCE, the Han emperor, Wudi, sent Zhang Qian
as his envoy to Bactria to seek cooperation of the Yueh-chih in their battles
against the Hsiung-nu. Zhang Qian was unable to convince the Yueh-chih
to enter into an alliance with Wudi against the Hsiung-nu and returned to
Xian empty handed. Zhang Qian provides interesting information about the
Bactria and the Yueh-chih tribes settled there:

> 'The Great Yueh-chih live north of the Oxus River. They are bor-
> dered in the south by Daxia (Greco-Bactria) and on the west by Anxi
> (Parthia). They are a nation of nomads, moving from place to place
> with their herds ... They have 100,000 to 200,000 archer warriors.'

> 'Daxia (Greco-Bactria) is located south of Gui (Oxus) River. Its
> people cultivate the land and have cities and horses. It has no ruler
> but only a number of petty chiefs ruling various cities. The people
> are poor in the use of arms and afraid of battle, but they are clever
> at commerce. After the Great Yueh-chih moved west and attacked
> their lands, the entire country came under their sway. The popula-

tion of the country is large (one million or more). The capital is a city called Lanshi (Bactra) and has a market, where all sorts of goods are brought and sold ...The men have deep set eyes, and are skilful at commerce and would haggle over a fraction of a cent.'

Kujula succeeded his father Heraios as Hsi-hou-wang (King) of Bactria when he was about 30 years. During the next two decades Kujula Kadphises destroyed the leadership of the other four Yueh-chih tribes and merged their territories with the territory controlled by his faction of the Yueh-chih, the Kuei-shuang. Kujula Kadphises, the King of the expanded kingdom of the Kuei-shuang (or Kushans as they are now generally known) was not content with subjugating the other four Yueh-chih tribes. Under the leadership of Kujula Kadphises the Kushans next conquered Eastern Parthia and Kabul Region (Kao-fu), but were prevented to move south of the Hindu Kush by the might of the Indo-Parthian ruler, Gondophares. The power of the Indo-Parthians in Greater Gandhara began to wane after the death of Gondophares in 50 CE. The successors of Gondophares were Pakores in Eastern Gandhara and Abdgases in Western Gandhara, and the Parthians were now a badly divided lot. Spotting the weakness in the Parthian regimes, Kujula Kadphises attacked and conquered Western as well as Eastern Gandhara and established himself firmly in Taxila sometime around 60 CE.

KUSHAN DYNASTY

Kujula Kadphises became the founder of an Empire, which was ruled by the Kushan Dynasty, at times with great pomp and flourish, at other times, especially after 230 CE in a subdued manner, for the next three centuries.

Kujula Kadphises: 60–80 CE.

A number of scholars interpret the writings in the Hou Han Shu to mean that Kujula did not conquer Western and Eastern Gandhara, and this was done by Kujula's son, Vima Taktu, or grandson, Vima Kadphises. The basis of their assumption is that the Chinese name Chipin or Jibin refers to the Upper Kabul Valley and not Gandhara. Therefore on the basis of what has been reported by Hou Han Shu, they believe that Kujula Kadphises did not cross into Gandhara and it was left to Vima Taktu or even Vima Kadphises to establish Kushan presence in Greater Gandhara. This is, however, not supported by archaeological evidence.

During the course of archaeological excavations in the Taxila Region carried out by Sir John Marshall from 1913–1934, 2633 coins of the Kushan emperors were recovered from the site of Takshasila-Sirkap, which was the first capital of the Kushans in Greater Gandhara. Out of the 2633 coins belonging to all the Kushan emperors, 2518 belong to Kujula Kadphises. And out of 4889 coins of all the Kushan emperors found from various sites in Taxila Region, 2590 belong to Kujula Kadphises.[52] Besides, the design of the coins issued by Kujula Kadphises also indicates that they were issued from Taxila. There are a large number of coins of Kujula Kadphises in the Lahore Museum. All of them are bilingual and carry Kharoshthi legends on one side.

This overwhelming dominance of Kujula Kadphises's coins at Takshasila-Sirkap leaves no doubt that Kujula Kadphises had firmly established himself in Taxila long before his death at the age of 80 years. Kujula could not have established himself in Taxila without conquering the Lower Kabul Valley, unless he chose the eastern route via Khunjerab Pass to enter Taxila. This seems highly unlikely. So the conquest of the Lower Indus Valley was in all probability also carried out by Kujula Kadphises. The reference in *Hou Han Shu* regarding the conquest of North-west India by Kujula Kadphises's son, probably refers to the Kushan conquests north of Malakand Pass in Swat, Dir and Bajaur, and perhaps consolidation of territories conquered by Kujula Kadphises in the Lower Kabul Valley.

Kujula ruled his vast Empire from Taxila for almost 20 years from 60 C.E to 80 CE. These dates can be fixed with reasonable assurance on the basis of the fact that Kujula Kadphises ruled Gandhara about a decade after the death of Gondophares, and there are quite a few references available to indicate that Gondophares's rule in Taxila extended till 50 CE.

At the age of 30, Kujula Kadphises was fired with an ambition to become the master of a mighty Empire. After his conquest of Gandhara, he had realized this ambition to a large extent. He was sixty years old when he conquered Taxila. Instead of engaging in further warfare he spent the last two decades in strengthening his position in this newly conquered region.

Kujala's early upbringing had been in an environment, in which the basic Hellenistic culture was tempered through Mesopotamian and Persian

---

52 Sir John Marshall. *Taxila- An Illustrated Account of Archaeological excavations carried out at Taxila*, Cambridge, 1951, and Dr. Saifur Rahman Dar in *Taxila & the Western World*, Lahore, 1998.

influences. As a result he developed a liberal and tolerant attitude towards all religions—an attitude that was adopted by his successors all through Kushan rule in Gandhara. In Gandhara, Kujula came into close contact with Buddhism. He had no hesitation in adopting a positive attitude towards the Buddhist beliefs and practices. The coins of Kujula Kadphises with seated Buddha in conventional attitude on one side and Zeus on the opposite side indicate that during his two decades rule in Gandhara, Kujula had struck the right chord with the Buddhist community in Gandhara.[53]

The close association of Kujula Kadphises with Takshasila-Sirkap is indicated by the large number of coins belonging to Kujula from the ruins of the city. They indicate that Kujula not only stepped into the shoes of the Indo-Parthians, securing maximum advantage in the beautifully laid out city left by the Indo-Parthians, he also laid the sound foundations of an economy based on trade with other regions of the Kushan Empire.

The conquest of Gandhara provided a great boost to the morale of the Kushans. For the first time in their history the Kushans began to look upon themselves as a great imperial power, in the nature of the Roman Empire. Kujula issued the first Kushan coins from Taxila, which were patterned on the Roman coinage.

Kujula Kadphises initially issued coins based on the coins of the Roman emperor, Augustus, and later, also in the early period of his reign, Kujula issued coins of the last Indus-Greek ruler of the Upper Kabul Valley, Hermaeus. This can only be explained by Kujula's fascination with the Greeks and the Romans. The coins of Hermaeus issued by Kujula are inscribed with his (Kujula's) name in Kharoshthi on the reverse side. There was no family connection between Hermaeus and Kujula Kadphises. There was a period of almost a century between the death of Hermaeus and the conquest of the Kabul Valley and Gandhara by Kujula. Perhaps Kujula Kadphises wished to indicate that his rule was in a way a continuance of the culture and policies of the Indus-Greeks.

In a typical design of the coins issued by Kujula on one side is the engraving of the bust of Kujula Kadphises on the pattern of busts of Roman emperors on the Roman coins. The legend in Greek mentions the name of Kujula Kadphises. On the reverse side were images usually of Greek gods with the legend in Kharoshthi. His coins project him as 'Savior' and 'the Pious'.

---

53   R.B. Whitehead. *Catalogue of Coins in the Punjab Museum Lahore.* Oxford 1914.

Vima Taktu: 81–100 CE.

Kujula's son Vima Taktu took over the reigns of the Government some-time around 80 CE. He is referred to as Yen-caochen in Chinese chronicles and identified as the grandfather of Kanishka-I through the Rabatak Inscription in Afghanistan. About 100 bronze coins of Vima Taktu have been found from various sites in Taxila and some more from other sites in Gandhara. His coins mention him by his title Soter Megas or the Great Savior.

Vima Taktu is credited with the additional conquests in the western region of Gandhara, probably northern regions of Swat, Dir and Bajaur. Thus already in the last decade of the first century the Kushans had become masters of the entire Greater Gandhara region, including the territories east of the Indus upto the River Jhelum, the entire valley of the Kabul and Swat Rivers, west of the Indus, and the Dir and Bajaur region west of the Swat River.

Vima Kadphises: 101– 127 CE.

Vima Taktu's son, Vima Kadphises, succeeded his father around 100 CE. Vima Kadphises was the first Kushan emperor to issue high standard gold coins on the pattern of the Roman Aurei. The coins with Greek and Kharoshthi legends, were issued in three denominations, and were based on an 8-gram standard adopted by the Romans.

Vima Kadphises' reign is also significant because it marks the period of increasing affluence (of which the gold coins were one manifestation), a sharp increase in trade with countries along the Silk Route, and acceleration in construction of Buddhist monuments all over Gandhara. His sympathetic attitude towards Buddhism is further indicated by the symbol of 'Triratna' on his coins.

Vima Kadphises laid the foundations of the new Kushan capital at Takshasila-Sirsukh. A large number of his coins are among the finds from this site.[54]

Vima Kadphises was also keen to establish diplomatic relations with the Romans and with this intention sent his ambassador to the court of the Roman emperor Hadrian sometime around 120 CE.[55]

---

54 Sir John Marshall. *A Guide to Taxila*, Cambridge, 1960.
55 *Historia Augusta: 'The King of the Bactrians (Kushans) sent ambassadors to him to seek his friendship'.*

Kanishka-I: 128–150 CE.

Vima Kadphises had secured Greater Gandhara. He had brought prosperity to the region and established good relations with the majority Buddhist Community. So, when his son Kanishka succeeded him as emperor sometime around 128 CE, he could look forward to building on the foundations laid by his predecessors with ease, and further strengthening the spiritual and cultural bonds with his subjects.

Extending and consolidating his empire was high on the agenda of Kanishka after he became emperor. During the last four decades his predecessors had spent most of their time in consolidating their position in Greater Gandhara. As a result the regions conquered by great grandfather, Kujula Kadphises, in Central Asia were neglected and were slowly slipping out of the hands of the Kushans. Kanishka could now easily find time to attend to these virtually lost possessions.

Kanishka took a number of administrative measures, which enabled him to spend a good part of his 23-year reign fighting wars in Greater Bactria (the region between the Hindu Kush and the Guissar Mountains), Eastern region of Chinese Turkistan (Tarim Basin), and in the Ganges and Jumna Plains. Kanishka was immensely successful in these campaigns, as a result of which all these territories either became a part of the Kushan Empire or became vassal states of the Kushan Empire.

The Kushan royal family was a close knit family. Unlike the Indus Greeks and the Parthians, there were no feuds within the royals, which would have created several contenders to the throne and existence of multiple political entities, each under the control of different princes belonging to the royal clan. This unity within the royal Kushans based in Gandhara permitted Kanishka to be extensively engaged in military conquests in Central Asia. Kanishka's sons and other family members, along with Kanishka's local advisors like Vasumitra, ensured stability. As a result Kanishka was able to play a very active role in the religious and cultural activities of Gandhara.

Several traditions indicate that Kanishka sponsored the Fourth Buddhist Council meeting at Jalandhar, which gave birth to Mahayana Buddhism.

During Kanishka's rule the capital of the Kushan Empire was transferred to Purushapura, and Purushapura developed into the greatest city in Kushan Empire.

Among the large number of coins issued by Kanishka were two gold Dinars and three gold quarter Dinars, all of which carry portraits of Buddha.

Vasishka: 151–155 CE.

Kanishka was succeeded by Vasishka-I, who ruled for just four or five years after the death of Kanishka. His coins are rare. Among the few coins found from various sites in Greater Gandhara, there are some gold coins also. Like his father, Kanishka, Vasishka issued coins with Bactrian legends in Greek alphabets on both sides.

Huvishka: 155–190 CE.

Huvishka's main area of concentration was Gandhara, Bactria and the vassal state of Mathura in the Jumna Basin. The remaining regions conquered by Kanishka, namely the regions north of the Amu Darya and western regions of Chinese Turkistan, remained neglected after Kanishka's death. Huvishka seems to have been as great a patron of the Buddhist establishment in Gandhara as Kanishka, but fell short in enthusiastically promoting Buddhism in the manner in which Kanishka had done through his very talented Buddhist advisors.

The foundations of a prosperous Gandhara laid by Kanishka, especially through active participation in the Silk Route trade, continued to be strengthened during Huvishka's reign. This continuous prosperity is reflected in the large number of Buddhist monuments constructed in Huvishka's reign and the large number of gold and copper coins belonging to his period found from all regions of Gandhara. The prosperity and cultural interactions with countries in the west and the east also elevated the personality of Huvishka. Huvishka sent his ambassador to the court of the Roman emperor Antonius Pius, who succeeded Hadrian to the Roman throne in 138 CE.[56]

Huvishka appears on his coins as a sophisticated well-dressed regal figure. On some coins Huvishka appears riding an elephant in the royal style with a scepter in one hand and elephant goad on the other. On other elegantly designed gold coins he appears in embroidered coats and fancy helmets or headdresses, either seated or reclining on a couch.

Like Kanishka, Huvishka only used Bactrian legends in Greek script. As many as 33 different Greek, Perso-Mesopotamian and Brahmanic deities appear on the reverse side of his coins. There are 23 gold coins among the collection of 93 coins of his coins at the Punjab Museum Lahore. In the Bactrian legend on his coins found from Taxila sites, he uses the title Sha-

---

56   Aurelius Victor. *Epitome XV.4* & Appian *Praef. 7.*

onano Shao Oeshko Koshano on one side and Oesho or Miro on the opposite side. This translates to 'King of Kings, Huvishka the Kushan' and on the reverse side, 'Siva or Mithra'. The title King of Kings was first used by ancient Persian emperors and this title was also used by modern Persian rulers (Shahinshah). The use of this by Huvishka is yet another indication of the tendency among Kushan rulers to emulate the emperors of the Persian Dynasties.

Vasudeva: 190–220 CE.

Vasudeva-I, who succeeded his father, Huvishka-I, sometime around 190 CE, continued to rule Greater Gandhara and Mathura on the pattern set by his illustrious predecessors. During his rule, which was spread over three decades, the Buddhist establishment continued to prosper, and so did the economy. There was an acceleration of the activities of the Buddhist missionaries and a large number of Buddhist monks moved to Bactria and western China.

In the six gold coins among the 22 available at Punjab Museum Lahore, Vasudeva uses the title Shaonano Bazodeo Koshano (King of Kings, Vasudeva, the Kushan). He is shown wearing a peaked helmet and chainmail, making an offering at a small altar. On the reverse are the legend Oesho (Siva) and a portrait of Siva with bull.[57]

Kanishka-II: 221–230 CE.

Kanishka-II became Kushan ruler in 221 CE when major political changes were taking place in Persia, which would in due course have a major impact on the politics and trade and commerce in the region. The Sassanians under Shahpur-I invaded Western Gandhara during the rule of Kanishka-II and caused large scale destruction to Buddhist monuments, and left the Kushans highly demoralized. Four gold coins in the Pumjab Museum carry his portrait and the Bactrian legend 'Kanishko Kushano' on one side and Oesho and a portrait of Siva on the reverse.

Minor Kushan Rulers 230–350 CE.

In 230 CE the Sassanians, under Shahpur-I, conquered Western Gandhara. However, Gandhara continued to be ruled by the Kushans till the second Sassanian invasion under Shahpur-II in the 4th century. In the intervening period, 230–350 CE, eight minor Kushan kings ruled Gandhara,

---

57   R.B. Whitehead. *Catalogue of Coins in the Punjab Museum*, Oxford 1914.

including Vasishka-II, Kanishka-III and Vasudeva-II. The deterioration of Gandhara's economy after 230 CE is indicated by the fact that the last eight rulers of the Kushan Dynasty issued copper coins only.

EXTENT OF KUSHAN EMPIRE

When Kujula Kadphises founded the Kushan Empire in 60 CE with Taxila as his capital, the Kushan Empire included Greater Bactria, Anxi (Indo-Parthia), Kaofu (Kabul Region), Puda (Paktiya), Jipin (Kapisa & Gandhara) and the Taxila Region. However, after establishing himself in Taxila, the entire focus of Kujula Kadphises was on the region around Taxila. He gave very little attention to the other territories he had conquered earlier.

During the rule of Vima Taktu and Vima Kadphises the entire region of Greater Gandhara including Uddhyana (Swat, Dir & Bajaur) and Upper and Lower Kabul River Valleys became a solid part of the Kushan Empire. North of the Hindu Kush, till the Guissar Mountains, Kushans exercised some influence; but these regions were not strictly under the political control of the Kushan emperors. Probably Mathura was also established as a vassal State of the Kushan Empire during this period.

After Kanishka's conquests in Central Asia and the Tarim Basin, the Kushan Empire included besides the territories of Greater Gandhara, Greater Bactria, part of Parthia and the Tarim Basin in Chinese Xinjiang.

The Rabatak Inscription discovered a short distance away from the southern Bactrian city of Surkh Kotal (in Baghlan Province) mentions a number of cities which Kanishka says formed a part of his vast empire. The names of these cities are given as Ozene, Zageda, Kasambo, Palabotro and Ziri tambo in the Rabatak inscription, which the translator of the Rabatak Inscription, Professor Nicholas Sims-Williams, has identified with the cities of Ujjain, Saketa, Kausambi, Pataliputra and Champa. The mention of these cities and these cities only seems rather strange. Professor Sims Williams himself remarks:

> The statement that he (Kanishka) ruled Northern India as far as Pataliputra is sufficiently striking.[58]

This identification, if it is correct, obviously gives a rather exaggerated account of the extent of the Kushan Empire during Kanishka's reign. This

---

58   Professor Nicholas Sims-Williams. *New Findings in Afghanistan—the Bactrian Documents Discovered in Northern Hindu Kush*, 1997.

statement in the Rabatak Inscription is not supported by reliable archaeo-logical or historical information from other sources. At best one could agree that Kanishka invaded these territories and forced the rulers to pay trib-ute, but such an arrangement could not have lasted for very long. These ter-ritories could therefore not be considered an integral part of the Kushan Empire.

During the rule of Huvishka it seems that the territories north of Amu Darya and the Tarim Basin again became independent but Bactria (south of Amu Darya) could have remained under Kushan control. After Vasudeva's reign, during the rule of the minor rulers, the entire Central Asian region became independent.

RELIGIOUS BELIEFS AND CULTURAL ORIENTATION OF KUSHAN EMPERORS

The religious beliefs and the culture of the Kushan rulers were very much influenced by the conditions prevailing in Greater Bactria when they migrated to that region in first century BCE.

Prior to Alexander's invasion of Bactria in fourth century BCE, the dom-inant influence in Bactria was that of the Persians. The spoken language was Bactrian, a close derivative of Persian, but there is no evidence of any script being employed to write this language. The Persian and Mesopota-mian influences were also quite apparent in the deities worshipped by the Bactrians. Bactria was where Zoroaster was born in late 7th century BCE, and he must have spent at least the early part of his life here. Therefore Zo-roastrianism may have been one of the prominent religions of Bactria.

The situation began to change after Alexander invaded Bactria some-time around 330 BCE. During the next 150 years after Alexander's invasion Bactria was ruled by the Greeks. First it was ruled by the Seleucids, then after the Seleucid satrap of Bactria, Diodotus declared independence from Seleucid rule, Bactria came under the rule of the Bactrian Greeks.

During the 150-year of rule by the Greek Dynasties a large number of Greeks settled in Bactria. Although the Greeks remained very much in mi-nority in Bactria, they exercised exclusive control over this region and they had a major influence in the culture of this region. Greek became the of-ficial language of Bactria, beautiful coins with portraits of Greek rulers and deities from the Greek Pantheon became the common currency, and Greek temples were constructed employing Greek styles of architecture and decorations. During all this period the Bactrian speaking ethnic Bactrian population remained in the background. Although they must have been influenced to a certain degree by Greek culture, by and large their lifestyle remained different to that of the Greek rulers.

This situation prevailed till mid-second century BCE, when the Sakas from the Tarim Basin moved to Sogdia and then conquered Greater Bactria and put an end to the Greek rule in this region. The end of Greek rule in Bactria, although it did not result in any major changes in the official set-up of Bactria, gradually increased the participation of the ethnic Bactrians in everyday affairs. The Sakas did not possess any culture of their own and lacked the ability to install a proper administrative system of their own. So they very conveniently they stepped into the shoes of the Bactrian Greeks and retained their system of administration.

But there was a major difference in the private lifestyle of the Sakas. They felt much closer to the ethnic Bactrians and adopted their language in their private lives. They also began to worship Iranian and Mesopotamian deities.

Around 100 BCE the Yueh-chih conquered Bactria and drove the Scythians southwards to Gandhara. During the period 100 BCE to 40 CE, conditions in and around Bactria remained unsettled as the five factions of Yueh-chih battled against each other for supremacy. But in this period all the Yueh-chih tribes had an opportunity to adjust themselves to the environment prevailing in the Bactrian region.

By the time Kujula Kadphises achieved supremacy over the other Yueh-chih tribes and established the Kingdom of the Kushans in Bactria, the Kushans had adopted Bactrian as their spoken language and started worshipping a number of Iranian and Mesopotamian deities. This was the cultural status of the Kushans when Kujula Kadphises established Kushan rule in Taxila in 60 CE. His bilingual coins issued from Taxila followed the pattern used previously by the Indus Greeks and the Indo-Scythians and Indo-Parthians. They carried a Greek legend on one side and a Kharoshthi legend on the opposite side. This practice was followed by the first three emperors of the Kushan Dynasty in Greater Gandhara.

Although by the time Kanishka had ascended the throne, the Kushans had already been well-established in Gandhara for almost 70 years, they had made no attempt to learn Gandhari-Kharoshthi. They were influenced by Buddhism to some extent but none of them actually converted to Buddhism. They patronized the Buddhist establishment and gave full respect to the Buddhist community and Buddhist religion, but continued to worship a large number Iranian, Mesopotamian, and even some Indian deities. Even Kanishka, who was the greatest patron of the Buddhist institutions and sponsored the Fourth Buddhist Council on the advice of his Buddhist advisors, did not convert to Buddhism, at least not in the sense such a conversion is understood in the sub-continent and in the west.

After Kanishka became emperor, a major change took place with regard to use of languages, scripts and portraits of deities on coins. Kanishka discarded the use of Greek as well as Kharoshthi legends on the coins and instead started using legends in Bactrian language employing Greek alphabets. Also portraits or symbols of as many as 33 different deities appeared on his coins. Portrait of Buddha also appeared on some of his coins.

This practice of employing only Bactrian language legends on the coins was continued by all Kushan rulers, who followed Kanishka, including Huvishka and Vasudeva.

Although the use of Gandhari-Kharoshthi on Kushan coins was discontinued starting from the reign of Kanishka, Kharoshthi was almost exclusively employed on various types of inscriptions in Gandhara and it was also exclusively and extensively employed for compiling Buddhist texts in Gandhara all through the Kushan period, as well as for a large number of donative inscriptions in Central Asia. Kharoshthi was also employed on a fairly large scale for writing non-religious texts, such as legal documents, land transfer deeds, official letters, etc. in various parts of Xinjiang Province of China, particularly in the Kashgar-Khotan-Niya Region.

Only two Kushan Period inscriptions in Bactrian script employing monumental Greek Script (as against cursive Greek script used later by the Kushano-Sassanians) have been discovered so far, both of them from Southern Bactria, and both belonging to Kanishka, These inscriptions were carved on rocks at Surkh Kotal and Rabatak in the Baghlan Province of Afghanistan.

The Rabatak Inscription is inspired by the Rock Inscriptions of Darius the Great at Behishtun in Persia. While Darius proclaims, "By the grace of Ahurmazda am I king, Ahurmazda has granted me this kingdom[59]," Kanish-

---

59   L.W. King & R.C. Thompson. *The Sculptures and Inscriptions of Darius the Great on the Rock of Behishtun in Persia,* London 1907. This is the source of all the references pertaining to Darius quoted above.

ka owes his kingdom to Nana: "Kanishka the Kushan...worthy of worship, has obtained the kingship from Nana and from all the gods...."[60]

On the question of genealogy, Darius states, "My father is Hytaspes, the father of Hytaspes was Arsames, the father of Arsames was Ariaramnes, the father of Ariaramnes was Terispes, and the father of Terispes was Achaemenes." Kanishka has something very similar to tell us, when he mentions that Kujula Kaphises was his great grandfather, Vima Taktu was his grandfather, and Vima Kadphises was his father.

Darius provides a list of satrapies under his rule, "Elam...Bactria, Sogdia, Gandara, Scythia...," and similarly Kanishka mention the names of cities in India where he rules.

These aspirations of Kanishka throw some light on why he had opted to use Bactrian, 'the Aryan language,' on his inscriptions and coins. It is also interesting to note that while Kanishka is including regions where different languages are spoken in his Empire, he uses only Bactrian language to write down his inscriptions, which are general in character. On the other hand Darius had identical inscriptions carved on the rocks of Behishtun in three languages—Old Persian, Babylonian and Elamite.

With regard to religious beliefs, it is obvious that the Kushan concept of religion was rather primitive. They saw nothing strange in simultaneously worshipping deities of the Greek, Perso-Mesopotamian, Zoroastrian and Hindu pantheon. The need for religion was to obtain favors from the gods and to avoid their wrath. Therefore by worshipping all the gods worshipped in the region they probably thought they could obtain the maximum assistance and avoid the maximum number of dangers and calamities.

Another advantage of worshipping the deities of all the regions over which they ruled or came into contact, they probably thought, was that they hoped to earn the goodwill and political support of all the people living in their empire.

Administrative Affairs of the Kushan Empire

The Kushans were great conquerors but poor administrators. They managed to rule Greater Gandhara for almost two centuries because they had the support of the Buddhist establishment. The Buddhist establish-

---

60   Professor Nicholas Sims-Williams. *New Findings in Afghanistan—the Bactrian Documents Discovered in North Hindu Kush*, 1997.

ment had grown steadily over a period of several centuries into a closely knit organization, which enjoyed considerable support in most regions of Greater Gandhara. The Kushans had learnt from the regimes, which had ruled Gandhara earlier that they needed to keep the Buddhist establishment on their side, if they were to avoid problems in administering this region.

The previous regimes had ultimately collapsed because of infighting among their own kith and kin. The Kushans would have faced the same problem in Greater Gandhara if a powerful personality like Kujula Kadphises had not emerged to create a deep sense of unity within their clan. Throughout their period of rule in Gandhara, Kushans remained a closely knit organization. Vima Kadphises, Kanishka and other Kushan emperors could undertake military ventures in distant lands for months at a stretch without a thought ever crossing their minds that someone within their family or within their clan would undercut them and usurp their throne. Transition of rule from one emperor to another was always smooth. This was certainly not the case with the Indus Greeks or the Indo-Scythians or the Indo-Parthians. .

But what worked for the Kushans within Greater Gandhara would obviously not work for them outside Greater Gandhara. The social conditions and the political and the physical environments were quite different. And there was no such organization like the Buddhist establishment in Gandhara to help them administer the conquered territories in Bactria, or Sogdiana or in Tajikistan or Turkmenistan or the Tarim Basin or in the Jumna Basin. They knew how to create terror in the minds of many of the petty rulers; they knew how to use their steeds and their quills to vanquish powerful enemies, but they did not possess the political acumen or the administrative capability to maintain control over the conquered territories.

The Great Kushan Empire was great because it had the civilized Gandharans behind it. The Kushans plundered other nations and the Gandharans put the wealth they brought back to good use. The Kushans made the the Silk Routes possible and the Gandharan traders followed in their tracks to bring back luxury goods, which the growing affluent society of Gandhara required to satisfy its appetite for fancy items. The system worked in Gandhara.

Kujula Kadphises conquered the entire territory between the Hindu Kush and the Guissar Mountains (Greater Bactria) before heading south to conquer the Kabul River Valley and Eastern Gandhara. He obviously left the administration of the conquered territories in Greater Bactria in the hands of his trusted lieutenants, but there is no evidence to suggest that he provided his representatives with sufficient military troops, or established an effective link with his own organization in Taxila. The obvious happened. The tribes that had been defeated by Kujula Kadphises soon regained control of their territories.

After Kanishka re-conquered Greater Bactria, he tried to solve the problem faced by his great-grandfather by shifting the capital of his Empire to Purushapura, which was conveniently located at a short communicating distance with the Bactrian heartland. In addition he made it his policy to spend the summers in Kapisa, the gateway to Bactria, and his winters in Purushapura. This system worked satisfactorily during the period of rule by Kanishka. However, the later Kushan emperors tried to control Greater Bactria from Purushapura, and this system did not work.

More than five centuries earlier the Achaemenids had introduced the satrapy system, which enabled them to rule over their vast Empire reasonably well, although they also encountered some problems from time to time because they spent too much time fighting the Greeks and did not give sufficient attention to their satrapies in the east. However, there was a good chance that the system would have worked for the Kushans because they were not involved in Western Asia, and Central Asia looked manageable with a powerful satrap, who was sufficiently well-equipped militarily and administratively to counter the threat from the enemies of the Empire. But putting in place an effective satrapy system was not within the capabilities of the Kushans. They were cast in a totally different mold compared to the Achaemenids.

At Kashgar, Kanishka installed a king of his choice, who enjoyed the support of a sizeable section of the population of Kashgar-Khotan-Niya Region. With Kanishka spending a lot of his time in the Kapisa (Begram) area, the vassal Kingdom of Kashgar survived, but after Kanishka's death, this kingdom also slipped out of Kushan control.

The case of the vassal Kingdom of Mathura was similar, but because Huvishka and Vasudeva devoted sufficient time and effort during their reign towards the control of Mathura, Mathura remained attached to the Kushan Empire till after the death of Vasudeva.

The Kushans may have conquered many lands and subjugated peoples of various nationalities, but in essence it was Greater Gandhara, which sustained the Kushan Empire. Without Gandhara there would have been no Kushan Empire, but minus the other territories, which for some time remained a part of the Kushan Empire, Kushan Empire still remained in force.

Greater Gandhara was at the root of all thatthe Kushan Empire stood for, as is indicated in the following paragraphs.

Core Area and Administrative Base

After Kujula Kadphises conquered Eastern Gandhara in first century CE, the political and administrative base of the Kushan Empire shifted from Bactria to Gandhara and it remained in Gandhara all through the three centuries during which Kushans Empire lasted.

Takshasila-Sirkap, which was already an important center of international trade, became the capital of the Kushan Empire founded by Kujula Kadphises. Kujula's entire focus was on setting up an administrative organization at Takshasila-Sirkap through which he could secure Gandhara and effectively govern this newly conquered region. He successfully managed to keep the Parthians, who were still active on the western borders of Gandhara, at bay, and generated a lot of political and economic activity in the newly established capital. Gandhara was the only region, which really mattered during Kujula Kadphises' reign. The regions north of the Hindu Kush went into oblivion as far as Kushan rule was concerned.

During the reign of Kujula's son, Vima Taktu, also Gandhara remained the political base of the Kushan Empire and the only region where Vima Taktu was politically active.

When Vima Kaphises succeeded Vima Taktu, the infrastructure available at Takshasila-Sirkap was not sufficient to handle complexities of an extended Empire, which included the politically active regions of Uddhyana and Upper Kabul Valley. Around 100 CE, with the Kushans firmly established in Gandhara, and only Greater Gandhara, Vima Kadphises decided to construct a new city at the site of Taxila-Sirsukh, which became the new political base of the Kushan Empire.

The location of the administrative capital of the Kushan Empire once again came under review when Vima Kadphises' son, Kanishka, succeeded him as emperor sometime around 128 CE. The focus of the new emperor was on further extending and consolidating the Kushan Empire. This meant that Kanishka would be spending a lot of time away from Gandhara in regions as far north as Sogdiana and Turkistan, and as far east as the Tarim Basin. It would have been difficult to remain in touch with the central administration at Takshasila-Sirsukh, which was located near the south-eastern boundary of his empire. Kanishka therefore decided to shift his capital from Takshasila-Sirsukh to Purushapura (modern Peshawar). Purushapura was centrally located between Gandhara and Bactria, and at the mouth of the Khyber Pass. Kanishka could therefore visit his capital during breaks in his military campaigns in Central Asia, and regularly keep in touch with his central administration.

All through the tenancy of the Kushan Empire, Greater Gandhara was the only region where peace and stability prevailed and which was permanently under the control of the Kushan emperors. The second most important region in the Kushan Empire was Greater Bactria (the extended Bactrian region from the Hindu Kush in the South to the Guissar Mountains in the Uzbekistan-Tajikistan region). All the Kushan emperors considered this region their home turf, but except for Kanishka, no other Kushan ruler was prepared to maintain a strong physical presence in the region. The result was that in extended Bactria a very tenuous situation prevailed and the region continued to pop in and out of the political control of the Kushan emperors.

It was only during the rule of Kanishka that the Kushans were able to exercise some degree of political control over regions in Central Asia. Kanishka may have spent an appreciable portion of his time in Central Asia but there is no doubt that his real political base remained Gandhara and Gandhara only. Gandhara provided the glamour to Kanishka's court. Gandhara absorbed most of the wealth Kanishka mustered through his conquests and it was only in Greater Gandhara that wealth accumulated through the lucrative Silk Route Trade was effectively put to use.

Kanishka also conquered the Tarim Basin during the early part of his reign. He did not establish even a regional capital of his regime in Tarim Basin. Instead Kanishka put in place a regime at Kashgar, which was answerable to him. The king of Kashgar also ruled over the Khotan region of the Tarim Basin. During Kanishka's reign and even after that, till end of second third century, cultural and trade links of this region with Gandhara remained strong. The political alliance worked out by Kanishka by installing a King of his choice in Kashgar, however, remained effective only during the rule of Kanishka.

In the east, the Indo-Scythian king of Gandhara, Azes-I had conquered Mathura some time around 38 BCE and placed Mathura under the Indo-Scythian satrap, Rajuvala. Mathura remained attached to the Indo-Scythian-Parthian regime based in Taxila, as long as this regime lasted. As a result the small Buddhist community, which existed at the time in Mathura, received sustenance from the fast developing Buddhist establishment in Greater Gandhara.

After the Kushans established themselves in Taxila, Mathura became a vassal State of the Kushan Empire. This position was reaffirmed after Kanishka extended his conquests to the Jumna Basin, and Mathura came under increasing cultural influence of the Buddhist establishment in Gandhara. The images of Buddha and various postures and symbols used in Buddha images, which were developed in Gandhara, were introduced in Mathura, along with the Kharoshthi language.

Mathura subsequently developed an art style, which showed influences of Hindu mythology. Some of these influences penetrated into Gandhara in the shape of portraits of Shiva and Nandi on the coins of Kushan emperors, mainly Huvishka and Vasudeva. The divergence in art styles and differences in religious beliefs in Mathura and Gandhara, indicate that Mathura never really integrated into the Kushan Empire or into the Buddhist civilization of Gandhara.

Huvishka and Vasudeva ensured that Mathura remained within the political ambit of the Kushan regime in Gandhara by increasing contacts with this region, and as was the Kushan policy, adopting some of the deities ingrained in the culture of Mathura. But Mathura was an isolated town on the banks of the Jumna River, separated by a distance of several hundred kilometers from the heartland of the Kushan Empire (Gandhara). Accordingly the bonds of Mathura with the Kushan Empire as well as with Greater Gandhara always remained very weak, and unlike Central Asia, where Buddhism spread over a very vast area, Buddhist activism in Mathura remained confined to a small community there in an environment dominated by the Hindu establishment.

Mathura only remained a vassal State of the Kushan Empire, and that also till 230 CE, when Vasudeva's rule in Gandhara came to an end and the Sassanians invaded Gandhara. There never was any question of Mathura

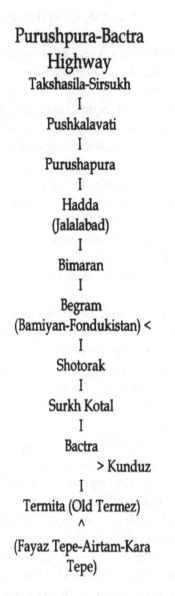

Purushpura-Bactra Highway

Takshasila-Sirsukh

I

Pushkalavati

I

Purushapura

I

Hadda
(Jalalabad)

I

Bimaran

I

Begram
(Bamiyan-Fondukistan) <

I

Shotorak

I

Surkh Kotal

I

Bactra

> Kunduz

I

Termita (Old Termez)

^

(Fayaz Tepe-Airtam-Kara Tepe)

Figure 5.2: Purushapura-Bactra Highway (*connecting Gandhara with important Budhist cultural and commercial centers in Central Asia in the Kushan Period*)

serving as one of the capitals of the Kushan Empire. While the Kushans were firmly established over the very substantial area of Greater Gandhara, Mathura was by comparison a very small political entity, a peripheral area of a regime based in Gandhara.

Cultural Center

Gandhara was by far the most culturally developed region in the Kushan Empire. The culture of Gandhara had the strength to influence the culture of all other regions included in the Kushan Empire and beyond. These cultural transmissions made up for the inability of the Kushan emperors to bind all the conquered regions together through physical force. The cultural influence which Gandhara exerted proved to be a much greater force in bringing the people of various regions together.

The dominating influence in the culture of Gandhara was that of Mahayana Buddhism. Mahayana Buddhism offered a complete package for healthy living. It appealed to the hearts and minds of the people and allowed the followers the flexibility to strike a proper balance between their spiritual and worldly lives.

To Gandhara goes the credit for developing progressive institutions, which gave practical shape to the spirit embodied in the Mahayana scriptures. The institutions developed by the Buddhist establishment in Gandhara catered to the spiritual as well as the social needs of the people. The sangharamas assumed the responsibility for promoting healthy lifestyles. This became the guiding principle for sangharamas developed in other regions of the Kushan Empire, and as a result lifestyles of the people living in other regions of the Kushan Empire were appreciably influenced by the culture of Gandhara.

In the large number of sangharamas, which were constructed all over Gandhara during the Kushan period, special attention was given to making these places physically attractive and entertaining for the visitors. To fulfill this requirement enormous attention was given to the development of beautiful stone sculptures, which were extensively employed to decorate the sangharamas. This special form of sculptural art developed in Gandhara, became popular in other regions of the Kushan Empire as well. Sculptors in far off places such as Termez in Uzbekistan and Ashkabad in Turkmenistan, and Fondukistan and Kakrak in Bamiyan Valley of Afghanistan adopted the styles, themes and compositions employed in the Buddhist sculptures produced in Gandhara. Gandhara developed images of Buddha and Bodhisattvas on the pattern of images of Greek gods and incorporated Greco-Persian features in the sculptures such as folds of robes and hairstyles. These styles and features strongly influenced the styles and features employed in images of Buddhas and Bodhisattvas, which were used in the stupas and temples in other regions of the Kushan Empire.

In the literary field also, Gandhara played the dominant role in the Kushan Empire. Most of the literature produced was in the form of religious texts and commentaries. These texts and commentaries were written in Gandhari language and Kharoshthi. As a result a lot of people in the Central Asian region of Kushan Empire became familiar with this language and script. This facilitated interactions between Gandhara and these regions at various levels.

Commercial Hub

Gandhara became a major commercial hub in the Kushan Period. During Kanishka's reign, the goods plundered during conquests in various countries of Central Asia found their way into Gandhara and added to the wealth of Gandhara. Also the tributes paid by local rulers filled the coffers of the Kushan Treasury and Gandhara reached the height of its prosperity.

As a result of the conquests of a large number of countries in Central Asia which were located on the Silk Route, the Kushans were able to exercise a certain degree of control over the goods passing through this route. This control enabled them to have a share in the profits in the lucrative trade between Rome and China.

Because of its geographical location, Gandhara also became much more actively engaged in trade with Central Asia and Western China. As Gandhara was located off the main Silk Route, most of the trade conducted by traders from Gandhara was through Exchange Stations.

In the third century another development took place on the political front which benefited Gandhara immensely. The Sassanids became powerful in Persia and, due to enmity with the Romans, created problems in passage of goods being traded by Rome with China. Due to the Sassanid blockade the goods being traded between Rome and China were routed through Gandhara and transported on the Indus Waterway to and from the Arabian Sea ports on the mouth of the Indus, which were connected by sea to the Near East, Egypt and Rome.

This arrangement generated enormous revenues for Gandhara and led to the strengthening of the trading infrastructure in this region.

The Purushapura-Bactra Highway was extensively used by traders, missionaries and random travelers during the Kushan Period, It contributed immensely to the political, cultural and economic integration of Greater Gandhara with Central Asia. A large number of towns and cities grew up or increased their stature when these regions became a part of the Kushan Empire.

Under the Kushans, Gandhara, for the first time in its history, became the center and the base of an Empire, which stretched beyond the Amu Darya, as far north as the Guissar Mountains of Tajikistan-Uzbekistan.

While in theoretical terms, after the conquest of Gandhara by Kujula Kadphises in 60 CE, Gandhara became connected politically to regions as far north as the Guissar Mountains, in practical terms the political unification of Gandhara with the regions north of the Hindu Kush was only effective during the rule of Kanishka from 128 CE till 151 CE.

However the cultural and trade relations between Gandhara and Central Asia were considerably strengthened after the conquest of Gandhara by Kujula Kadphises, and these close relations were maintained till the end of Vasudeva's rule in 230 CE.

Chapter 6: The Golden Age

> Art from that fund each supply provides,
> Works without show, and pomp presides:
> With spirit feeds, with vigor fills the whole,
> Each motion guides, and ev'ry nerve sustains;
> Itself unseen, but th' effect remains.
> —Alexander Pope

In the period 60 CE to 230 CE, the entire Peshawar Valley, Swat and Taxila regions sprung to life under the enlightened umbrella of more than a thousand sangharamas. These sangharamas were transformed into dynamic institutions through funds provided by the regime and the donors, and through guidance and control provided by the Buddhist scholars attached as advisors to the Kushan emperors. They played an effective role in taking care of the spiritual, social and cultural requirements of the population.

Through the patronage of the Kushan emperors a well organized and mature Buddhist fraternity emerged. The creative activities of almost 20,000 Buddhist monks working in the Buddhist institutions not only provided spiritual and administrative support to the Kushan regime, it also helped in bringing order, peace and tranquility into the lives of the Gandharans.

On the economic front the wealth pouring into the country through the Silk Route trade and conquests of the Kushan emperors resulted in a lot of new initiatives taken by the businessmen and entrepreneurs, which strengthened the Commercial and Industrial base of the country and brought about a very noticeable change in the living standards of the people.

Under the Kushans, for the first time in its history, Gandhara became the center and the base of one of the great Empires. This Empire stretched as far north as the Amu Darya, embracing the politically and culturally active region of Bactria. During some periods in the two centuries of rule by the main branch of the Kushans, the Empire also included the entire region of Sogdiana, western part of the Tarim Basin and north-eastern India as far as Bihar.

In the two centuries prior to establishing their control over Gandhara, the Kushans became 'semi-civilized'. They assimilated local culture, became familiar with the Greek language and script and were introduced to a number of Greek, Persian and Mesopotamian deities, who were supposed to protect them from the evil spirits and lead them on the path of salvation. However, during their rule in Bactria they could only savor the sophisticated environment of Gandhara from a distance. Their cultural background, their wild nomadic roots, limited exposure to the higher values in life, prevented them from fully adopting civilized ways, interact effectively with the masses, and partake fully in the rich spiritual experience, such as the one Gandhara had to offer. They remained somewhat confused, bewildered, embroiled in petty pursuits and military adventures.

After the Kushans became firmly entrenched in the Gandhara region, a major change came about in their outlook. They were impressed with the culture of Gandhara; they were dazzled with its wealth. They found the physical and socio-economic environment of Gandhara more to their liking than that of Bactria. They found Gandhara ideally situated for launch of their military ventures. They found the local Buddhist population peaceful and reclusive, morally strong and disciplined, and intellectually inclined.

The Kushan emperors could therefore not remain untouched for long by the great civilization, which was taking shape in Gandhara. Their relations with the local population, which were initially quite superficial and lacking in depth, gradually began to change. Kanishka and the emperors who followed him appointed local spiritual and administrative advisors to interface with the local population. They doled out bounties, flirted with, and extensively patronized the Buddhist establishment. The Kushans at the level of the ordinary citizens learnt Gandhari language and made limited use of the Kharoshthi script.

The struggle between the traditionalists and the liberals (also referred to as revisionists) is a phenomenon which has been witnessed over and over again in many religious and national movements. It was one such struggle which gave birth to Mahayana Buddhism in Gandhara.

The liberal factions of Buddhism initiated a process for reformation of Buddhism in Gandhara in fourth century BCE. The official approval of the Mahayana Sutras at the Fourth Buddhist Council convened by the Kushan emperor, Kanishka, around 100 CE, was the culmination of that process.

Early Development

The Mahasanghikas established the foundations of the Mahayana doctrine in Gandhara. The Mahasanghikas were isolated by the traditionalists in the core areas of early Buddhism around Bihar after disagreement between the traditional conservatives, the Sthaviravadins (Elders), and the liberal faction, the Mahasanghikas (Members of the Great Order), at the Second Buddhist Council meeting in Vaishali in 383 BCE. A large number of them moved to Gandhara, where they found the multicultural and relatively liberal religious environment much to their liking.

During the meeting of the Third Buddhist Sangha, another division took place among the Buddhist community. The divergent views of the Sarvastivadins were rejected by Third Buddhist Sangha, and the Sarvastivadins, following on the footsteps of the Mahasanghikas, began to migrate to Gandhara. These Sarvastivadins soon emerged as the major sect among the Buddhists in Gandhara.

About the same time as the Sarvastivadins began to emerge as a major sect among the Buddhists in Gandhara, members belonging to another sect, which professed very similar views, were also making their presence felt in Gandhara. These Buddhists belonged to the Dharmaguptika sect. The substantial, perhaps overriding, presence of the Sarvastivadin and Dharmaguptika sects in the pre-Kushan period in Gandhara is indicated by a number of donative inscriptions found from Sirkap, Kalawan and other monasteries in Taxila.

During the rule of the Saka-Parthians (90 BCE–60 CE) the Sarvastivadins were singled out for support by the Scythian and Parthian rulers, as their dominance among the Buddhist community in Gandhara had been virtually established. In this period the face of Mahayana Buddhism had already emerged in Gandhara. Starting with Sutras belonging to the Perfection of Wisdom series other main Mahayana texts were being compiled in the Gandhari language. However, the entire Buddhist community of Gandhara was not yet totally behind the basic Mahayana concepts advanced by the Sarvastivadins.

After the arrival of the Kushans under Kujala Kadphises, the process of compilation of Mahayana Sutras was accelerated. With the Sarvastivadins dominating the Buddhist movement in Gandhara, a much broader consensus began to emerge on basic Mahayana concepts and the texts of the Mahayana Sutras. The Sarvastivadins became officially associated with the Kushan regime and Kanishka appointed one of their leading scholars, Vasumitra, as his spiritual advisor.

Vasumitra was one of the shining lights of Gandhara Civilization. He was a Buddhist scholar par excellence, who played a very active role in the development of Mahayana Sutras. Vasumitra also wrote a treatise, *The Eighteen Schools of Buddhism*, on which an article was published by Rev. S. Beal in Journal of Oriental Research.[61] Rev. Beal refers to Vasumitra as 'one of the patriarchs who lived about the time of Kanishka and goes on to state that 'His aim was to reconcile the difference that existed in traditions, customs, and acknowledged scriptures, and it was under his auspices or by his influence that the Great Council (Fourth Buddhist Council) was held that rearranged the Buddhist Canon as it is known in the north (Mahayana Sutras).'

Establishment of Basic Mahayana Doctrines

Vasumitra's efforts on establishment of unanimity in view of the liberal Buddhists led the establishment of basic Mahayana doctrine of Trikaya and firmed up the basic concept of the Bodhisattva.

Quite early in the history of Buddhism in Gandhara the Sthavira concept of Buddha as just an enlightened human being did not satisfy a growing number of members of the Buddhist community. The speculations made by the followers of the Mahasanghikas in the fourth century BCE began to gain increasing support among the Buddhist community in Gandhara. Around 250 BCE the Sarvastivadins came up with a view that Buddha had a past, present and future, and the historical Buddha was just one manifestation of a divine being.

---

61 *The Eighteen Schools of Buddhism*, Rev. S. Beal, *The Indian Antiquary*, a Journal of Oriental Research, Vol. IX 1880.

This divine status of Buddha became the subject of intense deliberations by the later Sarvastivadins. The profound nature of the doctrine, which emerged to explain the true nature of Buddha, indicates that the subject must have been meditated, debated and discussed by Sarvastivadin scholar-monks before the final refined version of the Trikaya or three bodies doctrine emerged. Trikaya explains the threefold nature of eternal Buddha through the three bodies—a body of essence, a body of communal bliss and a body of transformation.

Mahayana Buddhists refer to the first of these bodies as Dharmakaya, the Dharma body or the body of essence. It represents the inner nature of Buddha, the absolute reality, the true nature of being, which can only be realized through transcendental wisdom (it is an experience of transcendence, a divine experience so to say, a something that cannot be perceived by the five human senses).

The second body, the body of Bliss (Sambhogakaya), is assumed by the five cosmic Buddhas. These eternal Buddhas are suppose to sustain the universe. They are perceived as spiritual fathers of the earthly Buddhas, like Gautama (and many others like him in other universes). It is a state that cannot be perceived by the senses but can be experienced spiritually.

The third body is the Nirmanakaya, or body of transformation. It refers to Buddha's presence on earth in human form. The divine being assumes the physical form of a mortal, as in the case of the historical Buddha, in order to preach the Dharma and lead human beings towards the path of enlightenment.

Besides the concept of Trikaya, the other concept, which the Buddhist scholars needed to agree upon, was that of the Bodhisattva. The seeds of the evolution of the concept of Bodhisattva were sown by the Mahasanghikas when they proclaimed that the path of enlightenment was open to all Buddhists, monks as well as other practitioners of the faith. The path of enlightenment, which essentially meant cultivating the lives according to the teachings of Buddha, was later elaborated by sects who held similar views to those of the Mahasanghikas, particularly the Sarvastivadins.

This led to the crystallization of the view that through the cultivation of the six perfections, namely generosity, morality, patience, vigor, meditation (contemplation) and wisdom, even a lay Buddhist could become a Bodhisattva. An example of a lay Buddhist, who had succeeded in this way was said to be Amitabha, who was initially a lay Buddhist, then a monk, then a Bodhisattva, and finally became a celestial Buddha.

Another Bodhisattva, who captured the imagination of the Buddhists of Gandhara, was Avalokitesvara. He represented compassion and was regarded as a manifestation of Amitabha, the Buddha of compassion. He came to be referred to in a number of Mahayana Sutras, including Heart Sutra and the Lotus Sutra.

The third Bodhisattva conceived by the Gandhara scholars was Maitreya, who was regarded as the future Buddha, waiting for his rebirth in the Tushita Heaven.

After agreement on these basic doctrines, the time was ripe for the Sangha to meet in order to give a final shape to the Mahayana scriptures. Accordingly Vasumitra advised Kanishka to convene the meeting of the Fourth Buddhist Council. This Council was convened by Kanishka in Jalandhar around 128 CE. The Council meetings led to the compilation and approval of the Mahayana Sutras by a Sangha comprising of 500 Buddhist Sarvastivadin scholars.

The convening of the Fourth Buddhist Council in Jalandhar is significant because this was the first time that the Sangha was called to meet in the north-western region of South Asia. This is an indication of the fact that that during the rule of Kanishka, Mahayana thought had achieved a certain level of maturity and the emerging Mahayana doctrines were accepted by majority of members of the Buddhist community in Greater Gandhara. Also, through the zeal and enthusiasm of the Sarvastivadins, who were concentrated in Gandhara, this region had become a fertile ground for the Buddhist movement, whereas in other regions of South Asia, the progress of the Buddhist movement was being checked by the Brahmans.

The Fourth Buddhist Council was obviously a watershed in the history of the Mahayana movement. It signaled the crystallization of core Mahayana philosophies after centuries of deliberations by individuals and at various schools of thought in Gandhara.

During the course of the proceedings at the Fourth Buddhist Council, Triptaka, the fundamental scripture of Buddhism, came under total review; the Sutra Pitaka, which contains the Discourses of Buddha, was amended and expanded to include core Mahayana Sutras, such as the Lotus Sutra, Perfection of Wisdom Sutra and the Diamond Sutra. Relative minor changes were made in the Vinaya Pitaka to bring it in line with Mahayana rules on monastic discipline; and the Abhidharma Pitaka, which contains commentaries on the Sutras and Vinaya.

Similarly, the Triratna, which defines three fundamental objects of worship in Buddhism, was reviewed and revised to accommodate all Buddhas recognized by Mahayana believers. Mahayana Sutras were made part of the Dharma and provision was made in the third Ratna for Bodhisattvas along with other community of monks.

SANGHARAMAS GALORE

An important feature of the Golden Age of the Gandhara Civilization was the uniform distribution of a large number of sangharamas over the entire region of Greater Gandhara. Several thousand sangharamas dotted the vacant spaces in inhabited areas. They were located in the plains, on plateaus and on flat surfaces created within mountains. Terraces were cut out on the slopes of mountains to construct stupas and the monasteries at different levels.

In the early years of Buddhism in Gandhara the general policy of the Buddhist priests was to locate the sangharamas away from the hustle and bustle of crowded settlements. This policy was revised. Sangharamas now began to be constructed within the urban limits as well as outside. New designs of stupa courts and monastic establishments emerged to minimize disturbances in crowded areas. High-walled viharas emerged, which ensured privacy to the monks and allowed various activities in the viharas to be conducted in relative seclusion. The stupas, which were located outside the viharas, were systematically arranged in several courts to conserve space. Small stupas were constructed in a concentric pattern around the larger stupas and also in niches created within the walls of the stupa yards.

While new sangharamas were being added to the existing ones to meet the demands of new settlements and of communities dispersed from the central location of existing sangharamas, a very large part of the construction activity consisted of expansion, renovation and repairs in existing sangharamas. Existing construction was strengthened through use of more durable materials and a major effort was made to decorate the sangharamas with sculptures and reliefs. Terraces were constructed around the stupas with plastered faces, which were divided into panels by Corinthian pilasters and the space between the pilasters was decorated with reliefs and statues. Similarly the chapels in the stupa yards as well as within the high-walled viharas were provided with magnificent images of Buddha and Bodhisattvas and decorated with sculptures.

The sangharamas assumed a different character during the Kushan Period. Plenty of funds were available, the regime was sympathetic to and highly dependent on the Buddhist establishment, and the overall environment was highly conducive for intellectual activities. All this brought about a major qualitative as well a quantitative change in the activities at the sangharamas. The activities at the sangharamas became more diversified and more focused. Apart from the provisions in the sangharamas for performance of its traditional functions of attending to the spiritual concerns of the general Buddhist population, the sangharamas now geared itself up for arriving at a consensus on major religious issues and for the spread of these ideas in an organized manner.

An assembly hall became a standard feature in the larger sangharamas, where scholar-monks met regularly to debate on various religious issues, which led to high degree of unanimity on basic Mahayana doctrines.

Training of Buddhist monks for educating the masses and for missionary work abroad became an important function of the Buddhist establishment and suitable arrangements were made at the sangharamas for this purpose.

Basically two categories of sangharamas emerged, one for performance of routine religious functions and the other where the focus was on specialized activities.

The simpler types of sangharamas were mostly located within the urban limits, where the people were more cramped for time and could just devote an hour or so before or after work to say prayers at the chapels located in the sangharamas or to make small donations in cash or place garlands or flowers in front of the deities.

The sangharamas belonging to the second category were meant for specialized activities, including celebration of festivals or for other gatherings of a social nature. In these sangharamas, such as the ones at Dharmarajika and Takht-i-Bahi, special provisions were made for scriptoriums, assembly halls, libraries and training institutes. Visiting scholars also spent some time at these sangharamas to consult the literature available at the libraries and to discuss various religious issues with the masters. These sangharamas were usually located some distance away from the urban centers.

Kharoshthi script had been increasingly used in Gandhara since the rule of the Mauryans, but the main application, besides inscriptions on coins, was for inscriptions made by devotees while making donations of statues or stupas to sangharamas. Making these inscriptions on hard surfaces such as stone or metals was a relatively simple affair, but the volume of these inscriptions was necessarily limited by the material. A more flexible and easily transmittable material was required for writing longer texts.

In the spurt of missionary activities, which followed the activation of the Silk Route during the Indo-Parthian period, the need for producing Buddhist texts in written form began to be increasingly felt, and the Sarvastivadin monks and monks belonging to other sects in Gandhara, found an innovative solution by writing Buddhist texts on birch bark leaves. So a medium for producing written Buddhist literature had been created before the powerful movement was generated by scholars such as Vasumitra and Asvaghosha for getting official approval of the Mahayana Sutras and for preserving the Mahayana Sutras in authentic form.

After the official approval given to the Mahayana Sutras at the Fourth Buddhist Council during Kanishka's reign, the established medium of compiling texts on birch paper began to be put to use in a very organized manner to produce large volumes of Mahayana texts for the use of missionaries and other scholars.

Sangharamas had by now been firmly established as the focal point of all Buddhist activities in Gandhara. It therefore came naturally to the scholars at the helm of Buddhist affairs in Kanishka's court to provide special facilities at the major sangharamas for producing authentic versions of Mahayana Sutras on a large scale.

The facilities established at the major sangharamas took the shape of Scriptoriums. Scriptoriums existed in several formats in the sangharamas of Greater Gandhara. Usually in the larger monasteries in Gandhara such as Dharmarajika, Jaulian, Mohra Muradu, Shahji-ki-Dheri, Takht-i-Bahi and Butkara, special provisions seem to have been made by employing some courts or cells exclusively for producing manuscripts. But producing Buddhist texts was not confined to formal scriptoriums. Even where such special provisions were not available, well-trained monks carried out such activities inside their living quarters or even in open spaces such as veranda's or inner quadrangle of the vihara.

Under arrangements overseen by the advisors in Kanishka's court, well-trained and literate groups of Buddhist scholars converged in the sangharamas, where they took upon themselves the huge and laborious task of producing in the Gandhari vernacular and Kharoshthi script, the Mahayana versions of the Tripitaka and the vast body of new scriptures known as Mahayana Sutras. Volumes after volumes of texts were compiled for the use of thousands of members of the Buddhist clergy and for missionary work. Well-stocked libraries emerged in each sangharama, which served to educate the resident trainee-monks as well as visiting scholars.

The period when largest number of volumes of literature in the Gandhari language using the Kharoshthi script were compiled in Gandhara, was 2nd century CE. Under Kanishka's patronage, and zeal of highly motivated scholars, the activities of the Buddhist Church in Gandhara reached their zenith. The favorable environment attracted Buddhist scholars from all regions of South Asia, China and Central Asia.

Evidence of scriptoriums at a large number of monasteries in Gandhara is provided by two main sources:

First, the evidence has been provided by the manuscripts of Buddhist texts in the Gandhari language written with black ink on birch bark, which have been found from several sites in southeastern Afghanistan and Xinjiang. Studies carried out by various scholars indicate that these manuscripts originated from scriptoriums located in Greater Gandhara.

Second, manuscripts of Buddhist texts in Chinese have been studied by different scholars who have come to the conclusion that the originals of these were composed in Gandhari-Kharoshthi. Obviously Buddhist missionaries from Greater Gandhara, and Chinese monks who visited Gandhara, brought these Gandhari manuscripts from Greater Gandhara to China, and translations of these manuscripts were carried out in the translation bureaus in places such as Luoyang and Xian.

The traditions linked to the visits of Chinese scholar-monks such as Xsiuen Tsang indicate that mule-loads of Buddhist manuscripts were carried back to China by these scholar-monks at the conclusion of their visits to Gandhara.

The existing original Buddhist manuscripts in the Gandhari language-Kharoshthi script include the Gandhari Dharmapada and fragment of

Gandhari Mahaparinirvana Sutra found from Khotan area of Chinese Turkistan, thirteen rolls of fragmentary Gandhari Buddhist texts on birch bark from Hadda, near Jalalabad, Afghanistan, and manuscripts from other sites which are now available in the Schoeyen and Seniors collections.

The fragments from Gandhari Dharmapada were found from a site in near Khotan in 1892. They are also known as the Dutreil de Rhins documents. They have been studied in detail by several scholars including John Brough of the Oxford University, and there is unanimity on the opinion of all scholars with regards to the origin of these manuscripts from Gandhara.[62]

The 13 scrolls of birch bark found from Hadda were examined by Prof. Richard Saloman, who believes that these manuscripts came from the library or scriptorium of a Gandhara Buddhist monastery and that "they represent a very small fraction of the total amount of literature in the monastery's library."

The preliminary study carried out by Prof. Richard Saloman indicates that the manuscripts comprise of Rhinoceros Sutra, Avadana texts, Canonical Sutra texts and Abhidharma texts. The examination of these texts led Prof. Saloman to the following conclusion:

> The new discovery thus confirms what already seemed likely, namely, that the Gandhara Buddhists in the early centuries of the Christian era did have a substantial corpus of written scriptures in the Gandhari language comprising of considerable variety of genres ranging from didactic poetry to scholastic Abhidharma.[63]

As the Buddhist monks of Greater Gandhara almost exclusively employed birch bark for inscribing the sacred Buddhist texts, this being a highly perishable material, hardly any manuscripts have survived in the climate and physical environment of Greater Gandhara. (The manuscripts from Hadda survived because they were stored in ceramic pots). Some charred birch bark manuscripts have, however, been found from Dharmarajika and Jaulian during excavations carried out by Sir John Marshall.[64]

---

62 John Brough's book *Gandhari Dharmapada* was published in 1962. He discusses all aspects of discovery, publication and language of the manuscript from Khotan.

63 Professor Richard Saloman: A preliminary survey of some early Buddhist manuscripts recently acquired by the British Library in The Journal of American Oriental society, Volume 117 No. 2, 1997

64 *A Guide to Taxila*, Ch.8 & 14, Sir John Marshall, Cambridge University Press, 1960

The writings of Chinese scholar Hsiuen Tsang also indicate that producing manuscripts was a common feature of sangharamas in various parts of Gandhara.[65]

Among the large number of Buddhist texts produced in the scriptoriums of Gandhara, and translated by Buddhist missionaries from Gandhara in China, the best known are:

• A collection of 'Perfection of Wisdom' Sutras (Prajnaparamita Sutra) and Pratyutpanna Sutra, which were translated from Gandhari into Chinese by a Gandharan monk named Lokaksema. Lokaksema was born in Gandhara during the period of rule of Kanishka. He then went to China as a missionary and preached at a monastery near Luoyang in the period around 180 CE Prayutpanna Sutra contains the earliest reference to Amitabha and his western paradise, the Sukhavativyuha or Pure Land.

• Lotus Sutra (Saddharma Pundarika Sutra), which was translated from Gandhari into Chinese by Gandharan monk Dharmarakasa around 230 CE. This Sutra introduced the Pure Land doctrine in China, Japan and Korea and is widely regarded as the inspiration behind the Tiantai/Tendai School, which acquired a substantial following in these countries.

• Pure Land Sutra (Sukhavativyaha Sutra): It was originally compiled in Gandhara in the Gandhari language in first century CE and was translated into Chinese by Kumarajiva early in the 5th century.

Original translations of Mahayana texts carried out into Chinese from Gandhari-Kharoshthi by Kumarajiva have been found during excavations carried out at various Buddhist sites including Kucha and Dunhuang (Tun-huang).

New Styles in Religious Architecture

In the field of architecture, new styles emerged all over Gandhara during various phases of the Gandhara Civilization, which give the religious buildings constructed during this period a very special character. The divergence

---

65 Ibid, Chapter 16. The treatises, which Hsiuen Tsang says were being composed in Bhallar Monastery, were not Mahayana Buddhist texts, but the reference does indicate that producing manuscripts was a common activity in monasteries of Greater Gandhara.

in architectural styles is mainly on account of the influence of Greek and Persian architects.

After the conquest of Gandhara by the Achaemenids, Gandhara continued to interact with Persia and with the surrounding regions where Persian influence was substantial. Although Persian architects did not contribute directly towards the religious architecture in Gandhara, there were in the cosmopolitan population of Gandhara a number of architects, engineers and technicians who were influenced by their style of architecture. Thus a number of architectural elements of Persian origin were incorporated in the religious buildings constructed in various parts of Greater Gandhara during various phases of the Gandhara Civilization.

Greek architects were of course directly involved in the construction of religious buildings in Gandhara. For centuries after the invasion of Alexander in the fourth century, the Greeks had a substantial influence in the art and culture of a very vast region extending from Asia Minor to Gandhara. Especially during the rule of the Hellenistic regimes, an environment prevailed in which the creative talents of Greek architects, engineers and artists could be fruitfully and effectively employed to enrich the traditional architecture of this region. Starting from the period of rule of the Indus Greeks, an appreciable Greek influence can be seen in the religious buildings constructed in this region. During the period of Kushan rule, the availability of funds and an environment that was highly conducive for the construction of religious monuments on a large scale, the talents of Greek architects were extensively employed. Therefore their influence is much more apparent.

The earliest surviving religious building in Gandhara which shows overwhelming influence of Greek architects and classical Greek religious architecture is the Jandial Temple near the Indus Greek city Takshasila-Sirkap. It was constructed during the rule of the Indus Greek ruler, Menander, sometime around 165 BCE. Everything about this temple is Greek except, perhaps, the provision of a Zoroastrian-style fire tower in the *naos* or sanctuary part of the temple instead of the statue of a deity from the Greek Pantheon. In its plan, "the resemblance to the classical temples of Greece is striking." Like the temples of Classical Greece it is surrounded by a peristyle of Ionic columns and pilasters, two of which in the center near the entrance, supported the architrave. It has a front porch (pronaos), a sanctuary (naos) in the center, and a back porch or opisthodomos in the rear.[66]

---

66   Sir John Marshall. *A Guide to Taxila*, Cambridge, 1960.

The Jandial Temple is unique among the temples of Ancient Gandhara in that it represents a place of worship of classical Greece. The overwhelming preponderance of religious buildings in Greater Gandhara, naturally, are Buddhist. They comprise stupas and viharas, most of which contain some elements which are obviously Greek in design. Except for the three or four early stupas in Gandhara, which were provided with the traditional round bases, almost all the stupas constructed in Gandhara have a square base, which was the standard practice in monuments constructed in classical Greece. In some stupas, such as the one at Kunala near to the Indus Greek city of Takshasila-Sirkap, the base takes the form of multiple terraces one above the other, with the face of the terraces elaborately decorated with sculptures and friezes. This again was a feature commonly employed in Greek architecture. Starting from the period of rule of the Hellenistic Indo-Scythians and Parthians, increasing use was made of Ionic and Corinthian style columns, pilasters and architraves in the construction and decoration of stupas and other Buddhist monuments. Acanthus capitals and foliated moldings were also used quite frequently to amplify the beauty and add grace to the monuments.

Architectural elements such as Ionic and Corinthian columns also came to be represented in the sculptures used to decorate the stupas and other religious buildings. In addition, a whole range of foreign motifs such as cupids, tritons, marine divinities, vine and acanthus leaves were prominently displayed in the sculptured panels.

There were two major motives for enormous attention given to decoration of Buddhist places of worship.

The first was purely spiritual. Images of Buddha and Bodhisattva and sculptural representation of scenes from the life of Buddha occupied a central position in the Buddhist faith. The sculptures were meant to convey the ideal of a supreme being—a being who represented all that was good in nature.

The second, a slightly more worldly motive, was to inspire and attract people (lay Buddhists and potential converts) with a view to ensuring and preserving their loyalty and sincere devotion to the Buddhist faith.

The stupas in the Kushan Period were constructed in more or less standard format, comprising of identical or similar constructional elements. They were viewed as symbols of the universe, and various architectural elements embodied in the stupa design began to represent different parts of the Universe.

In this 'universal' concept of the stupa, the mountain shaped hemispherical dome symbolized Mount Meru, the Buddhist Cosmic Mountain, the center of the world. The different umbrellas or chattras were conceived as different levels of heaven, occupied by different categories of gods. The Yasti, the rod on which the chattras were mounted, became the axis of the Universe. The open space above the chattras was viewed as the dwelling places of the celestial Buddhas and Bodhisattvas. It also represented the formless state attained by the Buddhist saints in the highest levels of meditation. The square-sectioned cubicle base, symbolized the Underworld, its four sides facing North, South, East and West.

According to this concept, the ritual of making rounds on the Pradakshinapatha by the devotees meant they were taking a walk through the Buddhist cosmos.

The dome always remained the principal and the most symbolic element in the Gandharan stupa. The casket containing the body relics was placed inside the Harmika, a separate cubic enclosure constructed on the summit of the dome. Above the Harmika, mounted on a Yasti or axial rod, were the chattras or parasols, several of them mounted one on top of the other. Symbolically these chattras 'protected' the sacred contents of the Harmika and provided them the respect and reverence. The number of chattras raised on a Yasti varied from one to thirteen depending on the status of the person whose relics were preserved inside the stupa. If the stupa was for a lay Buddhist, it would have no chattra; for different categories of Buddhas or Bodhisattvas, the number of chattras would vary from seven to thirteen.

GANDHARA SCULPTURES INSPIRED BY RELIGIOUS ZEAL

Gandhara art was not art for art's sake. It was art developed to serve a specific purpose—to educate and inspire the devotees on the salient features of Buddhist theology. It was a visual presentation of Buddhist scriptures, scrupulously developed to appeal to the minds and souls of the followers of the faith as well as potential converts.

In a society in which the literacy level was very low, the sculptures provided an alternate and effective medium of transmitting religious knowledge. Lectures, sermons and singing of hymns further elaborated what was being conveyed by the sculptures. For the literate the sculptures comple-mented and supplemented the knowledge acquired through reading reli-gious texts.

With a view to educating and inspiring the common folks, no effort was spared to make the sculptures "talk, speak, converse and listen." To make the sculptures look beautiful and attractive the skills of the Greek sculptors and artists were utilized; to build spirituality into the stone pieces the ser-vices of Buddhist monks, philosophers and thinkers were utilized.

The expressions on the faces of Buddha and Bodhisattvas were articu-lately contrived to convey the messages the images were meant to convey. Hand expressions, gestures, symbols, hairstyles, the way robes draped, seats, and standing postures were developed to convey the attributes and characteristics of Buddha and his associates; articles carried by the figures in a sculptural composition further helped in identifying Buddha's associ-ates and companions.

Gandhara sculptures presented the Buddhist faith through interesting presentations of Buddha's life. They portrayed the luxurious life of Gautama Siddhartha as a prince of the Sakya community; they portrayed scenes of his disillusionment and renunciation of the courtly life, and thereafter his enlightenment and his sermons on various aspects of Buddhist religion. An-other set of compositions provided guidance to the devotees through sto-ries about his previous lives. The messages were easy to understand and ap-pealed to the senses, providing religious guidance as well as entertainment.

The sculptural techniques and portrayals were refined during the rule of the Indo-Scythians and Indo-Parthians when Mahayana Buddhism was passing through its formative phase. They achieved maturity during the reign of Kanishka, when Mahayana concepts crystallized. The dynamism generated by these beautiful pieces of sculptures led to increased patron-age by the regime and sustained efforts from Vasumitra and other advisors attached to Kanishka's court, not only to maintain but to increase the mo-mentum. The power of the sculptural presentations to capture the hearts and minds of the devotees was well-understood and appreciated by the intellectuals and by the establishment. They became aware of the dangers of proliferation and took suitable measures to avoid this. As a result the im-ages of Buddha and the composition of the scenes from his life were virtu-ally canonized, resulting in a uniform style of art all over Greater Gandhara.

The second and third centuries of the CE was a particularly glorious period in the history of Gandhara art. The interest the vigor imparted to the Buddhist movement during the reign of Kanishka was sustained during the reign of his illustrious successors, Huvishka and Vasudeva. In this period the highly developed skills of Hellenistic artists and engineers were most effectively employed to produce beautiful icons of Buddha and Bodhisattvas as well as elaborately sculptured panels depicting scenes from the life of Buddha. The material initially used for these sculptures was almost exclusively grey schist, which was ideally suited for the intricate carvings. It was hard enough to allow fine, sharp and pointed carvings to remain in place and soft enough to produce smooth facial profiles. Later on the plastic quality of stucco was full exploited at sites such as Jaulian and Sahri Bahlol to achieve the same result through a different process.

Gandharan Buddhist sculptural art began to spread rapidly to other regions of the vast Kushan Empire. In Mathura images of Buddha and the symbols and hand gestures devised by the Gandharan artists became entrenched in local art forms. In Afghanistan and Central Asia almost identical sculptures began to appear. In the Xinjiang Region of China Gandhara art was adapted to suit local topography and traditions.

OPULENCE — OVERFLOWING COFFERS

The Kushan period was one of great affluence and prosperity. It was a period hectic socio-economic activity fuelled by plundered wealth from lands across the borders of Greater Gandhara and through high volume trade. The wealth brought into the country was put to good use. Physical infrastructure improved and there was a boom in the construction industry. Any one who had skills could make a fortune. The fruits of a booming economy trickled down to the level of the common man. Unlike the Parthian Period where wealth was confined to a few families, there were numerous families who after meeting their basic needs could spend their surplus wealth on luxuries and for making generous donations to the Buddhist institutions.

The wealth and prosperity is reflected in the type of artifacts recovered from hundreds of archaeological Kushan sites and the large amount of currency in circulation. The dresses, types of buildings, jewelry and domestic utensils and miscellaneous items illustrated in the panels decorating various sangharamas, give some idea of the living standards.

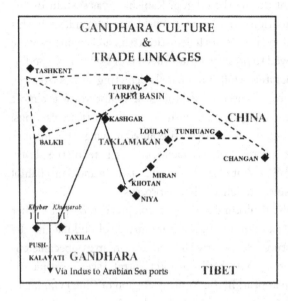

Figure 6.1: Gandhara linkages

Signs of substantial increase in wealth in the region began to appear quite early in the Kushan Period. During the rule of Vima Kadphises, Gandhara reaped rich harvests due to increased trade with China, Central Asia, Egypt and Rome. One indication of the growing prosperity during the rule of Vima Kadphises is that, whereas the two earlier Kushan rulers had issued only copper coins, Vima Kadphises issued both high standard gold as well as copper coins.

Another sign of growing prosperity during the rule of Vima Kadphises was Vima's decision to shift his capital from Sirkap site in Taxila to Sirsukh, about two kilometers to the west. The construction of Taxila-Sirsukh on a grand scale reflects the power and glory of the Kushan Empire during Vima Kadphises' period of rule.

But the most glorious period in Gandhara was during the reign of Vima Kadphises' son, Kanishka. Kanishka carved out a vast Empire, created a vast interacting region around Gandhara, and brought great economic prosperity to all regions of Greater Gandhara.

Within two decades of construction of the new Kushan capital at Takshasila-Sirsukh, Kanishka decided to shift his capital to Purushapura near the mouth of the Khyber Pass. While Purushapura was blossoming into a major administrative center as well as a great center for trade and commerce, Takshasila-Sirsukh also continued to prosper. Takshasila-Sirsukh controlled the other important trade route linking Eastern Gandhara and the Indus Plains with the countries along the Silk Route through the eastern Passes in the Karakorum mountains. The prosperity of Takshasila-Sirsukh is reflected in the construction of large number of Buddhist monuments around the city of Takshasila-Sirsukh.

The wealth brought into Greater Gandhara during Kanishka's reign was both through official as well as private channels. At the State level, the coffers of the State were filled by plundering conquered lands and by exacting tributes from the conquered nations. Private business houses brought wealth into the country through lucrative trade, made possible by easy access to the countries on the trade routes as a result of Kanishka's conquests. The increased trade created a strong class of businessmen, traders and landholders, who made a major contribution to the economy.

Funds provided by the State and the wealthy trading class resulted in sharp increase in socio-religious activities. There was a sharp increase in the construction of sangharamas and huge amounts were spent on the beautification of existing Buddhist monuments during Kanishka's period of rule.

After the death of Kanishka, the political control over the territories conquered by Kanishka in Central Asia and Tarim Basin became weaker. But interactions with countries in Central Asia and Tarim Basin continued and wealth continued to flow into Gandhara through active participation in the Silk Route trade. The economic prosperity was also promoted through investments in physical and economic infrastructure, which saw the growth of large number of businesses during the period of rule of the early Kushan emperors.

During the Kushan period river transport systems improved due to diversion of substantial Silk Route trade through Gandhara. Lots of people found employment to in the transport trade and allied professions. The construction industry was also organized on professional lines. With so many sangharamas being constructed, new cities being developed and existing towns being upgraded, the services of stone masons, carpenters and well diggers were in great demand.

Over a period of time Buddhist institutions also began to contribute towards the development of the economy. The increased availability of funds through State grants and private donations, led to the construction of elaborately decorated sangharamas, which created added interest and attracted larger number of devotees. The resulting boom in the demand for Buddha statues and other decoration pieces, led to emergence of specialized work-shops, where such items were manufactured on an industrial scale.

The economic prosperity continued till the end Vasudeva's rule in 230 CE. This is indicated by the large number of Buddhist monuments, which were constructed during the reign of Huvishka and Vasudeva, by the continuity in the practice of issuing gold coins, and very substantial increase in coins in circulation all through the Kushan Period. The huge hoards of coins belonging to Kushan period found from all parts of Greater Gandhara provide an indication of the surge in commercial activities during the entire Kushan period.

The flooding of Gandhara by goods produced in Roman colonies is also an indication of the prosperity in the Kushan Period. The Chinese historical chronicles pertaining to first and second centuries CE indicate that a large variety of Roman goods were found in Gandhara, ranging from luxury items to fine cloth and carpets to eatables and spices.

The flow of wealth into Gandhara resulting from the establishment of the Kushan Empire also had its impact on the lifestyle of the Kushan emperors.

Huvishka appears on his coins as a sophisticated well-dressed regal figure. On some coins Huvishka appears riding an elephant in the royal style with a scepter in one hand and elephant goad on the other. On other elegantly designed gold coins he appears in embroidered coats and fancy helmets or head-dresses, either seated or reclining on a couch.

MAGNIFICENT METROPOLISES

The increase in prosperity in Gandhara during the Kushan period gave rise to increase in urban population all over the region. Depending on their strategic locations, a large number of villages grew into towns and some small towns grew into major metropolises. The whole of Greater Gandhara became one great interactive region. Materials and skills available in one region were easily transported to other regions. There is a great uniformity in the type of construction and in the type of artifacts recovered from different regions of Greater Gandhara.

Purushapura

Figure 6.2: Kanishka's Casket (Courtesy Archaeological Department, Pakistan)

Purushapura (modern Peshawar), which probably existed as a small village as early as fifth century BCE, and was culturally linked to the Eastern Iranians, did not make much progress till first century CE. In the earlier period it was overshadowed by Pushkalavati (Charsadda), which enjoyed geographical advantage because of its link with Kabul through the Kabul River. Purushapura started gaining importance early in the Kushan period because of heightened political and commercial activity between Greater Gandhara and Bactria and other regions in Central Asia. It was located at the mouth of the Khyber Pass and the distance between Purushapura and Bactra was shorter by at least 30 kilometers as compared to the distance between Pushkalavati (Charsadda) and Bactra. An alternate route through the Khyber Pass provided a convenient connection between Purushapura and the Kabul region and beyond via Jalalabad.

Purushapura served Kushan Dynasty's strategic interests much better than any other settlement in the region. Buddhist monuments had begun to emerge in the surrounding areas of Purushapura even before the Kushan period. The Bara River, a tributary of the Kabul River met Purushapura's requirement of water for irrigation and domestic purposes, and a network of roads provided convenient connections from Purushapura to Pushkalavati

(Charsadda) and Takshasila (Taxila). Because of its central location, Purushapura became the natural choice for capital of the Kanishka's vast empire.

Purushapura went through rapid development during Kanishka's 23-year rule. Kanishka's capital was located at the site of Peshawar City and its boundary extended about 10 kilometers east of the Ganj Gate in eastern part of Peshawar City. A stupa complex *cum* vihara (Caitya) was constructed on two mounds just outside the eastern boundary of the city, at a site presently known as Shahji-ki-Dheri or the King's Mound.

Purushapura was a well fortified city in the Kushan period. According to general plans of new cities of Central Asia belonging to the period, it was rectangular in shape, with four Gates, one on each side. (Later, probably during the Mughal and Sikh Periods, the fortifications were rebuilt and sixteen gates were provided. These new fortifications and Gates existed well through the British period of occupation).

Purushapura, began to expand rapidly soon after its selection as the capital of the Kushan Empire. In the Kushan Period it was by far the largest and most impressive city in the Greater Gandhara. It became a great commercial and cultural metropolis and, a center for learning and an important base for Mahayana Buddhism.

Two important finds from Shahji-ki-Dheri identify this site of the great sangharama described by Fa-Hsien and other ancient Chinese Buddhist scholars.

The first is Kanishka's Casket, reputed to contain the relics of Buddha, and the second a begging bowl (Patra), which was used by the monks of the Patracaitya located at the site to collect offerings made by the devotees.

The intricately designed gilded copper casket of Kanishka is a piece of extraordinary beauty. It was found from what looked like a deposit chamber under the stupa commissioned by Kanishka at Shahji-ki-Dheri. It contained three bone fragments said to be of Buddha. On the lid of the casket are the three gilded statues of seated Buddha, flanked by Brahma and Indra. Kanishka is depicted in the lower part of the casket. The dedication statement in Kharoshthi mentions the name of Kanishka twice and ends with a statement by a Greek master mason "The servant Agisala (Agesilas), the overseer of works at Kanishka's vihara in the sangharama of Mahasena."[67]

The other important artifact recovered from the site was the Patra or begging bowl. Its walls were about 5 mm thick and were finished in bright

---

67 Ahmad Nabi Khan. *Gandhara- an illustrated Guide*, Karachi 1994.

glossy lustre. The ceremony involving the Patra is described by Fa-Hsien in his report written after his visit to Gandhara in the beginning of fifth century CE.[68] According to this account, there were about 700 monks in the monastery. The Patra was taken out daily at midday by the monks in the Patracaitya and then the monks and lay worshippers made offerings to it, after which they took their midday meals.

Kanishka's stupa at Shahji-ki-Dheri was an extraordinary piece of architecture and quite unlike any other stupa constructed in Gandhara in that period. It had been destroyed and rebuilt thrice before the Chinese scholar Sung-Yuen paid a visit to the site in 520 CE. Sung-Yuen mentions that the 125 meter high stupa was topped with a spire made of iron. The radiant spire, sparkling in the light of the sun, could be seen from a very long distance.[69] The superstructure was probably made of wood in the style of palaces constructed in that period.

To the east of the Grand stupa was a huge colony for Buddhist monks and scholars—the Patracaitya. Many famous Buddhist scholars spent a good deal of their time at this Patracaitya, consulting Buddhist texts available at its huge library. The Patracaitya was very much in place till the ninth century CE, when it was visited by Viradeva, a well-known Buddhist scholar.

Hsiuen Tsang visited Purushapura in 629 CE. He estimates the circumference of the city as 40 li, which is equivalent of 12 kilometers. He mentions two important religious foundations:[70]

"Inside the royal city towards the northeast is an old foundation. Formerly this was the precious tower of Patra."

"Outside the city about 8 or 9 li to the southeast is a Pipal tree about 100 feet in height, planted by Kanishka." Four past Buddhas sat in the shade of this tree.[71]

Buddhist traditions mention a Bodhi Tree, which was planted by Kanishka at the site of Pipal Mandi in the heart of the Old Sector of Peshawar city. Sung-Yuen describes the magnificent widely spread out tree with thick foliage under the shade of which there were four 17-foot high statues of seated Buddhas. Buddhist monks regularly cleaned the place and washed

---

68 [35] Fa Hsien. *A Record of Buddhist Kingdoms, being an account of his travels in India and Ceylon (AD 399-414)*, translation and annot. By James Legge, (Oxford 1886).

69 Samuel Beal: *Buddhist Records of the Western World*, London 1884

70 A. Foucher. *Notes on Ancient Geography of Gandhara: A Commentary on a Chapter of Hsiuen Tsang.* Translation by H. Hargreaves, Superintendent. Calcutta, 1915

71 Ibid.

the statues. In the period when Fa-Hsien visited Purushapura, lay Buddhists regularly stopped over at this site to pray and make offerings of garlands, food and money.[72]

PushkalavatiThe Lotus City

Pushkalavati, also known as Peuceloitus and Proclais, has a rich history commencing from the construction of the Achaemenid city in 6th century on the mound where the Bala Hisar Fort was constructed several centuries later. Several succeeding regimes added their construction within 5 kilometers distance of the Bala Hisar Mound. As all these sites were not totally disbanded, Pushkalavati assumed the shape of a central city with two or three adjacent sectors.

The first city of Pushkalavati on the mound known as Bala Hisar remained the regional capital of three regimes over a period of about two and a half centuries. It was occupied by Alexander's Macedonian Greeks after the defeat of the Achaemenids and a cantonment was constructed nearby by Alexander's generals. Subsequently the Mauryans used the same site for their regional capital.

In the second century BCE, the Indus Greeks constructed their city near the confluence of the Kabul and the Swat Rivers at a place called Shaikhan Dheri, which is about one kilometer from the Bala Hisar Mound. This city served as the regional capital of the Indus Greeks, the Indo-Scythian-Parthians and early Kushans. This is the city mentioned by the *Periplus of the Erythraien Sea* as the important metropolis in the period around 47 CE, where goods brought by the ships to the Arabian Sea port of Barbaricum were ultimately dispatched.

The excavations carried out by Professor A.H. Dani in 1963–64 revealed that Menander constructed Pushkalavati-Shaikhan Dheri on the Hippodamian pattern, and, as at Takshasila-Sirkap, this plan was maintained during the period of occupation by the Indo-Scythians, Indo-Parthians and the early Kushans. The Kushan city of Pushkalavati-Shaikhan Dheri was destroyed by floods in the early second century CE.

Vima Kadphises constructed a new city near the village of Prang, about 5 kilometers from Bala Hisar Fort. The Kushan city of Pushkalavati-Prang served as an important commercial and military center, from where Vima Kadphises conducted his operations in the Swat Valley. After Kanishka

---

72 Samuel Beal. *Buddhist Records of the Western World*, London 1884

constructed his capital city at Purushapura, 23-kilometer west of Pushka-lavati-Prang, Pushkalavati's importance was somewhat reduced, but it still served as an important cultural center for some time. Around the time of Hsiuen Tsang's visit in seventh century CE., Pushkalavati-Bala Hisar had once again assumed the premier status in the Charsadda region.

Sahri Bahlol

The Kushan city of Sahri Bahlol was located on a mound about 12 kilometers northeast of Mardan. The city was heavily fortified and fully equipped with all the necessary amenities for supporting a large Buddhist population.[73]

Sahri Bahlol was a major ceremonial and religious center during the peak period of the Gandhara Civilization. There was a large stupa on the city mound itself, which was constructed by Asoka in honor of a Buddhist saint. A large number of Buddhist sangharamas and stupas were located all round the city. The largest of these was the Takht-i-bahi sangharama complex, which was located about 4 kilometers north of the city. There was another large sangharama about 1.5 kilometers to the south of the city mound and several stupas a little further away. All these Buddhist institutions thrived on private donations from the affluent citizens of Sahri Bahlol and the local government organization.

The archaeological site of Sahri Bahlol and the Buddhist monuments around the city were extensively explored by Dr. D.B. Spooner in 1907 and by Aurel Stein about a decade later. The excavations yielded a large number of Buddhist sculptures, most of which are presently housed in the Peshawar Museum.

Sahri Bahlol was extensively damaged during the invasion of the White Huns in 6th century CE.

Shahbaz Garhi

Buddhist traditions indicate that Shahbaz Garhi was the site of the ancient city of Varusha. It began to develop into an important center of Buddhist culture in the third century BCE after Asoka selected Shahbaz Garhi for the location of his famous Edicts.

During the Kushan period, the Trade Route passing through Shahbaz Garhi acquired increased importance due to the linking of the Peshawar Valley with Xinjiang through Swat and the Khunjerab Pass. As a result

---

73 Ahmad Nabi Khan. *Gandhara – An illustrated guide*, Karachi 1994.

Shahbaz Garhi developed into an important commercial as well as cultural city in this period. It became a regular stop for all Chinese Buddhist scholar monks, who traveled on this route between fourth and eighth century CE.

Early Buddhist traditions linked Shahbaz Garhi with important events during the previous lives of Buddha. According to these traditions Buddha, in one of his previous lives donated a white elephant in charity here. After Shahbaz Garhi emerged as an important commercial and cultural city during the Kushan Period, two stupas were constructed on the outskirts of Shahbaz Garhi to commemorate the events pertaining to Buddha's previous lives. The stupa at Chanak Dheri commemorates the white elephant given by Buddha in charity, while the Salsi stupa honors Prince Visvantra for his noble deeds.

Shahbaz Garhi is located about 76 kilometers from Peshawar and 20 kilometers to the west of Mardan on the Mardan-Swabi Road. The Chinese pilgrim, Sung-Yuen, who visited this city in early 6th century C.E called this city Po-lu-sha. In the accounts of his travels, he makes special mention of the dazzling images of Buddha, which were located inside a nearby sangharama.

Archaeological excavations at the site were carried out the Japanese Archaeological Mission, which unearthed remains of buildings with typical Gandhara architecture.

Butkara

This was the principal city of the Gandhara Civilization in the Uddhyana region. It was located on the left bank of the Swat River in a very fertile area watered by two streams. The site, which is now called Gulkada, is located near the modern Swat city of Mingora.

Butkara developed in the Kushan period into a huge urban-cum-religious complex. The city was spread over a vast area towards the north and northwest of the sangharama designated as Butkara-I. Two other important sangharamas were located in the Jambir Valley around the Butkara metropolis. These are designated as Butkara-II and Butkara-III.

Prof. Giuseppe Tucci's archaeological excavations in the mid-1950s and early 1960s revealed an extensive period of occupation starting from 3rd century BCE, when Asoka was ruling over the Mauryan Empire (which included Gandhara), and covering all subsequent phases of the Gandhara Civilization. After reaching its peak in the Kushan period the city survived a prolonged lean period. The Chinese pilgrim, Sung-Yuen, who visited the city in early 6th century CE, was particularly impressed with the beautiful gilded images of Buddha and Bodhisattvas, located in the Butkara Sangharama (which he called Ja-Lo) south of the city.[74]

Udegram

This Gandharan city was located near the village of Udegram, 8 kilometers from Saidu Sharif, the modern capital of Swat. It was the second most important Gandharan city in Lower Swat Region, and, like Butkara, the site where this Gandharan city was located, also contains construction belonging to periods earlier as well as later than the Gandhara Civilization.

The construction during different periods of occupation is dispersed over three adjacent sites, referred to as Gogdara, Udegram Bazaar and Raja Gira's Castle. Gogdara the most ancient of these sites dates back to protohistoric period. Raja Gira's Castle dates to the post-Gandhara civilization period after 5th century CE. The ruins belonging to various phases of the Gandhara Civilization are mostly located at the site of Udegram Bazaar.

The archaeological excavations at these sites were carried out by the Italian archaeological mission, under the leadership of G. Gullini. These excavations reveal different layers of occupation belonging to the Indus-Greek, Saka, Parthian and Kushan periods. The coins of Gondophares and some Saka and Indus Greek rulers recovered from the lower layers indicates that this site was occupied for almost two centuries before the Kushans constructed their city here.

From the ruins belonging to the Kushan city located in the top-most layer, a large number of coins belonging to almost all the Kushan rulers from Vima Kadphises to Vasudeva-II have been recovered. They indicate the important part played by this city during the entire period of Kushan rule.

Chakdara

Chakdara, the major Gandharan city in Southern Dir, is located at the confluence of the Swat and Panjkora Rivers. During the Gandhara Civilization period it was the center of a large urban *cum* religious complex, which included about half a dozen sites located within a radius of about 15 kilometers. These sites include the villages of Damkot, Andan Dheri, Chatpat, Ramora, Jabagai and Amlukdara.

Archaeological excavations carried out by Prof. A.H. Dani in the 1960s, and various teams from the Archaeological Department of Peshawar Uni-

---

74   Samuel Beal. *Buddhist Records of the Western World*, London 1884.

versity, have revealed construction belonging to almost all the phases of the Gandhara Civilization at these sites.[75]

Takshasila-Sirsukh

Takshasila-Sirsukh was the largest of the three Gandharan cities in the Taxila Region. It was located about 2.5 kilometers northeast of Indus Greek and Saka-Parthian city of Takshasila-Sirkap, just off the road from Sirkap to Khanpur Dam. The area inside the boundary walls of the city was about 2 square kilometers. The site includes the present villages of Tofkian, Mirpur and Pind Gakhar.

The planning of this city commenced immediately after the Kushans under Kujula Kadphises conquered Gandhara and established their tempo-rary capital at the Saka-Parthian city of Sirkap. However the construction must have commenced around after 80 CE. Takshasila-Sirsukh was ready for occupation during the reign of Vima Kadphises. The large number of coins belonging to Vima Kadphises from the site indicates that the Kushan capital was shifted to this new city soon after Vima Kadphises succeeded to the Kushan throne in 100 CE. When Kanishka moved the Kushan capital to Purushapura around 128 CE, Takshasila-Sirsukh served as the capital of Eastern Gandhara. The city survived the attack by the White Huns in the 6th century CE. It was still a prosperous city and a major center of Buddhism when the Chinese pilgrim Hsiuen Tsang stayed here for some time during his visit to Gandhara in 630 CE.

The plains, where the Kushan city of Takshasila-Sirsukh was located, are presently occupied by thickly cultivated agricultural fields, while the mounds, where no cultivation of crops is possible, are occupied by vil-lages and graveyards. Therefore major parts of the Kushan city remain un-explored. The excavations carried out at two or three relatively accessible spots indicate the character of the city and the quality of its constructions. The archaeological explorations indicate that that the Kushans adopted the grid-layout of Takshasila-Sirkap, the city, which they occupied prior to constructing their new city at Takshasila-Sirsukh. At the same time they incorporated certain attractive features of Central Asian cities, with which they were familiar.[76]

---

75   A.H. Dani. *Ancient Pakistan*: Volume IV, 1968-69, Bulletin of Department of Ar-chaeology, University of Peshawar.

76   Sir John Marshall. *A Guide to Taxila*, Cambridge 1960.

As a result the essentially Kushan city of Takshasila-Sirsukh seems to have been better planned and it was more modern, and its buildings were stronger and more durable than those in the two earlier cities in Takshasila region. That the security issues were well addressed, is indicated by the selection of the site for the new city and the quality of it boundary walls.

The shape of Takshasila-Sirsukh was a rectangle with well proportioned sides to permit a smooth layout and avoid congestion. All round the city walls the natural features of the land are such that they would pose difficulties for intruders. The Lundi Kas River flows along the southern boundary walls of the city. On three sides surrounding the boundary are hillocks or raised ground. The boundary walls are much stronger than the ones at Sirkap. They employ heavy limestone blocks as the main construction material. They are about 6 meters thick and are provided with semicircular bastions at intervals of 30 meters.

Inside the city, among the few structures which have been exposed by archaeological excavations is a palatial building with two courts, a veranda supported by pillars, and several rows of chambers.

Takshasila-Sirsukh benefited immensely from the diversion of Silk Route towards the Arabian Sea via the Indus Waterway, due to blocking of the land routes by the Sassanids. All round the city, at short distance from the boundary wall, are some of the most elegantly designed and commodious sangharamas, which were no doubt heavily patronized by the rulers. Towards the southeast there is the impressive Mohra Muradu Sangharama, located in unusually beautiful surroundings. A little further to the east, are the famous stupa complexes and viharas of Jaulian. The Badalpur stupa complex is located east of Sirsukh and the Lalchuk stupa just outside the northern boundary walls of the city.

GLITTERATI IN KANISHKA'S COURT

Among the many special qualities possessed by the great Kushan emperor Kanishka was his knack of recognizing talent and his capacity to derive immense pleasure and satisfaction in the company of people with extraordinary skills. The greatness of the scholars around him ultimately reflected on his own personality and provided a major boost to his ego. Like Alexander, Kanishka was fired with an ambition to stamp his mark as a great emperor. Like Alexander, his successes got into his head and he began to claim divinity.

Vasumitra was one such luminary, who adorned Kanishka's court. He was not only the principal developer and promoter of Mahayana philosophy, but also the developer and administrator of the closely knit and disciplined Buddhist organization based on sangharamas. It was mainly due to his efforts that a broad consensus emerged on the Mahayana doctrines, and it was mainly due to his administrative skills that the vast amounts, which became available to the Buddhist establishment through royal grants and private donations, were properly utilized, and the local organizations responsible for running the sangharamas performed their tasks strictly within the guidelines provided to them.

Asvaghosha used his enormous artistic talents to spread Buddhist religious thought through the highly attractive medium of sensually provocative narrative poetry, music and Drama.

Charaka used the innovative medium of a question and answer session between a teacher, Atreya, and his pupil, Agniversa, to spread his knowledge pertaining to treatment of diseases through plant, animal and mineral resources.

SOCIAL TRANSFORMATION

When the Achaemenids conquered Gandhara in the 6th century CE. Gandhara had little to offer to the invaders in the shape of a united opposition. The whole region was divided into small clans under the control of a large number of petty chieftains. The whole system was restrictive and exploitative. The political integration by the occupying powers did not automatically lead to social integration because no effective medium for social integration was available.

The process for social integration in real terms started after the arrival of the Buddhist missionaries in Gandhara in 4th century BCE. The missionaries presented to a suffering population a goal—the goal of Nirvana. They also showed them the path to achieve Nirvana, as enunciated by the great master himself. The eight-fold path required to be followed by the devotees, had in it the ingredients for total transformation of society. Through right understanding, right thought, right speech, right action, right livelihood, right effort, right mindfulness and right concentration, the devotees could once and for all get rid of the miseries that plagued this world. The goal was clear, the path was clear, but disciplining life to follow the 8-fold path was lifelong exercise, which could only be achieved through persistent efforts in a congenial environment.

The process of motivating the people towards the goal of Nirvana remained painfully slow until Asoka introduced the stupa culture. The adoption of stupa culture was the first step towards institutionalization of the process for reforming society. The institutionalization through a complex network of sangharamas was set in motion and it was in the first and second centuries CE that these plans had matured to a large extent. An environment was now in place in which the people could reorder their lives according to the teachings of Buddha.

People from towns and villages visited the sangharamas in large numbers to partake in the spiritual activities. These visits provided the laymen escape from the humdrum of their daily routines in the dusty towns and villages. Here they prayed, sang hymns, made rounds of the stupas and performed other traditional religious rituals under the guidance of the Buddhist monks. In return for promises of a better life in this world and in the life hereafter, they made generous donations and offerings of food, garlands, and ornaments to the Buddhist institutions. They invited monks from the monasteries to bless their weddings and to perform funerary rites.

A new social order with strong moral overtones had taken shape. It infused discipline into the lives of the common man; it broke down social, ethnic and cultural barriers; it promoted fraternal feelings in the community as a whole, and it provided a platform in which all social needs of the community were taken care of.

From the point of view of social attitudes, social orientation and community development, 2nd and 3rd century Gandhara had come quite close to the structure of modern societies.

Chapter 7: Decline

> Religion blushing veils her sacred fires,
> And unawares Morality expires.
> Nor public Flame, nor private, dares to shine;
> Nor human spark is left, nor Glimpse divine!
> Lo! Thy dread Empire, CHAOS! is restored;
> —Alexander Pope

After the Achaemenids and the Mauryans had established the basic parameters of the physical and administrative infrastructure in Greater Gandhara, there were a number of political and religious elements, which propelled the rise of the Buddhist Civilization in Gandhara, and sustained the Civilization during its peak from 60 CE till 230 CE. After that the conditions began to change in Gandhara.

In 230 CE Vasudeva, the last of the great Kushan emperors died and shortly afterwards the Sassanians under Shahpur-I invaded Gandhara. The invasion of Shapur-I virtually brought an end to the Kushan Empire. The Sassanians caused major damage to the Buddhist monasteries all over Western Gandhara and badly shook the confidence of the Buddhist establishment all over Greater Gandhara. After causing widespread damage the Sassanians returned to their homeland without establishing their permanent presence in Gandhara.

After the return of Sassanian forces under Shahpur-I, Kushan rule was re-established in Greater Gandhara, but in a highly diluted form. The pomp and glory that prevailed during the rule of early Kushan emperors was now all gone. There was not much wealth pouring into Gandhara and all socio-economic and cultural activities registered a sharp decline.

Greater Gandhara once was once again invaded by the Sassanians in mid-fourth century CE. This time the Sassanids conquered entire Greater Gandhara, but as their rule was restricted to just three decades, no further damage was done to the Gandhara Civilization.

Gandhara Civilization registered a period of revival during the rule of the Kidara Kushans from 380 till 450 CE. After the end of Kidara Kushan Rule, the glory of the Buddhist Civilization in Gandhara became an event of the past. The hostile environment created by non-sympathetic regimes against the Buddhist establishment, the absence of patronage and paucity of financial resources led to a steady decline in the Gandhara Civilization during the next six centuries.

More than anything else, Buddhist civilization thrived on the backs of dedicated Buddhist scholars and their practical arm—the missionaries. All through the period from the embryonic phase till the mature phase of the Gandhara Civilization the Buddhist scholars and missionaries played an important role in the moral, spiritual and social development of the Gandharan society. The convergence of ideas of the scholars belonging to the Mahasinghakas, the Sarvastivadins and the Dharmaguptaka sects promoted harmony within the Buddhist communities and led to the universal acceptance of the Mahayana philosophy in Gandhara in late first century CE.

The activities at the sangharamas in the first two and a half centuries of the Common Era were built around a close working relationship between the Kushan emperors and the Buddhist establishment. Buddhist scholars serving as advisors to the Kushan emperors played an important part in maintaining a healthy relationship between the regimes and the Buddhist communities. They had a positive influence on the working of the Buddhist establishment and helped strengthen the social organization of the Buddhists.

The long era of cooperation between the ruling regimes and the Buddhist establishment in Gandhara virtually came to an end after the Sassanids under Shapur-I invaded Gandhara in 230 CE. Except for the period during which the Kidara Kushans ruled Greater Gandhara, even the healthy practice of appointing Buddhist advisors to interface with the predominantly Buddhist population was dispensed with. As a result the socio-political environment of Gandhara deteriorated rapidly.

Invasion of Sassanians under Shahpur-I

The invasion of Bactria and Gandhara by the Sassanid armies under Shahpur-I in 240 CE was part of the proclaimed mission of the Sassanids to capture 'lost territories' of the Achaemenid Empire. The Sassanids considered themselves as successors of the Great Achaemenid Empire. To assert his claim, the founder of the Sassanid Dynasty, Ardeshir-I at the very outset assumed the title of 'emperor of AiIran and AnIran', thereby implying that he was emperor not only of territories within Iran but also territories which were once a part of the Achaemenid Empire outside Iran.

Ardeshir-I did not live long enough to a give a practical shape to his claim. This task was left to his successor Shahpur-I, who launched a major assault soon after he came to power.

Shahpur-I initially took on the Romans, who were at that time in control of the whole of West Asia. Then he turned his attention to the east, towards Bactria and Gandhara.

Shahpur-I entered Western Gandhara during the rule of the Kushan king Kanishka-II. After crossing the Khyber Pass the Sassanid armies launched a blistering attack on the thriving Kushan capital of Purushapura. This attack caused considerable damage to the Relic Tower and the Mahavihara constructed by Kanishka in the outskirts of Purushapura about a century earlier. When Kanishka established Purushapura as the capital of his Empire, Purushapura was a safe haven, being protected in the north by the territories Central Asian regions of Kanishka's Empire and in the southeast by Eastern part of his empire. But this position had changed drastically after the Kushans lost their territories in Central Asia. Purushapura now became vulnerable to attacks because it was the first city in the line of attack of the invading armies.

The army of Shahpur-I, besides causing severe damage to the Buddhist monuments in Purushapura, plundered the rich capital of the Kushan Empire, and then went on to plunder other towns and cities all along the Kabul and Swat Rivers in the Peshawar Valley. The Sassanid army restricted it's conquests to territories west of the Indus River. Shapur-I appointed his son Hormuzd-I as Kushanshah of Western Gandhara and established his seat of Government in Seistan. Shahpur then returned to his capital, Ctesiphon (near Baghdad), with loads of plundered goods.

From his seat in Seistan Hormuzd-I could not exercise much control over Gandhara. Ultimately he was restricted to Seistan, where he was succeeded by other Kushanshahs also. In Gandhara Kanishka-II, who was earlier defeated by the armies of Shahpur-I and had fled to Taxila, once again established Kushan rule in the entire region of Greater Gandhara.

GREATER GANDHARA UNDER THE RULE OF MINOR KUSHAN LEADERS

The Kushans, who re-established Kushan rule in Greater Gandhara after the invasion of Shahpur-I faced a totally different situation from that prevailing during the rule of the earlier Kushans. The large-scale destruction of Buddhist monasteries in Western Gandhara by the armies of Shahpur-I totally shattered the morale of the Buddhist establishment. The Buddhist establishment looked for guidance and financial support from the new Kushan rulers. Because of altered economic and political environment in and around Greater Gandhara, this support was no longer available.

The trade of Greater Gandhara with countries on the Silk Route was reduced to a trickle due to obstructions created by the Sassanid emperors; the treasury of the Kushan emperors became virtually empty because the payment of tributes had stopped and Kushan plundering expeditions across the borders of Greater Gandhara were no longer possible with new powers in control. As a result construction of new sangharamas in Greater came to a stop and there were no funds available from the government treasury as well as private donations to take care of the upkeep of the existing sangharamas.

Including Kanishka-II, five minor Kushan kings ruled Greater Gandhara from 230 CE till 350 CE. Very few coins of these minor Kushan kings have been found from various sites, which is an indication of subdued economic activity. However, inspite of limited wealth available in the Kushan treasury during this period, most of these minor kings continued to issue gold coins. Gold and copper coins of Kaneshko (Kanishka-III) and Vasudeva-II reveal that they employed Bactrian and Brahmi on their coins.

SASSANID RULE IN GANDHARA

In 309 CE Shahpur-II (also known as Shahpur the Great) became the eighth emperor of the Sassanid Dynasty. Immediately after assuming power he went about completing the mission of his forefathers of establishing control of all the territories, which were once a part of the Achaemenid Empire.

Till the middle of fourth century, Shahpur-II was kept busy in West Asia. Around 350 CE, he found time to focus his attention on the Central Asian and Gandhara regions. Sassanian armies under Shahpur-II invaded Bactria, and after re-establishing their control there, crossed the Hindu Kush and established their temporary base in Kabul. From Kabul Shahpur-II launched a massive invasion of Greater Gandhara. While Shahpur-I had restricted his conquests to the region west of Indus, the armies of Shahpur-II crossed the Indus Region and brought the entire Greater Gandhara region under his control.

The Sassanians ruled Gandhara for just about three decades and because of the short period of their rule, the situation with respect to the Gandhara Civilization and the activities of the Buddhist establishment in Greater Gandhara did not deteriorate further beyond the state they had reached during the rule of the minor Kushan kings. Shahpur-II invaded Gandhara in 350 CE, when Shaka was ruling Greater Gandhara. Shaka was in no position to offer any resistance to the Sassanids. He fled to Taxila where he was followed by the Sassanid forces. Ultimately Shahpur-II succeeded in establishing Sassanid control over the entire region of Greater Gandhara.

Following the successful invasion of Shahpur-II, the entire region of Greater Gandhara was under the political control of the Kushanshahs, who were appointed by the Sassanid emperors. This situation continued to prevail till 380 CE

The title of the Sassanid Governor indicates that the change from Kushan rule to Sassanid rule in Western Gandhara was not abrupt. During the period 350–380 CE, the Buddhist establishment did not suffer any further upheaval. Because of absence of State patronage and cessation of income through Silk Route Trade, the economy and the activities of the Buddhist institutions remained subdued. However, the basic features of Gandhara Civilization remained intact.

With regard to granting political autonomy to the conquered regions, the character of Sassanid rule in Gandhara was similar to that of the Achaemenids. They delegated vast powers to their regional representatives, the Kushanshah, who maintained cordial relations with the local population. The principal objectives of the Sassanids was to earn revenues from the conquered nations, and to ensure security within the core area of their Empire, namely Iran and Iraq, by preventing Greater Gandhara from coming under the influence of Rome and other nations with which they were at war. As long as these requirements were met they did not interfere too much in the internal affairs of the region—least of all in cultural and social matters. The Kushanshahs saw to it that these requirements were met to the entire satisfaction of their masters, the Sassanid emperors.

About 32 coins of Sassanid rulers have been found from Eastern Gandhara. These coins, mostly belonging to Shapur-II and Shapur-III, carry Bactrian Cursive Greek and Pahlavi legends.[77] Two of these coins belonging to Hormuzd-II and Varahran-I are in the Punjab Museum, Lahore.[78] In addition about 202 Sassanid coins have been found near Hadda in the northwestern region of Greater Gandhara.

Almost all the above coins were standard coins of the Sassanid emperors and were minted in their Iran-Iraq homeland. Therefore Kharoshthi legends do not appear on these coins and the portraits and symbols appearing in the coins pertain to the emperors and their Zoroastrian faith. It can therefore be inferred that the Gandharan economy was exclusively controlled by the Central regime based in Ctesiphon.

KIDARA KUSHAN RULE (380–463 CE)

Bactria had remained a stronghold of the Kushans ever since they drove the Parthians out from this region in the closing years of last century BCE. The Sassanids achieved some success in the battlefield, but they were never really able to break the power of the Kushans.

Kidara was the Chief of the Bactrian factions of the Kushans in mid-fourth century CE. Around 360 CE, pressures were generated in this region by the Sassanids. This led to migration of Kidara Kushans southwards. Kidara crossed the Hindu Kush, wrested power from the Sassanid Kushanshahs and assumed control of Greater Gandhara, including the region around Kabul and Jalalabad, Charsadda, Mardan, Swat and Taxila. He established the Kidara Kushan Dynasty in this region in 380 CE.

The Kidara Kushan's rule brought an end to the status quo prevailing in Greater Gandhara since the death of Vasudeva in 230 CE. During the rule of Kidara Kushan rule in Gandhara, the Buddhist institutions all over Gand-

---

77   Sir John Marshall. *An Illustrated Account of Archaeological Excavations Carried Out at Taxila 1913–34. Volume II*, Cambridge: 1951.

78   R.B. Whitehead. *Catalogue of Coins in the Punjab Museum, Lahore. Oxford*, 1914.

hara were revived and rejuvenated. The sangharamas, which had blossomed up in Gandhara during the reign of his fellow Kushans several centuries earlier, and then went through a period of decay during Sassanid rule, were once again buzzing with life. Under Kidara the State once again identified itself totally with the Buddhist establishment, its institutions and the Buddhist population. State patronage and State funds were available in plenty to supplement the generous donations by lay Buddhists.

The Kidara Kushans ruled Gandhara for more than 80 years. Their rule was brought to an end by the invasion of the White Huns in 463 CE.

The pattern of Kidara Kushan rule was very similar to that of the earlier Kushans even though the economic and literary activities did not quite achieve the level of their illustrious predecessors. Kharoshthi was still the principal script employed in Greater Gandhara but Brahmi was also employed in donative inscriptions. The kings of the Kidara Dynasty used Bactrian and Brahmi legends on their coins.

During the rule of the Kidara Kushans very substantial additions were made to most of the major existing sangharamas. At the Sahri Bahlol Monastery most of the construction and a lot of the sculptures (especially those in stucco) belong to this period. At the nearby Takht-i-Bahi Sangharama the entire construction in the Court of the Three Buddhas was carried out during the rule of the Kidara Kushans. In the Taxila Region, the Jaulian, Mohra Muradu, Giri, Kalawan and Dharmarajika Sangharamas, a lot of the construction and quite a large number of sculptures, belong to the Kidara Kushan period, while the entire construction and decorations at the Pippala and Bhamala Sangharamas near Taxila were also carried out in this period.

Hundreds of coins belonging to the Kidara Kushans have been recovered from the monasteries at Dharmarajika, Bhamala, and Lalchuk, in the Taxila Region, and from other regions of Gandhara. Among these are four gold coins, which is an indication of prosperity during the rule of the Kidara Kushans. There were certainly other rulers in Gandhara belonging to the Kidara Kushan Dynasty, but only coins bearing the name Kidara and Kidara Kushanshah have been identified.

Firsthand information on the state of affairs in Gandhara during the rule of the Kidara Kushans is provided by the Chinese pilgrim Fa-Hsien. Fa-Hsien arrived in Swat sometime around 400 CE and traveled extensively to all regions of Gandhara. He visited more than 500 sangharamas in Swat alone and several hundred more in other parts of Gandhara, all of which were patronized by a very large number of pilgrims, devotees and lay Buddhists. The Great stupa built by Kanishka at Shahji-ki-Dheri, near Peshawar was intact when Fa-Hsien visited this place and he came across more than 700 priests at the Patracaitya nearby. He also describes the stupa of the Eye-Gift at Pushkalavati (Charsadda), which was adorned with gold and silver.[79]

STEADY DECLINE (463–845 CE)

The result of the break in socio-political link after the end of the rule of the Kidara Kushans was the collapse of the all powerful Buddhist establishment in Gandhara. The moral and spiritual guidance provided by the scholars-cum-advisors attached to the royal courts was no longer available to those responsible to execute these policies. Also the check was no longer there on the activities of the clergy responsible for running the sangharamas. This led to weakening of the moral and spiritual forces within the Buddhist establishment resulting in conditions described by the 7th century Chinese pilgrim, Hsiuen Tsang. "The monks took part in religious rituals in a routinish manner. Moral standards have declined and superstitions and magic play a prominent role in the daily lives of the Buddhists."[80]

The real downslide of the Gandhara Civilization began after the invasion of the White Huns or the Ephthalites. After destruction of Buddhist monasteries carried out by the Ephthalites the Buddhist Church never fully recovered. The confidence of the Buddhist communities was shattered, their enthusiasm wavered, and their closely knit social organization was now in tatters.

The huge social and economic infrastructure created during the rule of the Kushans began to crumble through deliberate acts of destruction by the Ephthalites and other regimes, which were opposed to the Buddhist ideology.

Destruction Wrought by the Ephthalites

The Ephthalites or White Huns were the nomadic Turkic people who had driven out the Kidara Kushans from Bactria and Southern Afghani-

---

79   Fa Hsien. *A Record of Buddhist Kingdoms, Being an Account of His Travels in India and Ceylon 399–414 C.E*, Chapter X, Translated by James Legge, Oxford 1886. Also in *Buddhist Records of the Western World* translated by S. Beal, 1884.

80   Hsiuen Tsang. *Buddhist Records of the Western World*. Translated by Samuel Beal, London 1884.

stan in the third quarter of fourth century CE. After driving out the Kidara Kushans, they first concentrated on consolidating their position in Afghanistan. Then in the second half of fifth century CE, they launched a series of attacks on Gandhara. They ultimately succeeded in vanquishing the Kidara Kushans and establishing their kingdom in Gandhara around 463 CE.

During their century long rule in Gandhara, the Ephthalites created a hostile environment in which the rulers were totally alienated with the local Buddhist population. The initial period of their rule is characterized by large scale destruction.

Chinese pilgrim Sung-Yuen, who visited Gandhara around 519 CE in the 6th century, provides details of the religious persecutions carried out by the Ye-Tha (Ephthalites) and large scale destruction of the Buddhist monasteries all over Gandhara "about two generations ago." Archaeological investigations at various monasteries in the Taxila Region also confirm the damages indicated by Sung-Yuen. The 32 silver Ephthalite coins found from Dharmarajika, Bhamala and Lalchuk monasteries in the Taxila Region indicate that almost all the damages to these monasteries were carried out towards the end of 5th century CE.[81]

Having established their total control through a wave of terror, the Ephthalites seem to have shown a high degree of accommodation to the conquered people in Gandhara, as indeed they did in other countries where they ruled, for example Persia, where they seem to have partially adopted Zoroastrian faith. The same attitude is indicated by inscription attributed to one of the later Ephthalite rulers, Toramana, which proclaims that he made a donation to one of the Buddhist monasteries in Gandhara.

However these tokens of respect by the Ephthalites for the Buddhist establishment came too late. The confidence of the Buddhist communities in the Ephthalite regime had been badly shattered. There was now very little dialogue between the Buddhist priests and the rulers.

Within the Buddhist community also major changes started taking place, which were to disturb the harmonious relationship between all members of the Buddhist Sangha. The priestly class became more powerful and assertive in religious matters. It began to distance itself from the lay Buddhists.

---

81   Sir John Marshall. *Taxila-An Illustrated Account of Archaeological investigations carried out in Taxila, 1913-34.* Cambridge 1951.

Second Period of Sassanid Rule 570–655 CE.

The tussle between the Ephthalites and the Sassanids continued in Eastern Persia, Afghanistan, Bactria and even Xinjiang all through the fifth and first half of the 6th century. In the mid-5th century the Ephthalites had got the better of the Sassanids in various regions including Gandhara. In the early 6th century it was again the turn of the Sassanids to regain at least a semblance of their past glory.

During the reign of Khusrau-I (also known as Anushervan the Just), the resurgent Sassanids were once again on the march to re-conquer all lands, which once belonged to the Achaemenid Empire. In the second half of the 6th century CE, they destroyed the Ephthalite Empire in Bactria and Southern Afghanistan. Then in 570 CE, they drove the Ephthalites out of Greater Gandhara and established themselves in this region.

Things were going well for the Sassanids as long as Khusrau-I was on the throne. Khusrau-I died in 579 CE, and the downslide of the Sassanids started once again. Khusrau-II, who ascended the throne, remained constantly engaged in battles with the Byzantines in Mesopotamia and West Asia, with the result that in this second period of Sassanid rule Gandhara remained neglected and could not recover from the damages suffered during the rule of the Ephthalites.

Hsiuen Tsang, who visited Gandhara during the latter part of the 80-year rule of the Sassanids, found that most of the 1400 sangharamas on the banks of the Su-po-su-tu (Swat River) were in total ruin and out of the 18000 monks, who once resided in these sangharamas, very few remained.[82] During his stay of about 19 years in Gandhara and places of pilgrimages in other parts of South Asia, Hsiuen Tsang had an opportunity to observe the working of the Buddhist community and the Buddhist establishment in great detail. He writes about the sharp decline in the moral standards of the Buddhists and about the deviation of the Buddhist clergy from the ideals which had inspired them during the days when Gandhara Civilization was at its peak.

The Sassanid involvement in wars with the Byzantines and later with the Islamic forces, created severe pressures for the Sassanid regime not only in their homeland, Persia, but also in their colonies, such as Gandhara. The

---

82   Hsiuen Tsang. *Buddhist Records of the Western World*. Translated by Samuel Beal, London 1884.

Sassanids were not opposed to the Buddhist establishment in Gandhara. Under a prosperous Sassanid regime, the Buddhist establishment in Gandhara would have survived even without direct patronage of the regime. The economy in Sassanid Gandhara, weakened by their wars with Byzantines, meant that less funds were available to the Buddhist establishment from donations of the devotees. As a result during the rule of the Sassanids the activities of the Buddhist establishment in Gandhara were severely curtailed and their downslide continued.

Minor Buddhist Revival during Turk Shahi Rule

In the unsettled conditions prevailing in various parts of the Sassanid Empire in the early 7th century, the Buddhist Turk Shahis seized power from the Sassanids in the Kabul Valley and shortly thereafter, also in Gandhara. Sometime around 655 CE, when the Islamic forces attacked Kabul, the Turk Shahis moved their capital from Kabul to Udhabhanda (modern Hund), about 20 kilometers north of Attock. This new capital of Buddhist Gandhara was strategically located on the west bank of the Indus River, approximately midway between the two ancient metropolises of Gandhara, Takshasila and Pushkalavati.

After the anti-Buddhist rule of the Ephthalites and lukewarm attitude of the Sassanids towards the Buddhists of Gandhara, the Buddhist community of Gandhara experienced a minor revival during the two centuries of rule by the Buddhist Turk Shahis. In the region surrounding the new Gandhara capital of Udhabhanda, some new monasteries were constructed and in other regions of Gandhara also socio-economic activity picked up.

Wu-Kung, the last of the important Chinese Buddhist pilgrims to Buddhist Gandhara, provides valuable written records of the revival of the Buddhist activities in Gandhara during the rule of the Turk Shahis. Wu-Kung was sent by the Chinese emperor as a political emissary to the court of Turk Shahis in Kabul. After completing his political mission Wu-Kung arrived in Gandhara in 751 C.E on a pilgrimage to holy Buddhist places in the Greater Gandhara region. In Gandhara, Wu-Kung became a Buddhist monk and spent some time in a monastery in Swat. His writings indicate that a lot of reconstruction work was carried out by the Turk Shahis on the monasteries damaged during the rule of the Ephthalites and that Buddhism was very much a living religion in this period.[83]

---

83   S. Beal. *Buddhist Records of the Western World*, 1884.

But the Turk Shahis worked within very narrow parameters. The world was closing all around them. Already isolated from the north, they now came under pressure from the Hindu revivalist forces in the northeast and south. The Buddhists after dominating the cultural scene in this north-western region of Gandhara for almost a millennium, now looked like a spent force. While Buddhism continued to gain ground in the Far East under missionaries who had their roots in Gandhara, in the land of its birth Mahayana Buddhism no longer generated the same degree of dynamism among the scholars and the general masses as it did under the Kushans.

Repression during Hindu Shahi Rule

Around 845 CE, the Hindu Shahis seized power from the Turk Shahis in Gandhara. This more or less sealed the fate of the Buddhists in Gandhara. Two important Hindu dynasties, the Kallars and the Bhima ruled Gandhara, one after the other. Their capital remained Udhabhanda. The rulers belonging to these dynasties, for the first time in the political history of this region, replaced Buddhism with Hinduism as the State religion. Buddhist culture virtually disappeared from this region.

CHAPTER 8: SANGHARAMAS

The remains of thousands of sangharamas in the northwestern regions of Pakistan and the bordering southeastern region of Afghanistan throw light on some of the special features of the great Buddhist civilization in ancient Gandhara.

The vast majority of the population comprised of dedicated followers of the Mahayana religion. Mahayana philosophy provided for a healthy mix of spiritual and worldly activities. Therefore the sangharamas were designed to function within such a system.

The dynamic economic environment prevailing in Greater Gandhara during the period of the Gandhara Civilization gave birth to a large number of urban centers, where the life was principally akin to the life of people in modern towns and cities. The businessmen, traders, craftsmen and construction workers in the urban centers spent a good deal of their time in the performance of their secular tasks and in the process created a lot of hustle and bustle that one usually associates with urban life.

The section of the population which catered to the spiritual and intellectual needs of the people of Gandhara required an atmosphere of peace for the performance of their duties. They required quietness and solitude to meditate, pray, compile religious texts, train missionaries and perform their exercises and rituals.

According to the spirit of the Mahayana religion the two sections of the population could not function in isolation. A via media was found for healthy interactions between the spiritual and the secular establishments by locating the larger sangharamas at a convenient distance from the urban centers. The location of the larger sangharamas away from the center of the cities served to separate the secular activities of the people at large, from the socio-religious environment of the sangharamas. The population in the cities comprised of practicing Buddhists, but the lifestyle of the people was not circumscribed by the traditional laws and practices governing the life of the monastic community in the sangharamas. The people would go about doing their daily chores under an administrative and commercial set-up, which did not provide for interference or influence from the high priest in charge of the sangharamas. Within the sangharamas, the authority of the high priests prevailed. The rulers gave due respect to the clerics and provided financial assistance for the upkeep of the sangharamas.

The larger sangharamas in Gandhara were invariably located at picturesque sites—cloistered in valleys, glens, slopes of hills and spurs of nearby mountain ranges. They presented a majestic spectacle—grand as well as serene, dignified and peaceful. Streams and rivers flowed nearby and the areas were usually surrounded by forests or thick vegetation. These pleasant surroundings provided stimulation to the people working in the sangharamas and provided immense attraction and enjoyment to the families from nearby centers, who visited the sangharamas for the performance of their religious duties and to take part in social and religious festivities.

The sangharamas of Greater Gandhara during the mature phase of Gandhara Civilization comprised of two distinct sections:

- A stupa complex built around one or more large stupas, each surrounded by a large number of smaller stupas donated by the votaries. As the stupa complex continued to expand, separate courtyards were added to house the new stupas.

- Viharas spread over one or more courtyards, where the monks resided, meditated, compiled religious texts, and underwent training for missionary work.

The main stupa in each sangharama enshrined the body relics of an important member of the Buddhist monastic establishment. The smaller stupas housed the body relics of other members of the monastic fraternity or the Sangha. In addition a large number of Votive stupas were constructed in the compound or placed in niches in the chapels or panels decorating the walls of the drum. Some of these may have contained body relics but a large number of such stupas were donated to the sangharamas purely for decoration purposes.

Basically all stupas, whether the larger ones containing relics or smaller votive stupas donated for decorative purposes, were constructed in more or less standard format, comprising of identical or similar constructional components or elements. The dome always remained the principal and the most symbolic element in a stupa. During the peak period of Buddhist religious architecture in Gandhara, the casket containing the body relics of the deceased were not buried directly inside the dome. Instead the casket containing the body relics was placed inside a separate cubic enclosure constructed on the summit of the dome. Above this enclosure, mounted on an axial rod, were the parasols, several of them mounted one on top of the other.

The low circular plinth, on which the domes of the early stupas were mounted, was replaced in the later stupas by a rectangular base with drums raised to a height of several meters. This development is generally attributed to Hellenic influence as similar Greek and Roman monuments were constructed on this pattern. Another development, also attributable to the influence of Hellenic culture, is the introduction of images of Buddha and Bodhisattvas in the decorative panels as well as freestanding images in various areas of the stupa complex.

The standard form of the viharas, which emerged in Greater Gandhara in the first century CE, comprised of a high walled rectangular courtyard attached to the stupa courtyard. When the monastic activity at the site increased, other vihara courtyards were constructed in the vicinity in a similar design to the original vihara.

All viharas in the mature phase of Gandhara Civilization contained an inner Quadrangle, constructed at a level of about two or three feet below the level of the surrounding area. The Inner Quadrangle was surrounded by passages or walkways. On all four sides of the outer periphery of the vihara Quadrangle, with their backs to the high stone masonry boundary walls, there were the monastic cells, chapels and service buildings of the monastery.

PROMINENT SANGHARAMAS IN GREATER GANDHARA

In each of the four major regions of Greater Gandhara, two or three sangharamas became the objects of special attention of the Buddhist establishment and the regime. They acquired regional status and served to inspire the people of each region with their grandeur and the range of their activities. In the Peshawar Valley, Shahji-ki-Dheri and Takht-i-Bahi, in the Uddhyana (Swat Valley) Butkara, in the Taxila region Dharmarajika, Jaulian and Mohra Muradu, and in South-eastern Afghanistan the Hadda complex stood out among the other monuments in their respective regions.

Shahji-ki-Dheri

This sangharama is closely associated with Kanishka. The finds from the site indicate that it was constructed on the orders of Kanishka, shortly after he moved the Kushan capital to Purushapura.

The ruins of this sangharama are located on two mounds about six kilometers outside the urban limits of Peshawar (ancient Purushapura). The stupa was located on one mound, while monastery complex was located on the other mound towards the east of the stupa Mound.

The sangharama was badly damaged during the Sassanian invasion in 240 CE, but it was restored to its original glory shortly afterwards. It was visited by all the important Chinese scholar-monks, who visited Gandhara in the period from 4th to 8th century CE. The accounts of these scholar monks provide most of the information pertaining to this most important sangharama.

According to the accounts of the Chinese scholar-monks, the sangharama at Shahji-ki-Dheri contained a 125-meter high stupa which was topped with a spire made of iron. The radiant spire, sparkling in the light of the sun, could be seen from a very long distance.[84] The superstructure, which was probably made of wood in the style of palaces constructed in that period, was surmounted by 25 gilded copper umbrellas.[85]

To the east of the Grand stupa was a huge colony for Buddhist monks and scholars—the Patracaitya. Fa-Hsien, who visited the sangharama early in fifth century CE, indicates that there were about 700 monks in the monastery at that time. He then goes on to describe the ceremony, which took place every day before lunch, when a bowl (Patra) was moved around and donations collected.[86] Various references indicate that the sangharama was very much in place till the ninth century CE.

---

84 Samuel Beal. *Buddhist Records of the Western World*, London 1884.

85 Ahmed Nabi Khan. *An illustrated Guide of Gandhara*, Karachi, 1994.

86 Fa-Hsien. *A Record of Buddhist Kingdoms*, translated by James Legge, Oxford, 1886.

Sahri Bahlol

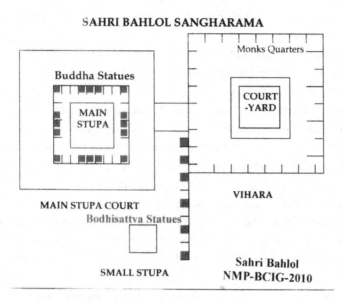

Figure 8.1: Sahri Bahlol Sangharama

The principal sangharama near the fortified Kushan town of Sahri Bahlol was located about one and a half kilometer from the city mound, about 12 kilometers from the modern city of Mardan. Major part of the construction at this sangharama belongs to the 3rd and fourth centuries CE, when, after a period of relative inactivity, sangharamas began to be constructed once again on a fairly large scale.

The sangharama was constructed on the standard pattern of most sangharamas belonging to the Kushan and Kidara Kushan period. There were two walled rectangular courts, one for the stupas and the other for the monastery. The two courts were connected through a passage taking off from the eastern wall of the stupa court.

The main stupa was placed in the center of the stupa court. The core of the stupa was filled with schist and stucco debris which was covered with stucco plaster.[87] The stupa was surrounded by an interior wall, which was provided with cells. Inside the cell were large statues of seated and standing Buddhas and Bodhisattvas. These statues, a large number of them more than a meter in height, were made from schist and stucco and were covered with gold paint.

Outside the stupa court was another stupa, smaller in size to the main stupa inside the court, but impressive nevertheless.

The wall of the vihara was made of schist and stucco. The interior was of standard design, with a sunken quadrangle surrounded by passages and small cells on the inside of all four exterior walls. Some of these cells served as residential quarters for monks, others as chapels. Large gilded statues of Buddhas and elegantly clad Bodhisattvas, very similar to the ones in the stupa court, were also provided inside the vihara.

The stupa wall of the vihara facing the stupa yard was extended to make provision for niches, inside which votive stupas and statues were placed.

The archaeological excavations at the site carried out by Dr. S.B. Spooner in 1907 and Sir Aurel Stein in 1915 yielded more than 300 sculptures, high reliefs and statues. They are rated among the most beautiful art pieces recovered from any one site. They include magnificent statues of Buddha seated in Dhyana as well as Dharmachakra Mudras under beautifully carved canopies, and standing Maitreya and other Bodhisattvas with long flowing tresses sprawled over the shoulders, scantly clad in lungis or loin cloths with beautifully executed folds, but wearing loads of jewelry. Another beautiful panel from Sahri Bahlol now in the Peshawar Museum, is that showing Kuvera and Hariti seated side by side.[88]

Takht-i-Bahi

About five kilometers from Sahri Bahlol and twenty kilometers from Mardan is one of most picturesque sangharamas in Western Gandhara— the Takht-i-Bahi Sangharama. It is located on a plateau, about 165 meters above the level of the surrounding plains. The sprawling mass of beautifully laid out monuments belonging to this sangharama is approached by a wind-

---

87 Francine Tissot. *The Site of Sahri Bahlol in Gandhara, Pakistan: Further investigations, South Asian Archaeology*, Curzon Press, The Riversdale Co. 1985.

88 Dr. D.B. Spooner served as Curator of the Peshawar Museum in 1909–10. The *Handbook of Sculptures in the Peshawar Museum* compiled by him provides elaborate description of sculptures recovered from Sahri Bahlol and Takht-i-Bahi.

ing path, which takes off from the Peshawar-Swat Highway, just before the Highway enters the Malakand Pass.

Takht-i-Bahi Sangharama was the largest and most impressive of the Buddhist sangharamas west of the Indus River, with construction spread over a period of 700 years from 1st century BCE to 7th century CE. It is located in a region, which abounds in Buddhist monuments belonging to the Kushan era. While most of these monuments suffered major destruction at the hands of Mihiragula, the White Hun invader from Central Asia in the 5th century CE, the Takht-i-Bahi Sangharama escaped damage in this period due to its location on a secluded hill, some distance away from the main highway linking Gandhara heartland with Swat.

Takht-i-Bahi Sangharama maintained close relationship with Sahri Bahlol, the nearest urban center. Sahri Bahlol was regularly visited by the monks (Bhikshus) of Takht-i-Bahi for food, donations and other necessities of life.

The foundations of the sangharama were probably laid in the first century BCE, during the period of Parthian rule. Additions continued to be made all through the Kushan period. Thereafter, when the Sassanids, who conquered the region in third century CE, withdrew official patronage, the construction remained temporarily suspended. After the Kidara Kushans conquered Gandhara, the expansion of the sangharama was undertaken with increased enthusiasm and vigor. The latest construction at Takht-i-Bahi dates to the period around 7th century CE, when the Gandhara Civilization had well passed its peak.

At Takht-i-Bahi, the major constructions pertain to a large monastery, and three main courtyards, where the stupas are located. These courtyards are referred to as the Court of the Main Stupa, the Court of the Three Stupas, and the Court of Many Stupas.

Centuries before the regular construction of the sangharama commenced at the site of the Takht-i-Bahi, a monastery may have existed there, which was in the style of monasteries of the early phases of Buddhism. Primarily it served as the residential quarters of a colony of monks who wanted to spend most of their time on meditation.

In due course a huge sangharama began to take shape in an unconventional pattern because the construction of different courtyards and auxiliary buildings was carried out at different levels.

One of the earliest constructions at the site is a regular monastery or vihara which was constructed during the reign of Kanishka-I. The quadrangle at the center measured about 20 meters square. Surrounding the quadrangle on three sides were two storeys of monastic cells, which provided accommodation to about 35 monks.

Towards the west of the monastery, separated by a narrow passage, was an Assembly Hall, where monks met from time to time to discuss various religious issues.

Belonging to the same period as the monastery, was a stupayard, which is referred to as the Court of Many Stupas. There were about thirty votive stupas at the center of the stupa court. The bases of the votive stupas were extensively decorated with narrative reliefs molded in stucco. The reliefs were framed by raking cornices, supported on Corinthian pilasters. Surrounding the group of votive stupas, on three sides, there were chapels with nine meter high walls behind them. There was no main stupa in the yard containing the relics of some important religious functionary and the medium sized votive stupas did not get much importance. Thus, all through this early phase of the Takht-i-Bahi Sangharama, the vihara continued to dominate. It was several centuries later, probably during the reign of Huvishka, when the main stupa was constructed in a separate yard that a proper balance was established between the public part of the sangharama, the stupayards, and the more private section, the vihara, where the Monks' quarters and chapels were primarily located.

The main stupa yard was constructed during the later period of Kushan rule, late second and third century CE. Unlike the more common layout pattern of stupa courts in which the main stupa is located in the center of the stupa court and is surrounded on all sides by walls decorated with statues and reliefs, the main stupa at Takht-i-Bahi is located at one end of a spacious courtyard, backed by one of the walls. The other three walls were lined with chapels, with graceful dome-shaped roofs. Inside the chapels were elegantly carved statues of Buddha and other decorations, some of which can now be viewed in the Peshawar Museum.

The main stupa was located on top of a three-tiered, square plinth, of the type which was in fashion in the Kushan period. The terraced plinth rises to a height of three meters in three steps. It measures about six and a half meters square at the lowest level and five meters square at the top. Above the plinth, the dome, about 4 meters in diameter, rose to a height of about

6 meters, leaving a space one meter wide around the dome for devotees to make their devotional rounds. Above the dome, there must have been the relic casket and the Parasols.

Figure 8.2: Takht-i-Bahi Sangharama (Photo: Paramount Archives, Karachi)

The Court of the Three Stupas belongs to still later period. It was constructed during in the late fourth and fifth centuries during the period of rule of the Kidara Kushans. It measures 21.5 by 15 meters. It was located towards the west of the main stupa court and separated from it by a passage. The six meters square base of the main stupa in this courtyard was heavily decorated with stucco reliefs showing Buddha in Dhyana mudra. These decorations were divided into panels separated from each other by Indo-Corinthian pilasters. Besides this large stupa, there were two smaller *stupas* in this courtyard. The decorations on the wall of the drum of these stupas were in two parts. The bottom layer was decorated with statues of Buddha in Dhyana and Abhaya mudras, while above these was a frieze with standing figures.

Jamalgarhi Sangharama

Jamalgarhi Sangharama ranks among the earliest in Western Gandhara. It belongs to the period when the main stupa used to be at the center of the sangharama and the monastic cells, smaller stupas and chapels were constructed round it.

The site of Jamalgarhi Sangharama is located to the north-west of Mardan. The archaeological excavations conducted at the site by Sir Alexander Cunningham in 1893 resulted in the retrieval of large number of Buddhist reliefs and statues. Along with Sahri Bahlol, Jamalgarhi ranks among the leading sangharamas in Western Gandhara from the point of view of concentration of beautifully carved decorations belonging to different periods.

Among the decorations from Jamalgarhi, carvings of scenes from the Jatakas are of a particularly high standard. Some of these are in narrative form with a series of related panels 'narrating' the story contained in a particular Jataka.

<small>TAXILA ENVIRONS</small>

The concentration of large number of Buddhist sangharamas belonging to all periods of Gandhara Civilization indicates that Taxila remained one of the major areas of intense Buddhist activity in Greater Gandhara for a very long time.

The sangharamas were located north and south of the Hathial Spur in the background provided by the Margalla Hills. This region comprises of green elevated areas and fertile valleys watered by the Haro River, Dhamrah Kas, Lundi Kas and numerous other seasonal streams. Descriptions of its rich agricultural produce and pleasant climate appear in the writings of a number of scholars belonging to the period of Gandhara Civilization, including the famous Chinese scholar-monk, Hsieun Tsang.

Among the important Buddhist sangharamas and stupas in and around Taxila investigated by Sir John Marshall, were Dharmarajika, Kalawan, Khader Mohra, Akhauri, Jaulian, Mohra Moradu, Sirkap, Kunala, Ghai, Giri, Pippala, Bhamala, Bhallar, Badalpur and Lalchuk.

Dharmarajika Sangharama

It is not the most beautiful, but certainly the largest and historically the most important of all the sangharamas of Buddhist Gandhara. Given the fact that it is the oldest of the sangharamas in Gandhara, and large scale repairs and expansion took place at this sangharama over the entire period of the Gandhara Civilization, one is left with the impression that extra-care was given for its maintenance and all the extensions were carried out in a very organized manner.

The Chir Tope site where the main Dharmarajika stupa is located is a huge complex where over a period of about seven centuries from third century BCE to 5th century CE, hundreds of stupas, chapels and monastic cells were constructed. This construction belongs to the Mauryan, Indo-Scythian, Parthian, Kushan, Indo-Sassanian and Kidara Kushan periods, but perhaps the contributions made in its expansion and maintenance were largest during the Kushan period, particularly in the period of rule of Kanishka, Huvishka and Vasudeva.

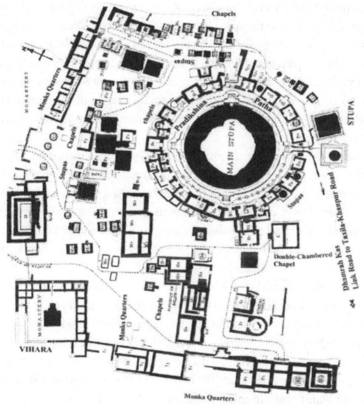

Figure 8.3: Layout of Dharmarajika Sangharama (Courtesy Archaeological Department, Pakistan)

The basic form of main Dharmarajika stupa replicates the form of the eight earliest stupas. It consists essentially of a low circular sub-structure, the medhi. There is no drum as such, only circular terraced platform round the base, serviced by four flights of steps. The circular periphery of this platform constitutes the ambulatory path, Pradakshina Patha. From the inner periphery of the ambulatory path rises the dome, which, unlike that in later stupas constructed in Gandhara, is not a semi-globe. Instead, it is slightly flattened and elongated. Also Dharmarajika stupa is different from most other stupas in Gandhara because it does not have a rectangular base and a platform or drum.

The main stupa had a diameter of 46 meters and its height must have been around 16 meters. To provide it strength major modifications to the core of the stupa were carried out in the post-Mauryan period. Sixteen walls, more than a meter thick were provided, which radiated from the center of the core, and the space between the walls was filled with rubble. During Kanishka's reign the circular terraced platform on which the stupa rested was completely redesigned. The face of the terrace was covered by decorated panels separated from each other by Corinthian pilasters. The Kidara Kushans also carried out large scale decoration of the base in the fourth century. The basic shape of the stupa remained unaltered during centuries of renovation.

During the post-Mauryan phases of the Gandhara Civilization a large number of small stupas were constructed through donations provided by the devotees, on raised ground all round the main stupa. Later a large number of chapels were constructed outside the inner ring of small stupas. In the entire area around the smaller stupas and inside as well as outside the chapels, statues of Buddha and other sculptures were provided during the Kushan and Kidara Kushans periods.

In the Mauryan Period, when the main stupa was constructed, the requirement of a large sized vihara to house a permanent group of monks engaged in writing sacred Buddhist texts, training new monks and holding regular religious meetings, was not there. Hence, only the basic accommodation was provided for the monks permanently residing at the site and perhaps some provisions made for hostels for visiting monks, who came here from time to time to spend some time at the sangharama.

However, the rapid growth of Buddhist population in the immediate vicinity of the stupa and reshaping of Buddhist institutions led to rapid change in the original plan. Besides the small votive stupas and chapels, which have been referred to above, linear barracks, containing more refined living accommodation for resident monks, were also constructed in large numbers. Around first century CE, a walled, rectangular shaped vihara was added in the outer periphery of the sangharama. As per standard practice, which emerged around first century CE, a courtyard was provided in the center of the monastery and residential cells and chapels were provided inside each of the four outer walls.

Inspite of its phenomenal growth, and the damage caused by a massive earthquake and by Sassanians and the White Huns, Dharmarajika maintained harmony in its layout and remained operational all through the Buddhist periods in Greater Gandhara, from its infancy in the Mauryan till its period of neglect in the period after the end of the rule of the Kidara Kushans.

The huge stupa complex *cum* vihara of Dharmarajika has yielded a very large variety of valuable artifacts. These include several hoards containing nearly 1000 coins of Indo-Scythian, Kushan, and Indo-Sassanian rulers. A large number stupas yielded gold and silver-bronze caskets inside which were calcined bones, ashes, and beads of gold and precious stones. The chapels also contained votive offerings of stone, stucco and terracotta sculptures. Also a silver scroll inscribed in Kharoshthi and a gold casket containing ashes said to be of Buddha, was found in side a vase placed in one of the chapels.[89]

Mohra Muradu Sangharama

The site of the Mohra Muradu Sangharama, in a verdant valley, a few kilometers from the village of Mohra Moradu, presents a rare spectacle of natural beauty. Surrounded on three sides by green hills, the valley, watered by a number of seasonal nallahs (streams), has a luxuriant growth of trees and shrubs, which have been sustained these days by additional water provided by the canals from the nearby Khanpur Dam.

The sangharama was constructed about the time Vima Kadphises had started the construction of the new city of Takshasila-Sirsukh. In the period 2nd century CE to 7th century CE, when Takshasila-Sirsukh was the principal center of political, religious and economic activity in the Taxila Region, a large number of new sangharamas were constructed near to it. Along with Jaulian, Mohra Muradu was the most spacious and well-decorated sangharamas in this part of Taxila.

---

89 Sir John Marshall. *Taxila- an Illustrated Account of Archaeological Excavations carried out at Taxila, 1913-34.* Volume I, Cambridge 1951 & *Journal of Royal Asiatic Society of Great Britain and Ireland,* October 1914. Known as the Silver Scroll Inscription of Azes, this important donative inscription refers the year 136 of Azes (78 C.E.), when Ursaka, a Bactrian donated relics of Buddha, which were enshrined in his Bodhisattva chapel at Dharmarajika.

Fig. 8.4: Mohra Muradu Sangharama (Photo: Paramount Archives, Karachi)

Mohra Muradu Sangharama was located less than 3 kilometers from the southern wall of Takshasila-Sirsukh. It is surrounded on three sides by tree-covered hills, which blend beautifully with the construction and have over the years provided protection against natural disasters as well as thieves.

In the foreground there is the main stupa. It was among the most profusely decorated stupas in the region. The cubic drum has six panels on each wall separated by pilasters. Each panel, about 4 meters high and two meters wide, was decorated with beautiful images of Buddhas and Bodhisattvas. Even the face of the pilasters had decorations of images of Buddha. These decorations represent the mature phase of Gandhara art, in which the skills of Hellenistic artists and sculptors were most effectively utilized to produce sharp life-like images with well-defined features. Above the drum is a circular ledge about a meter high, the outer surface of which was also provided with decorated rectangular panels.

Behind the main stupa is another stupa, slightly smaller in size but decorated in a similar manner to the main stupa.

The two stupas are connected to a spacious monastery through a common well-decorated passage. The layout of the monastery is very similar to that in other sangharamas in the Taxila Area. The sunken rectangular courtyard is surrounded by walkways, behind which, with their backs to the walls, are several spacious chambers, which served as residential quarters of monks, and chapels with large statues of Buddhas. The kitchen and other service buildings were located in the eastern portion of the monastery and were approached from the court of cells through a doorway.

The main stupa at Mohra Muradu ranks among the larger stupas of Greater Gandhara. In the Taxila Region it was smaller in size only to Dharmarajika stupa.

Excavations at the site have yielded a large number of statues of Buddha and Bodhisattvas and other decorative material, most of which have now been removed to the Taxila Archaeological Museum. Among the artifacts removed from the Mohra Muradu site, is a beautiful four meter high model of a stupa with soft limestone core and decorations made from stucco. The coins found from the site, mostly belong to Huvishka and Vasudeva.

Jaulian Sangharama

Jaulian Sangharama is located on the flat top of a hill, which rises to a height of about 100 meters above the adjacent Taxila-Khanpur road. The Haro River flows less than a kilometer away, towards the west of the Jaulian site.

Jaulian Sangharama belongs to the same period as the Mohra Moradu Sangharama and is located about two kilometers to the south of it. The construction styles of the two stupas are quite different but the viharas are very similar in design and layout, and there is evidence of close relationship between the two sangharamas.

The dominating feature of the stupas in the Jaulian Complex is the extensive, almost exclusive, use of stucco plaster in the outer surface of the rectangular-section bases as well as in the moldings of images of Buddhas, Bodhisattvas, and in other decorations. However, inspite of greater ease with which stucco plaster can be used to mould images and other decorations, the artistic quality of the decorations around the bases of the stupas is distinctly inferior to that at Mohra Moradu. The size of the stupas is also much smaller than the sizes of the main and other larger stupas at Mohra Moradu and Chir Tope (Dharmarajika).

The layout of the sangharama provides for an upper and a lower stupa court on the western part of the sangharama, and a spacious monastery towards the east.

The main stupa occupies a central position in the upper stupa court. All around it are a number of smaller votive stupas with images of Buddhas in various mudras, placed inside trapezoidal or triangular shaped niches on the walls of the stupa bases. In none of the stupas have the constructions above the stupa bases, survived.

Figure 8.5 (Top) Jaulian Stupa-yard, 8.6 (below) Vihara. (Photos: Paramount Archives, Karachi)

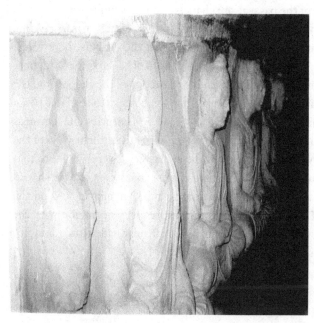

Figure 8.7: Buddha figures, Jaulian, Taxila (Photo: Paramount Archives, Karachi)

A passage from the main stupa court opens up at the end into a stupa quadrangle, the smallest of the three stupa quadrangles at Jaulian. A medium sized votive stupa was located at the center of the quadrangle. Only the base of the stupa has survived. The stucco decorations on the walls of the base are fairly well preserved.

Figure 8.8 Kunala Stupa.

On either side of the passage are chapels or shrines built through donations from the devotees. The surface of the plinth adjacent to the passage was decorated with stucco reliefs. Inside one of the chapels there was a statue of Buddha, which has now been removed. The superior stone masonry in the buildings indicates that the construction of the chapels and the votive stupa in this section of the stupa complex belongs to the later phase of the Kushan rule in Taxila—between 4th and 5th centuries CE. Towards the east of the stupa courts, is a large vihara with an excellent view of the lush green country side. The layout of the monastery is very similar to that at Mohra Muradu. In the western part of the monastey a square shaped sunken coutyard is surrounded by passages and 30 monastic cells on the outer periphery. The eastern wall of the court of cells is common with the Services section, in which three large halls are further divided into rooms for the kitchen, stores and toilets.

Figure 8.9 Vihara (Photos: Paramount Archives, Karachi)

Kunala

Located on high ground and approached by stairs rising from the eastern edge of the Indus Greek-Saka-Parthian city of Sirkap in Taxila, the Kunala Stupa is named after the son of Asoka Maurya. According to Buddhist traditions, blind pilgrims visited this stupa in ancient times in large numbers, because the stupa was said to possess miraculous powers of restoring the sight of the blind.

The stupa is particularly striking because of its magnificently sculptured drum. The three-tiered rectangular drum is constructed in the architectural style of Greek monuments. The profiling of the edges of the three terraces and the two-tiered base lined with brick-shaped cubicle stone blocks is of the type not found in any of the other stupas located in the Taxila Region.

Above the drum are the ruins of an oblong dome, much smaller than, but similar in shape to the dome of the Dharmarajika stupa.

The walls of the three terraces as well as the base were decorated with scenes from the life of Gautama Siddhartha. These decorations were made from molded lime plaster, a medium, which was increasingly used in the later phases of Gandhara art in the Taxila Region.

The major part of the construction at the Kunala stupa belongs to the period when the Kushan king, Vasudeva-I was ruling Taxila. Some additions were made during the reign of later Kushan rulers.

The magnificent vihara located to the west of the stupayard is surrounded by 4.5 meter high stone walls. It was constructed in the usual pattern; cells were constructed all along the inner side of the boundary walls and a sunken rectangular courtyard was provided in the center. The space between the cells and the courtyard was taken up by the beautifully decorated verandas and paved walkways.

Bhallar Sangharama

Perched majestically on a hill on the northern banks of the Haro River near the village of Usman Khattar, the Bhallar stupa provides an excellent view to travelers on the Taxila-Haripur Road. The Chinese pilgrim Hsiuen Tsang states that a stupa built by Asoka was located at this site; if there was such a stupa it has long disappeared. The stupa which we see these days belongs to the period around the 7th century CE.

Figure 8.10: Bhallar Sangharama (Photo: Paramount Archives, Karachi)

The most striking part of the stupa is its magnificent, multi-tiered circular drum, which rises to a height of about 15 meters above a rectangular base. The diameter of the drum is about 10 meters. This proportion between the height and diameter of the drum gives it a graceful cylindrical shape as against the more squat type stupas built in the earlier period in the Taxila region. Stupas of this type, belonging to the same period, are quite common in Swat e.g. the Shankerdar stupa, which was also visited by Hsiuen Tsang, and for which similar stories about its origin are also narrated by the Chinese pilgrim in his account of the visit to this region. (Hsiuen Tsang mentions that during the reign of Asoka, the body relics of Buddha were interred in both these stupas).[90]

Sculptured panels decorated the surfaces in the different tiers of the drum as well as on the walls of the rectangular base. Some fragments belonging to the scenes sculptured on these panels have been recovered from the site.

Of the dome, the lower portion has survived. Around the stupa the ruins of an adjacent monastery have been excavated. These include chapels, monastic cells and foundations of stone boundary walls. Hsiuen Tsang mentions that in the monastery the founder of the Sautrantika School composed his treatises.[91]

UDDHYANA REGION (SWAT-DIR-BUNER)

Uddhyana, 'Garden', the name by which Swat was known in ancient times was a very important part of Gandhara Civilization. In the peak period of this Civilization, there were more than 1000 Buddhist sangharamas in this region and more than 7000 Buddhist monks worked in these sangharamas.

Important Buddhist sites in his region are located at Butkara, Saidu, Udegram, Chakpat, Amlukdara, Gambat, Gumbatuna, Charbagh, Tokar Dara, Birkot, Nimogram, Panr, Sanghao, Nathu, Miyan Khan, Naogram, Ranighat, Loriyan Tangai, Shankardar, Chakdara and Andan Dheri.

The lush green hills and clear waters of the Swat River and its tributaries provided the ideal environment for meditation of the Buddhist monks, for their scholarly pursuits and for spiritual communion. Besides natural

---

90   S. Beal. Buddhist Records of the Western World, London 1884.
91   Sir John Marshall. *A Guide to Taxila*, Cambridge 1960

environment, it was necessary for the sangharamas to be located at a convenient communicating distance with the patrons. This was why some of the
largest and most elaborately decorated sangharamas in Swat were located
in the southern part of the valley, around Saidu Sharif, which was the most
thickly populated part of the region and was located at the confluence of the
Panjkora and Swat Rivers.

There were two major concentrations of large sangharamas in the Lower
Swat Valley and in the neighboring territory around Chakdara in Dir District. Among the well-known sangharamas in Swat and Dir were those
located at Butkara, and Nimogram in the Lower Swat Valley, and Andan
Dheri and Chakpat in Dir District.

Figure 8.11: Butkara Sangharama (Photo: Courtesy Archaeological Department, Pakistan)

Butkara

Butkara, presently known as Gulkada, is located near the town of Mingora on the left bank of the Swat River. Butkara Sangharama dated back to
third Century BCE, when a stupa was constructed here to bury the ashes of
Buddha distributed by Asoka. Additions to the sangharama continued to be
made till the 6th century CE.

Butkara was the largest stupa *cum* monastery complex in Swat with
more than 200 stupas, large and small, and an extended monastery area.
The excavations carried out at the site by the Italian Archaeological Mis-

sion have resulted in the recovery enormous number of artifacts of all types. They include thousands of beautiful sculptures, friezes as well as magnificent statues of Buddhas and Bodhisattvas. A large number of fancy architectural elements, including Hellenistic capitals, balustrades and cornices belonging to the period of rule of the Indo-Scythians and Parthians, jewelry, coins and pottery.

The Chinese pilgrim Sung-Yuen makes a special mention of the 6000 gilded images he found at this sprawling sangharama. [92]

Figure 8.12: Nimogram Monastery (Photo courtesy Swat Tourist Department)

Nimogram Monastery

The site of Nimogram Sangharama is located in a mountainous area about 44 kilometers from Saidu Sharif, the capital of Swat. Three impressive grey stone stupas, covered with lime plaster, were located in one line in the stupayard, along with more than fifty votive stupas and chapels. A monastery was located outside the western wall of the stupa-yard.

A large number of stone sculptures from this sangharama, depicting scenes from Buddhist Mythology and belonging to the Kushan period of rule in Greater Gandhara are on display at the Swat Museum in Saidu Sharif.

---

92 Hsiuen Tsang. *Buddhist Record of the Western World*, London, 1884. Sung Yuen calls the monastery at Butkara Ta-Lo.

Andan Dheri

The Andan Dheri Sangharama was located on a high mound near the point of confluence of Panjkora and Swat Rivers, about six kilometers from Chakdara in Dir District. The construction at the site covers the period from 1st century to 4th century CE.

The sangharama comprises of a main stupa at the eastern end of the site, a stupayard with 14 votive stupas in the middle, and a monastery at the western end.

The main stupa was constructed on a 38-meter-square plinth and was separated from the stupayard with 14 Votive stupas, by a wall. The monastery, measuring 60 meters by 30 meters, was surrounded by thick walls.

Archaeological excavations conducted at the site by Professor A.H. Dani, revealed four hoards of coins belonging to the period first to fourth century CE. The 440 coins included in these hordes mostly belong to the Kushan rulers Vima Kadphises, Soter Megas (Vima Taktu), Kanishka-III and Vasudeva-II. [93] They indicate considerable involvement of the Kushans in this area.

The earliest reliefs at the sites around Andan Dheri, belonging to the Parthian period, represent Hellenistic themes such as 'Soldiers and Lady Musicians' and 'A Drinking Party' and carvings of alien mythological figures such as the marine bulls and marine horses inside stone brackets/triangles meant for hanging votive garlands.

The Andhan Dheri sangharama was one of about half a dozen sangharamas located in the vicinity of Chakdara. Other important sangharamas in this area were located at Chatpat, Damkot, Ramora and Jabagai.

Amlukdara

The stupa at Amlukdara is located on the road from Swat to Buner. It is typical of the stupas constructed in the fourth and fifth centuries in the mountainous regions of Uddhyana.

Amlukdara Valley where this stupa was located is noted for its beautiful mountainous scenery. In the background of this stupa, Mount Elam towers to a height of 2811 meters. The picturesque historical village of Nawagai is

---

93 *Ancient Pakistan*, Volume IV, 1968-69, Bulletin of Department of Archaeology, University of Peshawar, 1968-69.

located about two kilometers from the stupa Site. Near to the main stupa a large number of votive stupas were constructed over a period of time.

Sir Aurel Stein, who visited the site in 1927, estimates the total height of the stupa, including the height of the drum and the triple base, to be around 31 meters. The lowest base measures 34.5 meter square, while the diameter of the hemispherical dome is 21.5 meters. The facing with stones provides a smooth surface to the dome.

Sir Aurel Stein mentions that during this visit he was approached by locals, who offered for sale a large collection of copper coins belonging to the Indus-Greeks, Saka-Parthians and Kushans, which they had gathered from the hill-sides around the stupa.[94]

Figure 8.13: Shingardar Stupa (Photo: Courtesy Tourist Department, Swat.)

Shingardar Stupa

The Shingardar stupa is also located in the vicinity of Mount Elam, about three kilometers from the historical village of Birkot, where Alexander fought one of his famous battles (about 18 kilometers from Saidu Sharif).

The stupa is very similar in size and design to the Amlukdara stupa, described above. The hemispherical dome has a diameter of 20.75 meters, just about 0.75 meters less than that of the Amlukdara stupa. The height above the road is 27.5 meters.

94   Sir Aurel Stein. *On Alexander's Track to the Indus*, Indus Publications, Karachi, 1995

The Upper Kabul River Valley, which presently forms a part of South-eastern Afghanistan, became an integral part of Greater Gandhara after the Mauryan Conquests and thereafter its status varied during the rule of various Hellenistic regimes. In the Golden Age of Gandhara Civilization, the Upper Kabul River Valley was an integral part of Greater Gandhara. Under the patronage of Kanishka and other Kushan rulers, Buddhist sangharamas were established in a big way all along the Kabul valley.

Around Jalalabad one large Buddhist monastery complex emerged in the second century CE at Hadda. Other well-known Buddhist sites located in this region were Bimaran, Fondukistan and Charar Bagh.

The region figures prominently in the accounts of the Chinese pilgrims, Fa-Hsien and Hsiuen Tsang. Fa-Hsien visited Hadda at the start of 5th century. He found 500 monks residing in the monasteries there. Hsiuen Tsang, who visited Hadda region around 630 CE, mentions that a 300-foot high stupa was erected here in the 3rd century BCE by Asoka. [95]

Hadda Sangharama

The Archaeological Site of Hadda is located about 10 kilometers from the Afghan South-eastern city of Jalalabad, in the Nangarhar Province. The archaeological excavations carried by the French Archaeological Mission under Jules Barthoux in the period 1926-28 revealed a cluster of eight monasteries, about 500 stupas and 15000 sculptures. The Monasteries include those of Chakhil-i-Ghoundi, Bagh Gai, Tapa-i-Kalan, Tapa-Kafriya and Tapa-i-Shotor. A large number of sculptures from this site are housed in the Guimet Museum in Paris, and the National Museum of Afghanistan in Kabul. They belong to the period from the 1st to the 6th centuries CE.

The excavations at the site of Hadda, have revealed Buddhist monasteries lavishly decorated with statues of Buddha, Bodhisattvas and sculptured panels depicting the life and teachings of Buddha. As in Taxila and Sahri Bahlol, most of the sculptures at Hadda produced in the early period were in schist, but over a period of time stucco became the more popular material used in these sculptures. Some artifacts were also produced in painted limestone.

The Buddhist sculpture at Hadda went through the same phases of development as Taxila and other sites in Swat and Mardan Regions. In the

---

95 Samuel Beal. *Buddhist Records of the Western World*, London 1884.

early period the Hellenistic themes dominated and a number of panels and statues depicting Greek deities and drinking orgies were produced. Later, with the emergence of Buddha statues and canonization of Buddhist texts the well-known styles of Gandharan Buddhist art began to dominate. Third century stucco heads of Buddha found from the site in large numbers, display the same exquisite facial expressions as the ones found from the Taxila and Mardan region—heavy-lidded eyes, an aquiline nose and wavy hair combed back to form an ushnisa.

Chapter 9: Gandhara Sculptures

The beautiful and peaceful surroundings, in which the Buddhist monks practiced their religion, sharpened the senses of the artists and elevated the spirits of the devotees. They provided the Gandhara artists the inspiration to produce works of art of extraordinary depth.

Images of Meditating Buddha produced in Greater Gandhara exude an air of inner peace and tranquility; lifelike scenes emerge from the reliefs depicting events from the life of Buddha; compassion shows in the faces of the Buddha and Bodhisattvas.

In the development of these extraordinary pieces of art, the Gandhara artists also derived benefit from the rich artistic traditions of Greece, Persia and South Asia. New styles, new types of compositions, new patterns, fabulous, new mythological creatures, new types of flora and fauna, new motifs, new symbols, new type of architectural elements, new fashions, new types of personal ornamentation and hairstyles and headdresses, new art materials and mediums for the artists to work on, all combined to bring about a revolutionary change in the prevailing art form.

Early Sculptures from Gandhara

Stone sculptures began to be produced in various parts of Gandhara during Indus Greek rule. The activity became more widespread during the rule of the Indo-Scythians and Indo-Parthians.

A substantial part of the sculptures produced during the Indo-Scythian and Indo-Parthian period were Toilet Trays, presumably used for preparing cosmetics, mostly portraying scenes from the Greek Mythology.

Figure 9.1: Toilet Tray from Sirkap (Photo: Courtesy Archaeological Department, Pakistan)

More than 150 toilet trays found from Takshasila-Sirkap and other Gandhara sites represent the earliest period of Gandhara Art (1st century BCE-1st century CE). The Toilet Trays are in the form of soft stone plates (9-18 cm. diameter). The fine carvings on these plates essentially portray motifs from Greek Mythology and Hellenistic traditions. A large number of portrayals comprise of aphrodisiac and Dionysian scenes. One such tray from Takshasila-Sirkap portrays the marriage of Adriane and Dionysus. The carving is divided into three sections, each section portraying a drinking scene. In one section a man holding a woman in tight embrace offers her wine; in the second section wine is being crushed, while the third section shows figures are shown lying drunk on the floor.

The toilet tray above was also found from the Indus-Greek layer at Takshasila-Sirkap. The upper register shows a reclining man pouring wine in the cup of a seated woman, while another woman with a garland is standing behind.

Some scholars believe that the trays with aphrodisiac and Dionysian scenes probably belonged to a Dionysian or similar Greek cult in which Bacchanalian rites played a significant part.[96]

---

96 Dr. Saifur Rahman Dar. *Taxila and the Western World*. Lahore, 1998.

Figure 9.2: Sculpture of drinking scene (Photo: Courtesy Archaeological Department, Pakistan)

Towards the end of the Indo-Scythian period and in the Parthian period, in the first half of first century CE, for the first time stucco figural reliefs began to used for decoration of stupas. The evidence comes mainly from the Apsidal Temple in Takshasila-Sirkap, where a number of stucco heads of Hellenistic nature, and also a few of Bodhisattvas, were found. These heads were probably part of the figural reliefs decorating the stupa.

In the mid-Parthian period, a somewhat bizarre development takes place in Gandhara Art. Stucco reliefs depicting male and female figures in drinking scenes appeared in the decoration of Buddhist stupas. Sculptures portraying drinking scenes were a favorite subject of the Hellenistic Indo-Parthian artists. These Hellenic Parthian artists, who had experience of producing such sculptures in their home country, produced these reliefs in Gandhara before they became familiar with Buddhist traditions. Very often the sculptures show mixed group of five to nine persons standing in a row with wine glasses or amphoras and stringed instruments in their hands.

One such relief is shown above. It comes from the stupa complex at Andan Dheri in Dir. The three men and three women included in the group are all wearing Greek dresses—the himation worn by the male members in the group is held in place by a girdle round their waist and one end of the cloth flung over the left shoulder. The women wear long sleeved chiton from neck to feet with shawls on their left arms.

Most of the reliefs depicting drinking orgies belong to the period from 1ˢᵗ century BCE to 1ˢᵗ century CE. They mostly come from stupas in the Uddhyana region of Greater Gandhara.

Figure 9.3: Composition of standing figures of Buddha and his companions derived from similar compositions belonging to Indo-Parthian period. (Photo: Courtesy Archaeological Department, Pakistan)

These non-Buddhist compositions were the forerunners of similar compositions in which the members of the drinking parties were replaced in the early period of Kushan rule (late first century CE) by a line of standing Buddhist deities, Buddha himself and Bodhisattvas (figure 9.3).

INTRODUCTION OF BUDDHA IMAGES IN GANDHARA

In the Greek cultural traditions, carved images of gods and other mythological figures always occupied a central place. These images continued to be the dominant feature of the Greek dominated hybrid Greco-Persian art, which emerged in West Asia after Alexander's invasion.

Therefore, when the Hellenistic sculptors were commissioned to produce Buddhist sculptures, the thought of introducing the images of Buddha must have come very naturally to them. The philhellenic Saka-Parthians and Kushans would have held similar views. Thus in the cosmopolitan cultural environment developing in Gandhara during the rule of the Saka-Parthians and the Kushans, the taboo on making images of Buddha was finally removed and Buddha images began to get their proper place in the Gandharan Buddhist sculptures.

Buddhist images first began to emerge in Gandhara during the rule of Saka-Parthians initially in the form of heads of Bodhisattvas. A number of such sculptures have been found from the Apsidal Temple in Sirkap, Taxila. The earliest statue believed to be that of Buddha dates to around 25 CE. This coarse, headless sandstone carved figure, recovered from the Dharmarajika stupa complex in the outskirts of Taxila, was identified by Sir John Marshall as that of Buddha on the basis of the chin-mudra position of the hand and fingers.

Figure 9.4: Buddha Statue (Peshawar Museum) (Photo: Paramount Archives Karachi)

Under the Kushans, Buddha's statues and sculptured images in reliefs and panels began to appear in ever-increasing numbers in Taxila as well as in other regions of Gandhara. During the reign of Kanishka and Huvishka images of Buddha modeled on Greek gods and dressed in Greek style, became the most prominent feature of Gandharan Sculptural Art.

The statue shown in figure 9.4 represents a hybrid design, in which the features in statues of Greek gods have been modified to emphasize the spiritual qualities of Buddha. The bold straight looking features of Greek gods have been replaced by the cool and calm figure, with half-closed eyes looking downwards. The statue obviously belongs the later period of Gandhara Art when most of the important features of Buddha statues were canonized. Unlike the earlier statues produced in Gandhara, in this statue Buddha has no moustache, his hair are in the form of tight ringlets instead of the sun-rays type of wavy hair combed backwards, and beneath Buddha's feet is a beautifully decorated pedestal.

BUDDHA ICON

> "What is there, Vakalli, in seeing this vile body? He who sees the
> Dharma sees me; he who sees me sees the Dharma."

Samyutta Nikaye

After the emergence of the images of Buddha in the Gandhara region
during the Saka-Parthian period, considerable emphasis was placed in the
succeeding Kushan period, on developing an image, which would do justice
to Buddha's special and exalted status.

Special attention was given to ensure harmony in the physical proportions of all parts of Buddha's body, so as to achieve an image, which reflected the physical beauty, grace and dignity of 'the Great Being'.

To bring out the spiritual qualities attributed to Buddha, appropriate
facial expressions and dignified postures were required to be devised.

The Gandhara artists made endless efforts on harmonization of the
physical proportions of all parts of Buddha's body; they selected appropriate dresses and hairstyles, and they developed facial expressions and postures, which reflected Buddha's attitudes on different occasions, and also
provided grace and dignity to Buddha's personality.

The incorporation of spiritual attributes of Buddha in the Buddha Icon
became a major challenge for the Hellenistic artists of Gandhara, who were
required to become familiar with the local traditions and basic teachings
of Buddhism before they could incorporate Buddha's spiritual attributes
into his image. Through the joint efforts of the clergy and the artisans, the
Buddhist sculptures the Buddha Icons began to be ultimately produced in
Gandhara, which faithfully and forcefully projected Buddha's spiritual personality and conveyed the essence of his teachings to his devotees.

The essential characteristics of the Buddha image which came to be
standard in Gandhara were:

   • Almond-shaped eyes representing Buddha Sakyamuni's descent
from the Licchavi clan. With half-closed eyes, the eyelids are shaped like
the leaves of the lotus or lily.

   • The Ushnisha, the 'bouffette' or bun, into which Buddha's hair was
tied at the top of his head, to reflect the enlightened nature of Buddha's
personality.

Figure 9.5: Buddha Icon Symbols

• The Urna, the small circular mark in the center of the forehead, called the Eye of Wisdom.

• The exaggerated length of the ears due to extended earlobes.

• The Nimbus, a symbol of deification, located behind the head of Buddha.

• The use of hand gestures to present Buddha in various modes.

Development of Symbols Used in the Buddha Icon

To bring out the spiritual qualities attributed to Buddha, besides appropriate facial expressions and dignified postures, specific symbols were developed and incorporated into the images.

The Ushnisa or bun of hair at the top of Buddha's head is part of all images of Buddha produced in Gandhara. It is the symbol of Buddha's Enlightenment. It is viewed as a source of power that remains in spiritual contact with the heavens and in this way enlightens the mind of Buddha.

Figure 9.6: Eternal Flame Ushnisa

To make the symbol more expressive, Gandharan sculptors used the analogy of the eternal flame derived from the Zoroastrian religious beliefs and practices. Wavy hair resembling flames emerged from the forehead, terminating in a bun at the top of the head, 'towards the heaven'. The wavy hair thus reinforced the idea of enlightenment.

Figure 9.7: Ringlets Ushnisa

In the later phases of Gandhara art, with Buddhist traditions and skills of locally trained artists dominating the artistic styles, other designs were developed to make the Ushnisa aesthetically more attractive, while still employing the analogy and symbolism of the original design. One of the designs which became popular in this phase of Gandhara Art was the representation of hair in form of tight ringlets, which some scholars believe represent cups holding the wicks of an oil lamp.

The solar disk or nimbus behind the head of Buddha was used by the Gandhara sculptors as a symbol of deification—probably an allusion to the Persian practice of Sun-worhip.

The Persians (Achaemenids), who ruled Gandhara as well as Bactria for more than two centuries before the arrival of the Greeks, practiced the Zoroastrian faith in which the sun, fire and flames served important purposes. Both before and after the birth of Zoroaster sun worship was an important part of the religious beliefs of the Persians and other West Asians. The solar disk was an important religious symbol for the Persians. For almost the entire period during which Buddhist religious art dominated the art scene in Gandhara, the Nimbus remained a simple plain round solar disc—a symbol of purity and enlightenment. The incorporation of the solar disc singled out Buddha or Bodhisattvas within a group of figures, emphasizing the special status of these deities.

The circular mark at the center of the forehead, referred to as Urna in Buddhist texts, was introduced by the Gandharan sculptors to highlight the wisdom of Buddha. Based on local traditions, the circular mark was seen as the Eye of Wisdom.

Use of Hand Gestures (Mudras)

Symbolic hand gestures were most effectively employed by Gandhara artists to recall events in the life of Buddha and to convey the deeper meaning associated with the event. These hand gestures, referred to as mudras, were readily understood by the common devotees to denote Buddha in the meditating, preaching, wish granting, protection and other such modes.

Three hand gestures dominate in the statues of Buddha in the Gandhara Region. These are the Dharmachakra Mudra, Dhyana Mudra, and the Abhaya Mudra.

Dharmachakra Mudra statues of Buddha begin to appear in the Gandhara in a relatively later phase—end of third century and early fourth century CE. The gesture indicates Buddha in a preaching mode. This pose is associated with one of the most important events in Buddha's life, The First Sermon.

In this Mudra (Figure 9.8), the two hands are folded in front of the breast, the right hand above and the left hand touching the fingers of the right hand. The palms of the hands are normally facing inwards in the statues from the Gandhara region, but in some other regions the palms are facing outwards.

Figure 9.8: Dharmachakra Mudra (Photo Paramount Archives, Karachi)

Figure 9.9: Dhyana Mudra (Photo: Paramount Archives, Karachi)

The sculpture in Figure 9.9 shows the youthful figure of Buddha in Dhyana Mudra. The two hands are folded in front of the navel; the ends of the thumbs touch each other, and the index finger of the right hand rests on the index finger of the left hand. The gesture represents Buddha in the Meditating Pose.

The statue of seated Buddha shown in the sculpture provides an excellent example of the overall impression required to be conveyed by sculptures of Buddha in the Dhyana Mudra. The expression on Buddha's face is one of serenity and calmness and single minded devotion.

Figure 9.10: Abhaya Mudra.

In the sculpture shown in Figure 9.10, standing Buddha is shown in Abhaya Mudra. The right hand of Buddha is in the elevated position, the fingers point upwards and the palms face outwards.

This sculpture portrays the Dipankara Jataka. The expression on the face reinforces the gestures of the hands to convey beautifully the thoughts and feelings associated with this pose.

BUDDHA STATUES

The statue of Buddha sets the tone and provides heart and soul to all pieces of Gandhara Buddhist Art. Whether in isolation as a single statue, or as a small sculptural piece fitting into niche or arches made in walls, or as one of the figures in an elaborate composition, the Buddha statue dominates the sculptural scene. It breathes life and spirit. The entire essence of Buddhist religious thought is built into the Buddha statue, hence the preoccupation with details. The facial expression, the posture, the position of the hands, the hairstyle, the dress, and individual features, they all tell a story.

Figure 9.11: Standing Buddha (British Museum London) Photo: Paramount Archives, Karachi

The figure above shows a fine schist stone carved standing figure of the Buddha in Greco-Roman robes. The hands, now detached from the statue, provide support to the ends of the chadar covering both shoulders. The eyes looking straight and the elongated moustache show confidence and grace.

The figure of Buddha in this statue is tall and stately; the build heavy and robust, of the type commonly associated with people in the northwestern regions of Pakistan. Each feature on Buddha's face is exquisitely carved—arched eyebrows above heavy lidded eyes, aquiline nose, prominent chin, and elongated earlobes. The wavy hair style swept backwards give the impression of flames rising from the forehead and terminating into a rather flattish ushnisa, in the typical style of Buddha statues belonging to the period 2ⁿᵈ–3ʳᵈ century CE.

This high quality piece comes from the heartland of Gandhara in the region around Mardan. The statue is presently housed in the British Museum.

Figure 9.12: Seated Bodhisattva (National Museum of Pakistan, Karachi) (Photo: Paramount Archives, Karachi)

Figure 9.12a: Standing Bodhisattva (National Museum of Pakistan, Karachi) (Photo: Paramount Archives, Karachi)

IMAGES OF BODHISATTVAS

The Mahayana sutras, which form the basis of the Buddhist sculptural art in Gandhara, began to appear in the last century BCE. In the two centuries intervening between the initial appearance of the Mahayana sutras and the appearance of the Bodhisattva images in Gandhara, a vast body of scriptures was compiled by the scholar-monks, which provided the characteristics of the Bodhisattva. It was left to the artists and artisans of Gandhara to develop a physical image of the Bodhisattvas, which reflected the appearance and spiritual qualities ascribed to the Bodhisattvas in the Mahayana sutras.

The statue shown in the figure 9.12 is that of a young mustached Bodhisattva seated with his ankles crossed. He wears a beautiful turban studded with precious stones, a lot of jewelry all over his body and sits gracefully, with drooping eyes on a well-decorated seat. The statue comes from the Taxila region and belongs to 2nd century CE.

The images of Bodhisattvas produced in Gandhara in the period first century CE to fifth century CE emphasize their two major attributes— Compassion (depicted by a suffering personality) and Wisdom. As in the case of the Buddha images, the Bodhisattvas are usually shown with extended earlobes and a halo behind the head, but otherwise there were important differences, as indicated in the Gandhara sculptures shown in the photographs.

As against the images of Buddha, who are invariably shown in monastic robes, the Bodhisattvas are shown in princely garbs and wearing a wealth of jewelry—earrings, necklaces, armlets, bracelets, scarves and belts. Instead of being tied in the form of ushnisa, the tresses are often shown flying around or falling on the shoulders.

According to the Mahayana School of Buddhism, there are numerous Bodhisattvas, human as well as divine. The Bodhisattvas most frequently represented in Gandhara sculptures are Maitreya, Avalokitesvara, and Vajrapani.

Maitreya occupies a very special position among the Bodhisattvas by virtue of the fact that he is the future Buddha and the last Buddha of this age in the world. In most of the large statues of Bodhisattva Maitreya from the Taxila-Gandhara Region, he appears as a very musculature person with broad shoulders, a prominent wavy moustache and drooping eyes. Maitreya is resplendent, ostentatious and in his full glory when he appears as a lone figure or as a central figure in a preaching mode in Tushita Heaven. He is usually shown with a long flowing toga thrown over his left shoulder and a thick circular necklace decorated with stones set in geometrical or floral patterns. Maitreya also appears in Gandhara sculptures in a subordinate position, as an attendant, standing to the right of a seated Buddha, with a kamandalu (a type of a flask) in his left hand.

Bodhisattva Avalokitesvara, also frequently appears in Buddha panels, standing to the left of the seated Buddha. Avalokitesvara represents Buddha's infinite compassion. His earliest images in Gandhara appeared in the second century CE in which he is shown in a varada mudra, with the left hand holding a stem of a lotus. His popularity increased with time. He became highly popular in the post-Gandhara period around 7th century CE, when his images appear with increasing frequency all along the Silk Route, particularly in China, but also in different Buddhist monasteries in India.

The third important Bodhisattva, Vajrapani, frequently appears as an attendant-companion of Buddha Sakyamuni, particularly in the early Gandhara sculptures. He is mature and robustly built, and bears a vajra or thunderbolt in one hand.

LOTUS IN GANDHARA SCULPTURES

> As a lotus born within a lake
> By water is nowise defiled,
> But growth fragrant, beautiful,
> So is the Buddha in this world.[97]

The sacred lotus is an important spiritual symbol in Buddhism. It represents purity, divine wisdom, and progress from the lowest to the highest state of consciousness.

In Gandhara sculptures, the Enlightenment of Buddha is symbolized by the emergence of lotus from the murky darkness at the bottom of the pond. As the lotuses grow out of the water pure and clean, bringing beauty, so does the Buddha seated on a lotus pedestal transcend the troubles of human existence, leaving behind the sea of pain in human existence. The lotus pedestals beneath the statues of Bodhisattvas symbolize another important concept embodied in Mahayana Buddhism. It suggests finding a

---

97   Udayin. *The Psalm of Brothers.*

release from worldly affairs by taking the path of a Bodhisattva through the troubled areas of the world.

Figure 9.13: Preaching Buddha on lotus throne (Jamalgarhi Sangharama)

In figure 9.13, Buddha is seated gracefully on a carved seat placed above a lotus throne. The Bodhi-sattva on the right of Buddha is Avalokitesvara shown here in the feminine form. On the left of Buddha is the ever glamorous Maitreya in his common Abhaya Mudra posture. The flask (kamandalu) in his left hand has been broken.

As per Mahayana traditions, the Bodhisattvas, when taking the Bodhisattva vow before Buddha, carried a lotus flower or a stem of the lotus in their hand, the lotus signifying the Bodhisattvas commitment to seeking enlightenment. Based on this tradition, numerous images of Bodhisattvas were produced in the Gandhara Region in which the Bodhisattva is shown holding the lotus in his hand. Out of the three celestial Bodhisattvas, who dominate the panels and reliefs of 2nd to 5th century Gandhara, two frequently appear on either side of the Buddha in a representation of the Buddha Trinity. The lotus became the major attribute of Bodhisattva Avalokitesvara, and this Bodhisattva is almost always shown carrying the lotus in his hand; the other two Bodhisattvas, Bodhisattva Maitreya and Bodhisattva Vajrapani have as their main attributes, the kamandalu (a type of flask) and the vajra (thunderbolt) respectively, but both of them frequently also carry the lotus in their other hand.

Another Buddhist tradition refers to Amitabha, the best-known celestial Buddha. According to this tradition, Amitabha on becoming a Buddha established a paradise, the 'Pure Land' or the 'Land Of Bliss'—Sukhavati-vyuha. The Larger Sukhavati-vyuha Sutra describes the Land of Bliss as 'carpeted in every direction with lotus flowers, made of seven semi-precious substances'.

GANDHARA SCULPTURES BASED ON JATAKAS

The stories of Buddha's previous incarnations, generally referred to as Jatakas, are presented with a great deal of imagination in a number of sculptures mostly belonging to the early period of Buddhist art in Gandhara (around first century CE). Three panels based on Jatakas are described by Sir John Marshall.[98]

The first is a panel depicting Dipankara Jataka from Sikri near Mardan. It is one of the 13 panels, which once decorated the drum of the Sikri stupa and are now in the Lahore Museum.

The Dipankara Jataka presents the Buddha in one of his earlier lives, before he was born as Siddhartha Gautama in his last existence. According to the legend Sumeda borrowed a bunch of lotuses from a flower girl and threw them in the air as an offering to Dipankara Buddha. These flowers, instead of falling down, formed a ring around the head of Buddha.

In one of the panels from Sikri, Sumeda appears in four forms or postures before Dipankara Buddha. The four forms in sequence build into a narrative which tells the story of the incident described in the Jataka—first Sumeda is shown bargaining with a flower seller, next he throws the lotus flowers in the air, then he prostrates himself in front of Dipankara Buddha, spreading his hair on the floor so that Buddha will not soil his feet, and lastly he is suspended like the lotus flowers in the air. According to this Jataka, Dipankara predicted that Sumeda would appear in future birth as Siddharta Gautama and would ultimately achieve enlightenment.

The second is a panel from Dharmarajika stupa, Taxila. It narrates the story of a boy, Syama, who is killed by an arrow and is restored to life by Indra. This panel is presently in the Taxila Museum.

The third panel, presently in the British Museum, illustrates the Visvantara Jataka. It shows the Bodhisattva seated inside a royal chariot with his wife and two children. He is shown giving away his purse to a Brahman.

98 Sir John Marshall. *The Buddhist Art of Gandhara.* Orient Books Reprint Corporation, New Delhi

SCULPTURES DEPICTING EVENTS FROM THE LIFE OF BUDDHA

The life story of Buddha from his impending birth till his death is illustrated through a large number of sculptured panels in hundreds of monasteries spread over different regions of Gandhara. They decorate the walls of the drums and bases of stupas, walls of monasteries, and bases of Buddha and Bodhisattva statues. Also included in this category are panels illustrating various legends pertaining to events which are believed to have taken place in the lifetime of Buddha.

Some of the more common events illustrated in these panels are described below.

Maya's Dream

According to the story of Buddha's life, Buddha's royal parents lived in a palace on the foothills of the Himalayas. There, one day, Buddha's mother Queen Maya dreamt that a Bodhisattva, who had assumed the form of an elephant, carrying a white lotus in his trunk, descended from the heavens and after circling her royal bed, thrust his trunk into her womb. This, the story goes, led to the conception of Buddha, or Siddhartha Gautama, as he was known before receiving enlightenment.

This event was portrayed by the Gandhara artists through sculptures which were used in the decoration of Buddhist monuments. One such relief, carved in a stone panel, was recovered from the Kalawan Monastery in the Taxila Region.[99]

The central part of the panel 'Dream of Queen Maya' from Kalawan, shows the beautiful figure of the queen lying on a couch with her head resting on a raised cushion, her eyes closed, and the calm expression on her face suggesting that she was pleasantly absorbed in her dream. Four female attendants, two on each side of her bed, are shown in different casual postures contributing towards the realism built into the scene. There is a gallery on the top right hand corner of the panel, above the head of the queen, where two seated figures are absorbed in watching the scene unfolding towards their left. In the slightly defaced face one can make out a descending figure with a prominent nimbus behind his head. He is obviously the Bodhisattva in the shape of an elephant.

Some idea of the excellent skills of the Gandhara artists can be gleaned from the well-preserved figure of Queen Maya and the two graceful and

---

99 Sir John Marshall. *An Illustrated record of Excavations at Taxila.* Cambridge 1951

dignified figures of the female attendants, one standing near the headrest, facing the observer, and the other with a bent knee posture and her back towards the observer. The composition is well balanced with symmetrically placed arches at the two ends of the frame and two Persepolitan columns on either side of the queen's couch.

Interpretation of Maya's Dream

The interest generated by Maya's strange dream led the king to seek an interpretation. This event is portrayed by the artists in a panel from Swat referred to as 'The Interpretation of Maya's Dream'.

In the panel King Suddhodana is shown seated in his royal splendor on a highly decorated throne, with the royal parasol held above his head. On either side of King Sudhodana, are figures seated on stools. The one on the right is the sage, Rishi Asita, with his raised right arm and face expression suggesting that he is explaining the meaning of this dream. His companion sitting on the left and another standing figure are listening intently to what the sage is saying.

The panel is on display at the Peshawar Museum.

Figure 9.14: Birth of Siddhartha Gautama (National Museum of Pakistan, Karachi) (Photo: Paramount Archives, Karachi)

Birth of Siddhartha Buddha

According to the legend, Maya gave birth to Siddhartha Gautama under a Sal Tree in Lumbini Gardens Siddhartha Gautama (Buddha in later years) was born out of the right side of Maya.

Panels portraying the Birth of Buddha come from several sites in Greater Gandhara. The one shown above comes from Mardan and is presently on display at the National Museum of Pakistan. The panel is carved in grey schist and belongs to the period second or third century CE.

Queen Maya stands beautifully poised with her wasp-like waist and rounded hips tilted towards the right side, from where Siddhartha has just been delivered and received by the god Indra. To strike a proper balance Queen Maya obtains support through her right hand by clasping a branch of the Sala tree, while her anxious-looking sister provides support from the left side. Two female attendants carrying a water vessel and a flywhisk appears on the extreme right of the panel, while behind Indra on the left of the picture there is another deity with folded hands, probably Brahma. Behind Brahma is a male attendant, who has his hand raised in amazement. Above among the branches of the trees are celestials looking down at the royal birth in admiration.

First Seven Steps of Infant Buddha

> Bodhisattva having thus been born without any assistance and support, he forthwith walked seven steps to each quarter of the horizon: as he walked, at each step there sprang from the feet beneath his feet a lotus flower.

Romantic Legend of Sakya Buddha

Another Buddhist tradition states that as Siddhartha took the seven steps, he cried, "I am supreme in this world. This is my last birth." On seeing the infant Buddha perform this miracle, an ascetic named Asita predicted that the child would achieve Buddhahood in this life.

In a panel from Swat belonging to the early Gandhara period and presently housed in the Peshawar Museum, infant Buddha, with a halo behind his head and a parasol held above his head by attendants, occupies the central position. He is about to take the next step and is being eagerly watched by the gods Indra and the Brahma and the attendants.

Life in the Palace & Renunciation

This composite panel from National Museum of Pakistan, Karachi, displays two scenes. The upper part of the panel depicts Life in the Palace in the early period of the life of Prince Siddhartha. The sculpture shows the prince making merry in the company of dancing and singing and dancing girls.

Figure 9.15: Life in the Palace & Renunciation (National Museum of Pakistan, Karachi) (Photo: Paramount Archives, Karachi)

The lower part of the panel presents the Renunciation scene. Siddhartha is seen quietly slipping away from the palace after having decided to give up his life of luxury to adopt a monastic way of life. Siddhartha's wife Yasodhara is shown fast asleep on a couch, while the other ladies are shown in a drunken state, not quite able to realize the gravity of the situation.

The Great Departure

This legend is continuation of the scenes of Life in the Palace and Renunciation, portrayed above. As the Bodhisattva (Siddhartha Gautama) steps out from his Palace for the flight from Kapilavastu, he is met by his groom, Chandaka, who is accompanied by Gautama's horse, Kanthaka.

The scene is described in the lower panel of the Photograph. The panel shows Gautama, with a Nimbus behind his head and a parasol above his head, getting ready to mount his horse. The groom, Chandaka is standing behind the horse, Kanthaka, holding the parasol above Gautama Siddhartha's head. As Gautama Siddhartha gets ready to mount the horse, two yakshas (holy spirits) bend down to lift the feet of the horse to make the horse float in the air.

Enlightenment

Gautama in his search for enlightenment wanders about from place to place until he lands under a Bo tree on the side of a river in Bodh Gaya. Here he goes into deep meditation and passes through various levels of consciousness. During this meditation he is attacked by Mara, the powerful god of evil, but Gautama succeeds in defeating Mara and finally achieves enlightenment. He becomes Buddha or the Enlightened One and the tree under which Buddha achieved enlightenment came to be known as the Bodhi tree or the Tree of Awakening.

Figure 9.16: Scenes in Palace and the Great Departure (National Museum of Pakistan, Karachi) (Photo: Paramount Archives, Karachi

This event is illustrated in a panel from the Mardan Region which is now in the Peshawar Museum. In this highly accomplished work of art, Buddha, seated under a canopy of leaves, is calling the gods to witness his strict adherence to the principles leading him to enlightenment. The cool, calm and unperturbed posture of Buddha in the face of the ugly situation developing around him has been beautifully conveyed by the sculptor. On the right side of Buddha, Mara armed with a sword is being prevented by Brahma from proceeding with his aggressive designs, while on the left side of Buddha Indra is shown foiling the attempt by another warrior of Mara to inflict harm on Buddha.

Panels describing various events in the life of Buddha after he has received Enlightenment. Some of the more popular portrayals in this category include the following.

The First Sermon

After receiving enlightenment, Buddha delivered his first sermon to his five disciples in Deer Park at Sarnath.

This important event was a favorite subject of the Gandharan artists and sculptors. A relief from Loriyan Tangai (presently housed in the Calcutta Museum) shows Buddha sitting under a mango tree. His calm and dignified figure towers above all the other figures in the composition. He is in the Abhaya Mudra pose. His five companions are sitting on either side of him, their hands folded in front of them and looking very attentive. Buddha's faithful companion, the Bodhisattva Vajrapani, is seated behind Buddha. A number of celestials are also included in the composition.

Mara and His Warriors

Mara, an evil god of the kamavacara heavens, was one of the favorite subjects of Gandhara sculptors. His role of a Satan in Buddhist religious literature has been projected in several different ways in several life-like sculptured panels. This relief from the Gandhara Region represents one of the scenes portraying Mara and his warriors in an extremely aggressive mood. After Mara tried in vain to deflect Gautama Siddhartha from seeking enlightenment by offering him all sorts of attractions, his army is shown here getting ready to attack Gautama Siddhartha. Mara and his warriors are shown armed with swords, javelins, clubs and shields. Some of them have masks of animals such as lions, boars and asses. The aggressive postures of Mara's warriors, their dresses and the expressions make their intentions all too clear.

Figure 9.17: Mara and his warriors (Photo: Courtesy Archaeological Department, Pakistan.)

Miracle of Sravasti

A number of panels depicting the Miracle have been recovered from various sites including Sahri Bahlol, Loriyan Tangai and Muhammad Nari.

According to Buddhist texts, in order to convince the unbelievers of his special status, Buddha performed a number of miracles at Sravasti. In one of the first miracles Buddha, while preaching the Dharma, caused multiple images of himself to appear in all directions, some rising towards the heavens. A number of beautiful sculptures have been found from various sites in Gandhara to portray this event.

In an intricately carved panel from the site of Muhammad Nari, presently on display at the Lahore Museum, Buddha is shown seated in the Dharmachakra pose. On either side of him are two of his disciples. The upper part of the panel is divided into about half a dozen sections. In each section there is a statue of Buddha sitting in various poses under an arch or under a canopy of flowers.

In the second miracle of Sravasti, Buddha caused flames to emerge from his shoulders and water simultaneously started flowing beneath his feet.

A sculpture from Gandhara portraying this event shows a large sized dominating image of Standing Buddha. The flames emanating from his shoulders have formed a huge halo around the head of Buddha, while water is gushing out from beneath his feet. Surrounding Buddha are a number of his devotees with folded hands and expressions of amazement written all over their faces. The frieze belongs to 1st or 2nd century CE, when Gandhara Art was at its peak.

Mahaparinirvana

According to Buddhist texts Buddha died peacefully at the age of 80, under a Sal tree near Kusinagara, in the presence of thousands of his devotees.

This event has been portrayed in panels composed by different Gandhara artists and sculptors. All these artists and sculptors preserved the presumably canonical features of Buddha's corpse shown lying on a couch in a particular posture. However, the details of the composition varied from panel to panel and the emotional make up of the event was interpreted by the artists and sculptors according to their own interpretation of the information conveyed by the ancient Buddhist texts.

Figure 9.18: Mahaparinirvana (Photo: Paramount Archives, Karachi)

In the panel shown above, the body of Buddha lies as if in eternal peace, on a sloping bedstead with pillared legs of the type which are common in traditional furniture of most regions in Pakistan. At the head of the bedstead is the familiar figure of a rather youthful Vajrapani without his beard. In front of Vajrapani, Kasyapa is seen sharing his thoughts with an ascetic. At the top left of the picture is the sala tree with a tree spirit seated comfortably between the branches. Behind the bedstead is a group of four smartly dressed devas with bejeweled turbans. In front of the bedstead in Dhyana Mudra, is Subhadra, the last convert to Buddism in the life time of Buddha, with a tripod on his right supporting a water bag.

The scene is one of resigned acceptance of Buddha's passage to the other world—no grieving tearful figures, which were portrayed in the Parinirvana panels belonging to the early period of Gandhara Art, no display of rejoicing on Buddha's return after accomplishing his mission on earth.

The carvings of various figures are exquisite, but otherwise the panel does not have the trappings of the mature period of Gandhara art—no lavish decorations at the top or bottom of the panel, no crowded figures of floating celestials or monks. The panel belongs to the late Gandhara period, the period of rule of the Kidara Kushans—perhaps fourth century CE.

While spacious Buddhist sangharamas are a common sight in broad valleys around Mardan and Taxila, in the more hilly regions the Buddhist monuments were designed to fit into the surrounding landscapes.

Huge rock carvings of Buddha and Bodhisattvas served as a practical, and visually attractive, form of Buddhist religious devotion and expression in the hilly regions not only of Swat but also Afghanistan, Central Asia and China, where the sculptural materials more commonly used in the heartland of Gandhara, schist or stucco, were not so easily available.

Rock Carvings in Swat Region

9.19: Rock Carving of Buddha Statue at Jehanabad, Swat (Photo: Courtesy Tourist Department, Pakistan)

Numerous statues of Buddha, Bodhisattvas (in particular Avalokitesvara) and scenes from the life of Buddha were also carved on the cliffs on the trade routes connecting the Southern Swat Valley to the mountain passes in the north. These carvings mostly belong to the Kushan and post-Kushan period, when numerous pilgrims and missionaries traveled between Swat and Chinese western regions and Bactria. Due to extensive contacts with China, most of the rock carvings belonging to this period follow the trends which were developing in this extended region after the end of the Kushan Period. Avalokitesvara (the Chinese Guanyin) became an ever increasingly popular subject among the new Buddhist cults and Tantric Buddhism was on the rise.

Typical examples of huge carvings of Buddha are provided by the engravings at Jehanabad and Ghaligay in Swat, Satpara in Baltistan and Kargah near Gilgit.

The Jehanabad Rock Carving shown in the picture above was carved on a broad face of a brownish colored rock about 10 kilometers from the modern town of Mingora. It dates to the period around 8th century CE. The three dimensional carving is technically very similar to the carvings of Buddha at Bamiyan in Central Afghanistan. Like the carvings at Bamiyan, it is huge—about 7 meters in height.

The artist has captured the essence of similar carvings of Buddha in Dhyana Mudra in the sangharamas in the Peshawar Valley. The composure in the face of Buddha, the pleats in his dress, the sun-rays type of streaks in the hairstyle and the boufette, all go to make the statue a very attractive piece of art.

The rock carving at Ghalagai, about 20 kilometers from Mingora, although executed in a different style compared to the carving at Jehanabad, is equally impressive. This carving also portrays Buddha in Dhyana Mudra and is four meters high. It belongs to the late Gandhara Period between 7th and 8th century CE.

Rock Engravings along Karakoram Highway

The Buddhist Rock Carvings at Satpara cover an extensive area and present a whole composition with Buddha seated in the center and a number of devotees standing with folded hands on either side of him. Both above and below the main carving of Buddha are rows of several images of Buddha in Dhyana Mudra. The carvings are located on a narrow valley connecting to the main trade route from Gandhara to Xinjiang. It belongs to the 8th century CE.

In the narrow valleys of Gilgit, Chilas, Skardu Hunza and Swat the material of the cliffs bordering the main routes taken by the travelers was of just the right hardness to permit carvings, which could withstand the vagaries of weather. Here the art forms of Gandhara found expression in huge dexterously carved images on the side of the cliffs.

Most of these decorations appear over a length of about 100 kilometers on either side of the village of Chilas along the Karakorum Highway, which connects the Gandhara Region with the Xinjiang Province of western China. These inscriptions have been chiseled into the dark brown varnished surface of the boulders scattered on the river banks and the terraces of the valley.

Figure 9.20: Buddhist Rock Carving at Satpara, Baltistan (Photo: Courtesy Tourism Development Corporation of Pakistan.)

These carvings span the entire period of the development of Buddhist religious art in Greater Gandhara. The stupas, images of Buddhas and Bodhisattvas and other Buddhist symbols, date to the period between 1st and 9th century CE.

As the ancient paths along the Indus valley became feeder channels on the extensive Silk Road system, the carvings on the cliffs fulfilled the spiritual needs of devout Buddhist travelers along these routes. The carvings were visible from a distance and very often served as billboards for Buddhist stupas and monasteries located nearby. Thus the pilgrims on the look out for temporary residential accommodation and for fulfilling their religious duties enroute, found these attractive carvings not only satisfying their religious appetites but also serving as guideposts on their laborious long distance travels across difficult terrains and varying climes.

The valley created by the Indus River as it makes its way between the mountainous regions towards the Plains of Punjab became a highly interactive region; it has catered to the trade between the Indus Valley and China and Central Asia since ancient times. The type of people, who traversed through this Valley along the Indus River, their customs and beliefs, is documented for us by the large number of inscriptions and carvings on the surface of mountains on either side of the Valley.

Left: Figure 9.21: Carving of a Stupa and Buddha near Thalpan (Photo: Courtesy of Heidelberg Academy for the Humanities and Sciences, Germany)

An extensive study of the rock engravings in the northern areas of Pakistan has been sponsored by Heidelberg University, Germany. Under this sponsorship a Pak–German team has been engaged since the 1980s in the documentation of the Rock engravings and inscriptions along the Karakoram Highway.

The more than 30,000 figural drawings and over 5000 inscriptions cover many different subjects belonging to the period from pre-historic till the 9th century CE. The majority of the rock carvings and Inscriptions were made between 300 BCE and 300 CE. A very large number of engravings belonging to the 1st to 9th century were made by or for the Buddhist pilgrims traversing this road. They provide evidence of impact of Buddhism in this area.[100]

The Buddhist engravings cover the entire gamut of Buddhist Art, from stupas to images of Buddhas and Bodhisattvas to scenes from Buddha's life, before and after he achieved enlightenment. However, engravings of stupas are more numerous, presumably because donation or construction of stupas is considered a highly pious act in Buddhist religion and donating engravings of stupas could lead the devotees towards achieving Nirvana.

---

100 Ditte Bandini-Koenig, Martin Bemmann and Harald Hauptmann. *Rock Art in the Upper Indus Valley*, Islamabad 1997.

Chapter 10: Gandhari & Kharoshthi

We are putting the language [Gandhari] on the map of major languages of the ancient world, which it really was. —Prof. Richard Saloman[101]

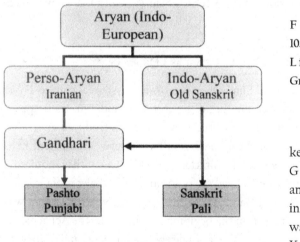

Figure 10.1: Aryan Linguistic Groups

The spoken language, Gandhari, and the script in which it was written, Karoshthi, were specific products of the Gandhara Civilization. They emerged in the embryonic phase of the Gandhara Civilization, matured into rich literary

---

101 Quoted by Peter Monaghan in his article "A Lost Buddhist Tradition is found." *Chronicle of Higher Education*, October 4, 2002.

languages in the mature phase of Gandhara Civilization, and they ceased to be employed in Greater Gandhara or in any other region in South Asia after the demise of the Gandhara Civilization.

Texts in Gandhari language were only written in the Kharoshthi script and Kharoshthi script was not employed for writing any other language. Therefore the exclusive relationship between Gandhari language and Kharoshthi stands firmly established.

Early Development of Gandhari Language

The original source of Gandhari language is Indo-European. The carriers of the Indo-European languages were Aryans, who began to move southwards from Central Asia around 10,000 BCE. Around 4000 BCE due to the gradual movement of the Aryans southwards in the form of small nomadic tribes, two groups of Indo-European languages emerged. One was the Perso-Aryan (Iranian) and the other Indo-Aryan (Sanskrit). Perso-Aryan languages became dominant in Persia, Afghanistan, Gandhara and other regions of the Indus Valley. Indo-Aryan languages began to dominate in the region south of the Indus Valley. Gandhari was born out of interaction of Perso-Aryan (Iranian) with Indo-Aryan (Sanskrit) as shown in diagram above.

Emergence of Gandhari Language as a Lingua Franca

The Achaemenid Empire was the world's first great empire. For the governance of the large number of territories included in its Empire, and to optimize the tax collection, the Achaemenids introduced an institutionalized system of administration and infrastructure development in all parts of their empire. For the facilitation of such a system they required a single spoken language and a local script. A number of dialects of Gandhari were probably spoken in Gandhara at that time. No writing system was being employed. So right from the beginning of their rule, the Achaemenid rulers concentrated on developing a single spoken language and a single script in their two satrapies in Greater Gandhara.

At the time of Achaemenid invasion of Gandhara in 535 BCE, all evidence points towards the existence of a totally disintegrated society in the Gandhara Region. The Achaemenids set in motion an integrating process by establishing a single satrapy West of the Indus River, and later during the rule of Darius the Great, another satrapy in the whole of Taxila Region. The environment for the emergence of one language, which could serve as the lingua franca in the core region of Gandhara, was thus created during the consolidation process initiated by Achaemenids in Gandhara in the 6th century BCE.

Because Gandhari was related to both the Perso-Aryan (Iranian) as well as Indo-Aryan (Proto-Sanskrit) group of languages, the process leading to the dominance of a single Gandhari dialect over all the dialects spoken languages in the Gandhara Region was relatively short. During consolidation of the region in the first century of Achaemenid rule, the Gandhari dialect firmly established its pre-eminence over the other dialects spoken in the Achaemenid satrapies of Gandhara and Sindh (Taxila). This process of synthesization was facilitated by promotion of interactions in the Greater Gandhara region through strengthening of the physical infrastructure and increase in commercial activity in the region, thus removing physical barriers to communication among the sub-groups speaking different dialects.

The second major element in the evolution and enrichment of Gandhari appeared quite early during their rule in Greater Gandhara, when the Achaemenids began to employ Gandhari as one of the two languages (the other being Aramaic) in their official communications. Local officials involved in the Achaemenid administration obviously received orders, and exchanged information in the Gandhari language. They introduced procedures for such activities as tax collection, maintenance of law and order, and infrastructure development employing Gandhari language. The Aramaic language, the language used by the Achaemenids, was far richer in vocabulary than the original Gandhari dialect, so quite a lot of words from the Aramaic language were probably incorporated into the vocabulary of the Gandhari when the Achaemenids interacted with the local officials or when the two languages were simultaneously employed in official correspondence. Thus the Gandhari language would have acquired an expanded vocabulary through incorporation of a large number of words from Aramaic.

Asoka's edicts, inscribed in the third century BCE in Gandhari on rocks at two places separated by distance of more than 100 kilometers in Greater Gandhara, indicate universal use of Gandhari in Greater Gandhara region at that time. Between the end of Achaemenid rule in Gandhara and the time Asoka's edicts were written, no major forces were acting which have brought about the integration of different dialects in Greater Gandhara.

Therefore it looks almost certain that Gandhari had emerged as a universal spoken language in Gandhara during the rule of the Achaemenids.

Evolution of the Kharoshthi Script

Figure 10.2: Document in Kharoshthi Script (Xinjiang Museum)

The rapid development of Kharoshthi as the common script all over Gandhara (and the first indigenous script in South Asia) also took place due to the pressing need felt by the Achaemenid regime to transmit written messages to the Gandharan officials in the Achaemenid administrative service, and to the Gandharan population at large.

The Achaemenids may have contemplated using Aramaic script for communications in Gandhari language. This was found to be impractical because Aramaic was phonetically incompatible with Gandhari because it had acquired some vocabulary from the Indo-Aryan (Proto-Sanskrit) languages also. Therefore Kharoshthi script emerged as a derived form of Aramaic script by introducing a set of alphabets in which all the sounds in the Gandhari language were accommodated.

Like Aramaic, Kharoshthi was alphabet based; both the languages employed square and rounded alphabets (as against the wedge-shaped alphabets used in some West Asian languages). Aramaic employed 22 alphabets; Kharoshthi employed about half a dozen more to accommodate the particular sounds of the Gandhari language. Both scripts were written from right to left. Kharoshthi remained the only script in South Asian sub-continent which was written from right to left until the Arabs introduced Arabic in eighth century CE. after their conquest of Sindh and Southern Punjab.

Greater Gandhara was the only region in the South Asian sub-continent where the Kharoshthi script was employed. (Outside South Asia, Kharoshthi was employed in areas which had come under the influence of Gandhara Civilization). This distinguishes Kharoshthi from all the written scripts which evolved in the South Asian region in due course, and sheds some light on the character of the Gandhara Civilization.

Gandhari continued to be employed on an increasing scale after the cessation of Achaemenid rule. The administrative infrastructure built by the Achaemenids continued to be employed during the brief rule of Alexander's Greek-Macedonians, and after that the Mauryans continued to benefit from the same systems. This means that Gandhari-Kharoshthi continued to be used in official communications.

During the rule of his father, Bindusara, from 298–273 BCE, when Asoka served as the Mauryan governor of Gandhara Province, he observed first hand the effective use of Gandhari-Kharoshthi in both official and private circles. With the full knowledge of the extent to which Gandhari-Kharoshthi was understood in Greater Gandhara, Asoka used Gandhari-Kharoshthi to address the people of Greater Gandhara when he had his 14 edicts inscribed on rocks at Shahbaz Garhi and Mansehra after his conversion to Buddhism in 261 BCE. Exactly the same texts were used in Asoka's edicts at Kandahar and other places in Afghanistan, which were inscribed in Aramaic and Greek languages. This led to the deciphering of Gandhari-Kharoshthi, and subsequently scholars had very little difficulty in translating Gandhari-Kharoshthi texts and inscriptions into English and other languages.

The Seleucid envoy in Chandragupta Maurya's court at Pataliputra, Megasthenes, has stated that no script was being employed in Magadha during Chandragupta Maurya's reign. Asoka's tenure of governorship in Gandhara brought home to him the need for an effective script to meet the administrative needs of the Mauryan rulers and bureaucracy at Pataliputra in distant Magadha. The principal language and dialects spoken in Magadha had a different base and employed different phonetics than those of Gandhari. Therefore Asoka faced the same difficulty (albeit on a much larger scale) in using Kharoshthi script for written communications in Magadhan language as the Gandharans had faced in using Aramaic to write Gandhari. To overcome these difficulties Kharoshthi influenced the evolution of a new script which came to be known as Brahmi. Kharoshthi's role in stimulating the creation of Brahmi has been attested by a number of scholars, among them the noted Frenchman Gerard Fussman. Fussman comes to the conclusion that Kharoshthi was developed in the northwest (Gandhara) before the Mauryan Empire, and it provided both the model and the inspiration for the development of Brahmi.[102]

---

102 Gerard Fussman. *Les premieres systemes d'écriture en Inde.* Quoted by Professor Richard Saloman in "The origin of early Indian Scripts," in *The Journal of the American*

Gandhari-Kharoshthi were put to much more diversified use after the Bactrian (Indus Greeks) established their rule in Greater Gandhara in 195 BCE and thereafter, during the next five centuries Gandhari-Kharoshthi were extensively employed in various formats.

Gandhari-Kharoshthi Legends on Coins and Medals

An important field of application of Gandhari-Kharoshthi was for legends on coins. Gandhari-Kharoshthi legends appeared on coins for the first time after the Indus (Bactrian) Greeks conquered in Greater Gandhara in 195 BCE. Demetrius-I, the founder of Indus Greek rule in Gandhara, was the first to issue bilingual coins in Gandhara. His coins typically carried an engraving of his portrait (bust) with the Greek legend 'Great King Invincible Demetrius' on one side and an identical inscription in Kharoshthi on the opposite side of the coin with engraving of the favorite deity, usually Heracles, Pallas or Zeus. In the period 195 BCE to 75 BCE, 33 Indus Greek Kings ruled over Gandhara or parts of Gandhara. Every one of them with two exceptions issued bilingual coins with Kharoshthi inscription and portrait of their favorite deity on one side.

In 95 BCE Indus Greek rule in Greater Gandhara was replaced by the rule of the Indo-Scythians. In the period 95 BCE–60 CE, ten Indo-Scythians and their kinsmen, Indo-Parthians, ruled Greater Gandhara. All of them issued bilingual coins with Kharoshthi legend on one side of the coin.

Likewise the early Kushans, who ruled Greater or part of Gandhara from 60 CE–128 CE issued bilingual coins. The first three Kushan rulers used Kharoshthi legends on their coins. Kanishka conquered the Bactrian speaking territories of Bactria and Sogdiana in the early part of his rule. In order to assert his position in these regions Kanishka began to use Bactrian legends using Greek alphabets. He did not use any South Asian language or script on his coins. This practice was followed by all later Kushan rulers.

Tens of thousands of bilingual coins issued by the Indus Greeks, Scythians, Parthians and Kushans, carrying Gandhari-Kharoshthi legends on one side have been found from various locations in Greater Gandhara as well as from a number of sites in Central Asia. The use of Gandhari-Kharoshthi on an exclusive basis in Greater Gandhara, and quite commonly in Central Asia indicates the status of this language and script in Gandhara Civiliza-

---

Oriental Society, 1995.

tion and the influence of Gandhara Civilization in adjoining areas of Greater Gandhara.

It is interesting to note that during the rule of the Chinese in the Khotan area, some bilingual coins were issued which carried a Chinese legend on one side and a Kharoshthi legend on the opposite side. Forty such coins were found at Yotkan, near Khotan, belonging to the period after 73 CE when the Kushans were ruling Gandhara. These coins have been mentioned by Dr. Hoernle in Part-I of the Report on British Collection of Central Asian Antiquities.[103]

Gandhari-Kharoshthi Inscriptions from Greater Gandhara

Another important field of application of Gandhari-Kharoshthi was inscriptions on stone, gold, silver, copper and other metals by common citizens of Gandhara. Stephen Baums and Andrew Glass have published a list of 600 inscriptions from various sites related to the Gandhara Civilization. The list includes Kharoshthi inscriptions found outside the boundary of Greater Gandhara in regions under influence of the Gandhara Civilization.[104] This list is by no means complete.

The inscriptions cover a period of about 700 years staring from the period of Mauryan rule in Gandhara. The later inscriptions mainly come from the Central Asian sites. The inscriptions found within the boundaries of Gandhara are related to the customs traditions and practices of the Buddhist population of Greater Gandhara. They indicate that Buddhism was a living religion in Greater Gandhara all through the period when this region was ruled by the Mauryans, Indus Greeks, Scythians, Parthians and Kushans. Secondly they indicate Gandhari and Kharoshthi were almost the universal language and script in all phases of the Gandhara Civilization.

Most of the inscriptions mentioned in the list were recovered from the sites of Buddhist monuments. The vast majority of them are very short, just a few words or one or two lines They indicate that it was a common practice among the monks and lay Buddhists to donate stupas containing relics, decoration pieces and jewelry to the monasteries with a view to achieving Nirvana. The inscriptions often provided useful historical information such as the name of the ruler, the date when the donation was made and the Buddhist sects which were in charge of the monasteries. The inscriptions survived because, unlike the Buddhist manuscripts, which were written

---

103 Aurel Stein. *Ancient Khotan*, 1907.
104 Stephen Baums and Andrew Glass. *Catalogue of Gandhari Texts.*

on birch bark, they were made on durable material such as gold, silver and copper plates, or stones and ceramics. The type of information conveyed by these inscriptions is provided by the texts reproduced below:

> In the year 134 of Azes, on the twenty-third -23- day of the month of Sravana, on this date Candrabhi, the female worshipper [upasika] daughter of Dharma, the householder [grhapathi], wife of Bhadra-pila, establishes relics in Chadasila, in the Stupa shrine, together with her brother Nandivardhana, the householder, together with her sons Sama and Sacitta and her daughter Dharma, together with her daughters-in-law Raja and Indra, together with Jivananandin, the son of Sama, and her teacher, in acceptance of the Sarvastivadas, having venerated the country-town; for the veneration of all beings; may it be for the obtainment of Nirvana.[105]

(The above inscription was engraved on a copper plate attached to a casket at a shrine in Kalawan Monastery, near Taxila. The year 134 of the Azes era translates to 78 CE.)

Another inscription comes from the Takshasila-Sirsukh, where the Kushan's constructed their capital several centuries later. It refers to the rule of the Scythian King Moga (Maues) in Taxila and records the name of Satrap Liaka Kusulka and his son Patika, and of the principalities of Chukh-sa, and Kshema.

> In the seventy eighth, -78th- year, [during the reign] of Great King Great Moga, on the fifth -5- day of the month of Panemos, on this first [tithi] of the Kshatrapa of Chukhsa Liaka Kusuluka by name— his son Patika—in the town of Takshasila, to the north, the eastern region, Kshema by name—in this place Patika establishes a [for-merly] not established relic of Lord Sakyamuni and a sangharama through Rohinimitra Buddhas, worshipping his mother and father, for the increase of life and power of the kshatrapa, together with his son and with worshipping all his brothers and blood relations and kinsmen.

> At the jauva-order of the great gift lord Patika.

> To Patika the kshatrapa Liaka.'[106]

Kharoshthi Manuscripts from Khotan-Niya Region of Xinjiang

Hundreds of Kharoshthi manuscripts written by the locals in the area of Khotan have also been found by Sir Aurel Stein[107] and other scholars from

---

105 Sir John Marshall. *A Guide to Taxila,* Cambridge University Press, 1960
106 S. Konow. *Corpus Inscriptionum Indicarum* No. XIII.
107 Sir Aurel Stein. *Ancient Khotan,* detailed report of archaeological explorations in Chinese Turkistan, 1907

a number of sites in Chinese Xinjiang Province. They indicate the extent to which Gandhari-Kharoshthi penetrated into these far flung areas. Gandhari had become "the Buddhist missionary dialect par excellence" and "a kind of lingua franca comparable to Latin of the European Middle Ages." [108] Daniel Boucher believes that "Gandhari had a noticeable impact on other languages it encountered in Central Asia."[109]

The manuscripts mostly cover legal, customs and other official issues. They were written on wood and sheepskin and were mostly found from large residential buildings near the town of Niya. The wooden pieces on which the manuscripts were written were either wedge shaped or in the form of rectangular plates, 3.75 to 8.75 inches in length and 2.25 to 4.5 inches in width. They belong to the 3rd and 4th centuries CE. They provide useful information on socio-economic environment. A sample of the manuscripts from Niya is reproduced below:

> Concerning the son of Tsina, a novice and an adopted child, to be carefully preserved by Simema....in the 7th year of his majesty Citughi Mahiriya, the son of heaven, in the 3rd month, 5th day, on this date. When the Khotanese plundered the kingdom of Cadota [Niya], at the time three young men of Khotan carried off the woman Tsinae. They came and gave her as a present to the mother of cozbo [functionary] Somjaka in the house of kitsayitsa Luthu. They gave the woman Tsinae along with her sons and daughters....That woman Tsinae gave her son, a novice, five distis high, as an adopted child to the man Kacana. As milk payment a vito horse was given. The transaction was made in the presence of the cozbo Somjaka.....[110]

Buddhist Religious Texts in Gandhari-Kharoshthi

The most extensive use of Gandhari-Kharoshthi was in the writing of Buddhist religious texts on birch bark. Well-trained and literate groups of Buddhist scholars converged in the sangharamas where they took upon themselves the huge and laborious task of producing in the Gandhari vernacular and Kharoshthi script the Mahayana versions of the Tripitaka and the vast body of new scriptures known as Mahayana Sutras. Volumes after volumes of texts were compiled for the use of thousands of members of the Buddhist clergy and for massive requirements of missionaries operating

---

108 Franz Bernhardt. *Gandhari Hypothesis,* 1970

109 Daniel Boucher. "Gandhari and Other Translations Reconsidered: The Case of Saddharmapundarika Sutra. *The Journal of the American Oriental Society,* Vol. 118 No.4, October 1998.

110 T. Burrow. *A translation of Kharoshthi Documents from Chinese Turkistan,* Royal Asiatic Society, London, 1940.

in places like China. Well-stocked libraries emerged in each sangharama, which served to educate the resident trainee-monks as well as visiting scholars.

The Buddhist texts compiled by monks in the scriptoriums of Gandhara were carried by missionaries to Central Asia and to various places in China. Chinese monks, such as Hsiuen Tsang also took large quantities of Buddhist texts in Gandhari-Kharoshthi with him on his return to China. Some originals of Buddhist texts in Gandhari-Kharoshthi, written on birch bark, have been found from Southern Afghanistan and Xinjiang. These include:

> Manuscript of Gandhari Dharmapada purchased by Dutreuil De Rhins from someplace near Niya in 1892.

> Fragments of Gandhari Mahaparinirvana Sutra found from Khotan area of Chinese Turkistan by Aurel Stein during the 1901–1905 excavations in the Khotan area.

> Thirteen rolls found near Hadda in Southern Afghanistan and acquired by the British Library. Preliminary examination of the manuscripts by Professor Richard Saloman revealed that the eleven rolls of fragmentary Gandhari Buddhist texts on birch bark from Hadda include fragments of the Rhinoceros Horn Sutra and other discourses of Buddha, Avadana texts describing past lives and karmic background of Buddha, Canonical Sutra texts and Commentaries and Abhidharma texts.

> The Schoeyan Collection and the Seniors Collection which include a number of canonical Sutras in Gandhari-Kharoshthi.

These documents provide an indication of the part played by the Buddhist missionaries from Gandhara in spreading Mahayana Buddhism in China and other countries in the Far East. According to Peter Monaghan,

> The Gandhari Canon may prove to be the crucial link to understanding the way Buddhism moved northwards along the Silk Road into Central and East Asia even as it died out in India, where it was born in the fourth or fifth century BCE.[111]

The manuscripts found in South Afghanistan and Xinjiang point to presence of institutions where production of texts was being carried out in a very organized manner. The few documents on highly fragile material, which have survived in highly protected environment are enough to con-

---

111   Peter Monaghan. "A Lost Buddhist Tradition is found." Article published in the *Chronicle of Higher Education*, October 4, 2002.

vince Professor Saloman that "the monasteries had well-organized scriptoriums and large libraries even at an early age."[112]

After examining the variety of material in the manuscripts of the Buddhist texts found from various places in Afghanistan and Xinjiang, Professor Richard Saloman states:

> The new discovery thus confirms what has already seemed likely,
> namely, that the Gandharan Buddhists in the early centuries of the
> Christian era did have a substantial corpus of written scriptures in
> the Gandhari language, comprising of considerable variety of genres
> ranging from didactic poetry to scholastic Abhidharma.[113]

The original manuscripts represent only a very small fraction of the
texts being produced in Gandhara. These texts were meant essentially for
missionaries and scholars, whose task it was to translate these texts into
the languages of the people in the lands where the missionaries traveled.
The translations of the texts in Gandhari-Kharoshthi were carried out at
centers like Luoyang, Dunhuang and Xian, where scholars and missionaries, who had basic knowledge of Gandhari-Kharoshthi as well as Chinese
worked with Chinese monks to translate the original manuscripts into Chinese. There was a whole array of translators who were actively working on
these translations from 2nd–7th century CE.

Lokaksema, a Gandharan Buddhist monk who embarked on his mission
soon after the approval given to Mahayana texts by the Fourth Buddhist
Council, was the first of these great translators. He established his base at
the Han capital of Luoyang in the second half of 2nd century CE and along
with equally motivated monks, like Zhi Yao, translated many basic Mahayana texts including the Prajnaparamita Sutra (Perfection of Wisdom Sutra),
and the Pratyutpanna Sutra (which contains the first known mention of
Amitabha and his Pure Land). The Han capital attracted a large number of
other Gandharan translators also in the second century CE, including two
monks of Parthian extraction, An Stigao and An Xuan.

In the third century CE, Dharmaraksa established a monastery at Dunhuang, where he preached the Dharma. The monastery became a major
translation center, where Dharmaraksa translated the Lotus Sutra, the Perfection of Wisdom Sutra and other Mahayana texts.

---

112 Quoted by Peter Monaghan, ibid.
113 Richard Saloman. "A preliminary survey of some early Buddhist manuscripts
recently acquired by the British Library." *The Journal of the American Oriental Society,*
Volume 117, No.2, 1997.

Kumarajiva, another great scholar of Gandharan extraction, established his base in Xian in the fourth century CE. He translated 72 important Mahayana texts into Chinese, including the Diamond Sutra, Amitabha Sutra, and the Lotus Sutra.

Hsiuen Tsang returned from Gandhara around 645 CE with 657 Gandhari-Kharoshthi texts contained in 520 packages, which were preserved in Xian's Golden Goose Temple. He spent the rest of his life in various monasteries around Xian translating Gandhari-Kharoshthi texts into Chinese, and is reported to have translated about 1300 volumes of Sutras into Chinese.

A large number of translations carried out by the above scholars in various parts of China were discovered by the European and Japanese Archaeological Missions, which carried our archaeological excavations at various sites. The Otani Mission in Japan, during its explorations from 1902–1914 at Turfan, recovered several manuscripts including those of Chapter 21 of the Lotus Sutra, a translation of Lotus Sutra by Kumarajiva dated 406 CE, Mahaprajnaparamitra Upadas (Treatise of the Great Perfection of Wisdom) translated by Kumarajiva in 405 CE and the Li Bao Document.

Among the Mahayana texts recovered through excavation of caves in the Dunhuang Valley is a scroll containing a copy of the Heart of Perfection of Wisdom Sutra, which is a translation by Hsiuen Tsang, and a printed copy of Kumarajiva's translation of the Diamond Sutra, both of which are now in the British Library.

These are just a few of the copies of translations available in libraries in China, Japan and Korea.

The Chinese translations of Buddhist texts have been studied closely by a large number of Western scholars, including H.W. Bailey, Franz Bernhard and John Brough, who have all come out for the support of the *Gandhari Hypothesis*, which is summarized in the following statement issued by John Brough:

> Sufficient evidence, however, has now accumulated to establish that the originals of these early Chinese translations were mostly, even if not exclusively, texts written in North-western Prakrit (read Gandhari).[114]

Thus it is more or less established that the main, perhaps the only, source of written Buddhist texts in the first few centuries of the Common

---

114 **John Brough.** *Gandhari Dharmapada,* 1965.

Era were the texts compiled in the scriptoriums of Gandhara in Gandhari-Kharoshthi. These texts were almost exclusively written on birch bark. Their Chinese translation written on paper became available in the 2nd century CE. After wood block printing was introduced in the 8th century CE. in China, the printed versions of these texts started being available. Among the earliest existing printed Chinese Buddhist text is the Kumarajiva's translation of the Diamond Sutra, dated 868 CE, which was the world's first complete printed book.

From these printed Chinese translations of texts originally written in Gandhari-Kharoshthi, translations of Buddhist texts into other languages commenced. Sanskrit, which virtually remained an oral language till the 17th century, acquired the Devnagri script around the 17th century. Thus the earliest published Buddhist Text in Sanskrit was probably a translation from the texts available in the Chinese language, which may have been carried out in the 17th or 18th century.

As a result of these dynamic processes taking place in the Greater Gandhara Region during various phases of the Gandhara Civilization, Gandhari emerged as one of the leading languages in the world. It became the common spoken language of a sizeable majority of the population in the entire region of Greater Gandhara, and because of very substantial trade and missionary activities involving Gandhara in Central Asia and Chinese Turkistan regions, Gandhari also began to be increasingly understood in the extended region, which subsequently became a part of the Kushan Empire.

CHAPTER 11: THE LITERARY ENVIRONMENT

The cultural environment prevailing in Greater Gandhara, particularly in the mature phase of the Gandhara Civilization, provided encouragement to intellectuals to use their creative talents to produce works of great literary merit. In the beginning the main focus was on producing Buddhist religious texts. Subsequently literature began to be produced on a large variety of subjects including biographies, and folk tales and medicinal treatises, in a large variety of styles ranging from epic poetry to drama.

ASOKA'S EDICTS

The inscriptions of Asoka's Edicts in Gandhari-Kharoshthi at Mansehra and Shahbaz Garhi belong to the period 260 to 252 BCE. They are the oldest surviving texts in Gandhari-Kharoshthi.

The subject matter of the 14 edicts (identical at all these sites) can be classified into three groups:

(1) Exhortation to the people at large to follow the Dharma and adopt the righteous path:

> In the past for many hundreds of years, killing or harming living beings and improper behavior towards relatives, and improper behavior towards Brahman's and ascetics has increased. But now due to the beloved of gods, king Piyadasi's Dharma practice the sound of the war drum has been replaced by the sound of dharma. (Extract from Asoka's Fourth Edict)

(2) Administrative announcements:

In the past state business was not transacted nor were reports delivered to the king at all hours. But now I have given this order that at any time, whether I am eating, in the women's quarters, the bed chamber, the chariot, the palanquin, in the park or wherever, reports are to be posted.

(Extract from Asoka's Sixth Edict)

(3) General announcements:

The beloved of the gods, King Piyadasi, conquered the Kalingas eight years after his coronation. One hundred and fifty thousand were deported, one hundred thousand were killed, and many more died from other causes. After the Kalingas had been conquered, the beloved of the gods began to feel a strong inclination towards the dharma, a love for the dharma, and for instruction in dharma. Now the beloved of gods feels deep remorse for having conquered the Kalingas.

(Extract from Asoka's Thirteenth Edict)[115]

MILANDAPANHA

Milandapanha is the text of the famous question and answer session between Menander, the Indus Greek ruler of Gandhara, and the Buddhist monk Nagasena. It was faithfully recorded by Nagasena's assistant. It is an excellent piece of literature in which key issues of Buddhism are presented through thought provoking questions articulately raised by Menander:

Master of words and sophistry, clever and wise
Milanda tried to test great Nagasena's skill,
Leaving him not, again and yet again
He questions and cross questions him, until
His own skill was proved foolishness'
(Extract from preamble to Chapter 1 of Book IV of Milandapanha)

The meeting took place "in the country of the Yonas [Indus Greeks], a great center of trade, a city that is called Sagala, situated in a delightful country, well watered hills, abounding in parks and gardens...."

(Milandapanha, Book I: The Secular Narrative)

---

115 Translations of Asoka's Edicts by Ven S. Dhammika.

The nature of the language of *Milandapanha*, and its logic, can be gauged from the following question and answer:

> "The King said, 'What is the root Nagasena, of past time, and what of present and of future?'"

> "'Ignorance. By reason of Ignorance came the Confections, by rea-son of Confections comes Consciousness, by reason of Conscious-ness Name-and-Form the six organs of senses, by reason of them contact sensation, by reason of sensation thirst craving, by reason of craving becoming, by reason of becoming birth, by reason of birth old age and death, lamentation, sorrow, pain and despair. Thus it is that the ultimate point in the past of all the time is not apparent'."

(Milandapanha, Book II, Chapter 3)[116]

ASVAGHOSHA

Asvaghosha's birthplace was near the Kushan capital of Purushapura. He served as the court poet of Kanishka when the Buddhist civilization was at its peak in Gandhara. His most famous work, *Buddhacarita*, was composed in this period.

Buddhacarita was originally composed in Gandhari and later translated into Chinese by Gandharan monks based at Kucha and other places in China. Centuries afterwards only the Chinese version survived, which was subsequently translated into Sanskrit. (Sanskrit remained basically a multi-dialect oral language for a very long period. The earliest form of written San-skrit emerged several centuries after Buddhacarita was composed.)

Asvaghosha's *Buddhacarita* is a sacred document for the followers of Ma-hayana Buddhism; it is also a document of outstanding literary merit. Es-sentially a biography of Buddha, Asvaghosha uses a lofty narrative style of poetry to describe various events in the life of Buddha. He often uses highly sensual, seductive phrases in his descriptions.

Asvaghosha was a versatile genius. Besides writing the life of Buddha in a most entertaining lyrical style, he is also credited with a number other poetic works and dramatic compositions. He also possessed extraordinary musical skills, which combined well with his poetic skills to produce an extremely pleasing effect in religious gatherings.

Asvaghosha's vivid and colorful description of scenes from the life of Buddha no doubt provided the inspiration to artists to produce the ex-

---

116 T.W. Rhys Davids. *The Questions of Milanda*, 1890.

quisite and masterful sculptures, which decorate the stupa complexes and sangharamas in Gandhara and elsewhere.

Buddhacarita

Asvaghosha's *Buddhacarita* was the greatest literary work produced during the Gandhara Civilization, not only in Greater Gandhara, but also in South Asia.

Buddhacarita is a biography of Buddha but written in an altogether different style from other biographies. Rhys Davids calls it 'a book of didactic ethics and religion, contritely cast into the form of historical romance.'[117]

Asvaghosha describes various events in the life of Buddha, such as the life in the palace, excursions from the palace, renunciation and flight from the city (The Great Departure), the returning of the horse to the palace without its master, fasting and breaking of the fast, enlightenment and Mahaparinirvana, in a flowing narrative style of poetry employing "striking imagery and polished language."[118] He often uses highly sensual, seductive phrases in his descriptions:

> Lying on the floor, another still clung to her flute,
> unaware that her white robe had fallen from her bosom —
> like a river whose banks were laughing with foam;
> its lotuses swarming with a straight flight of bees.
>   —*Buddhacarita*: description of a scene in the hall of sleeping dancers and musicians before Siddhartha's departure from the palace.

.....

> Her delight was enhanced by faith,
> and her lotus-blue eyes opened wide, as,
> doing obeisance with her head,
> she persuaded him to accept the milk rice.
>   —*Buddhacarita*: Description of the scene of breaking of the fast, when Sujata offers food to Siddhartha.

....

> At that time, just as in Paradise,
> mandrava flowers, lotuses and water lilies of gold and beryl
> fell from the sky and bestrewed,
> the place of the Sakya sage.

117 Ibid.
118 E.H. Johnstone. *The Buddhacarita*, Calcutta, 1939.

—*Buddhacarita*: Scene of Buddha's Enlightenment[119]

....

Thus the company of women,
asleep in various attitudes,
according to their disposition and breeding,
bore the aspect of a lake whose
lotuses were bent,
fractured by the wind.

—*Buddhacarita*, 'The Great Departure'.[120]

Saundarananda, Religious Dramas & Mahayana Texts

Asvaghosha's *Saundarananda* is a legendary tale based on Buddha's half brother Nanda and his quest for beauty. Ultimately Nanda's conversion to Buddhism leads to his salvation. Like Buddhacarita, Saundarananda is written in the style of court epic.

Asvaghosha wrote *Sariputra-Prakarana* and two other religious Dramas. The existence of these three dramas is indicated in the Gandhari Manuscripts on palm leaves, discovered by Prof. Luders from Turfan in Western China.

The major portions of the manuscripts found from Turfan are of the ninth and tenth chapters of the drama Sariputra-Prakarana, which pertain to the conversations between two of Buddha's disciples Sariputra and Maudgalyayana. Another disciple of Buddha, Kaundinya also appears in the texts, along with Buddha himself. The disciples ultimately join together on the stage to sing a verse in honor of Buddha.

Asvaghosha's *Discourse on the Awakening of the Faith* is regarded as an important text of Mahayana Buddhism. The text seeks to harmonize 'Buddha Nature' with 'Yogcara' into a synthetic version 'One Mind in Two Aspects'.

CHARAKA

Charaka was another famous character who adorned the court of Kanishka. The work for which he is best known is *Charaka Samhita*.

---

119 Dr. Edward B. Cowell. *Buddhacarita*, Cambridge 1893
120 Ibid.

Samhita

Charaka Samhita is a medicinal treatise based on a system of medicine in which the dominant Buddhist practice of meditation plays a central role. The therapies aim at restoring the 'energy balance' in a patient through a diet of herbs coupled with a series of mental and physical exercises. The book is divided into eight parts which deal with plant, animal and mineral resources for treating diseases.

VASUBANDHU'S *ABHIDHARMA*

Vasubandhu, who was born in Purushapura, was closely associated with the development of Mahayana Sutras. Earlier he composed Abhidharma of Sarvastivadin School, which was followed by the Abhidharmakosa (The treasury of Abhidharma) in which he introduced Sarvastivadin ideas.

VASUMITRA

Vasumitra served as advisor in Kanishka's court. He is said to have played a key role in bringing the Buddhist factions together and getting the Mahayana Sutras approved at the Fourth Buddhist Council. After the approval of the Mahayana Sutras he oversaw the compilation of these texts for use by the Sangha and the missionaries. In the early part of his life Vasumitra wrote the treatise, *The Eighteen Schools of Buddhism*, which was translated into Chinese by three Chinese authors. From Chinese it has been translated into English. Vasumitra also wrote Prakaranapada-Sastra, one of the seven Abhidharma Buddhist scriptures. It was translated into Chinese by Hsiuen Tsang. It is regarded as one of the major texts of Abhidharma.

The Eighteen Schools of Buddhism

The treatise is in the form of questions raised by Manjusri and the answers provided by Buddha. It is the history of Buddhism. Hardy Spence calls it "a great desideratum."[121]

According to Rev. Samuel Beal, "His aim was evidently to reconcile the differences that existed in traditions, customs and acknowledged scriptures."[122]

---

121 Samuel Beal. *The Eighteen Schools of Buddhism*, an article published *The Indian Antiquary* Volume IX 1880.
122 Ibid.

MAHAYANA SUTRAS & ALLIED TEXTS

A large number of religious texts in Gandhari-Kharoshthi were produced in the pre-Kanishka period by the pre-Mahayana sects such as the Sarvastivadins and Dharmaguptika sects. They include a substantial part of the manuscripts on birch bark and palm leaves found from various sites in Afghanistan and China. These manuscripts cover a broad range of religious subjects including Discourses of Buddha, collections of stories describing previous incarnations of important Buddhist personalities (including Buddha), commentaries on Abhidharma and pieces of early Buddhist Dramas.

The period when largest number of volumes of literature were compiled in Gandhara was the 2nd century CE. This was the period when a number of outstanding scholars flocked to the court of Kanishka and composed works of very high merit. These texts include the Varacana or Revelations of Buddha, which were compiled under the supervision of Vasumitra, and which lie at the heart of Mahayana Buddhism. The prominent Sutras (Discourses) which form a part of the Varacana texts include the Saddharmapundrika Sutra, popularly known as the Lotus Sutra, Avatamsaka (Garland) Sutra, Lalitavistara Sutra, Lanka Vitara Sutra, Diamond Sutra, Mahaparinirvana Sutra, Amitabha Sutra and a collection known as Prajnaparamita or Perfection of Wisdom Sutra.

A large number of these texts, which were translated from Gandhari to Chinese, are presently available in the form of original translations. These include 154 translations carried out by Dharmaraksa in third century CE, including the translation of Saddharmapundrika Sutra (Lotus Sutra). The Saddharmapundrika Sutra, which is one of the more important of the Mahayana Sutras, had a major influence in Chinese as well as Japanese and Korean cultures. It comprises of a long volume of poetry, sermons and stories, which projects the Mahayana view of Buddhist revelation. One of the famous parables included in the Sutra is that of the burning house, in which Buddha is compared to a rich man, whose loved ones are trapped inside a burning house, which represents the world.

In the fourth century CE, Kumarajiva translated the Diamond Sutra, Amitabha Sutra, Lotus Sutra and 60 other Sutras from Gandhari to Chinese. The original Chinese translations of Kumarajiva are also available.

CHAPTER 12: INFLUENCE IN CENTRAL ASIA

The artistic manifestation of the religion, as created in Gandhara, materially strengthened the bonds and deeply influenced even the later Buddhist Art of Central Asia, China and Japan.
—Alfred Foucher

Greater Gandhara shared a long history with countries in Central Asia dating back at least to the time when these countries became a part of the Achaemenid Empire.

In the mid-6ᵗʰ century BCE, along with Gandhara and the Taxila region, countries in Central Asia such as Bactria and Sogdia also became satrapies in the Achaemenid Empire. They were linked by highways and a vast network of roads to each other. They interacted with each other and with the Achaemenid regime on cultural and commercial planes. They developed a similar administrative system and went through similar process of physical infrastructure development.

In the early 4ᵗʰ century, Greater Gandhara as well as the erstwhile Achaemenid satrapies in Central Asia, became a part of Alexander's Empire and remained so until Alexander's death in 323 BCE. As part of Alexander's Empire they received their first exposure to Greek culture.

After the demise of Alexander, Greater Gandhara and Central Asian countries such as Bactria and Sogdia were successively ruled by the Hellenistic Bactrian (Indus) Greeks, Scythians, Parthians and Kushans. As a result this entire region came under strong Hellenistic cultural influences. On account of similarities in culture, the interactions between these countries increased considerably and trading activity picked up, especially after the opening of the Silk Route.

In first century CE, the successful military campaigns of Kanishka in Central Asia and in Chinese Turkistan extended the boundaries of the Kushan Empire to the regions beyond Amu Darya, in the north, and beyond Khotan and Kashgar in the east. These conquests opened up avenues for Gandhara traders and missionaries and strong cultural and commercial relations were established between Greater Gandhara and the Central Asian countries.

The important highway connecting the Kushan capital of Purushapura (Peshawar) and Pushkalavati (Charsadda) with Bactria (Balkh), Termez and Tashkent through the Khyber Pass became increasingly active as Greater Gandhara made steady progress towards the mature phase of Gandhara Civilization. The more frequent use of the Silk Trade routes by Buddhist missionaries, traders, and other travelers had the overall effect of extending the cultural influence of Gandhara to all regions of the extended Kushan Empire.

After the rule of Kanishka, some conquered countries in Central Asia gradually began to secede from the Kushan Empire and the political boundary of the Empire (and of Greater Gandhara) became confined to the regions south of the Hindu Kush. But the cultural and economic relations established between Greater Gandhara and the Central Asian Region north of the Hindu Kush, continued to grow because of the strength of the Gandhara Civilization.

Thus from the heartland of Buddhist Civilization in Greater Gandhara, art, culture and Buddhist religion spread via different trade arteries to a number of regions along the Silk Route. From the commencement of the mature phase of Gandhara Civilization in first century CE till the demise of Gandhara Civilization, an extended cultural union emerged, which included the Tarim Basin of Chinese Turkistan, Kapisa-Bamiyan and Balkh regions of central and northern Afghanistan, Southern Uzbekistan, Tajikistan, south-eastern Kyrgyzstan, and the regions around Merv and Ashkabad in Turkmenistan. All around the principal trading towns in each region clusters of sites began to emerge where monasteries and stupas of the type found in Gandhara, were located.

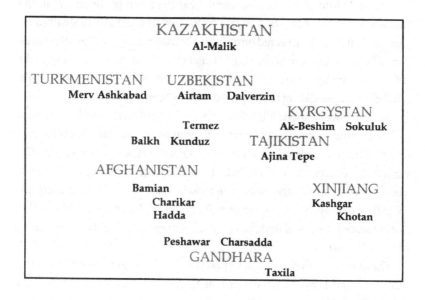

Figure 12.1 Gandharan Sites in Central Asia

GANDHARAN INFLUENCE IN CENTRAL AFGHANISTAN

North of the Hindu Kush in the region between Kabul and Begram, mountains continue to dominate the physical horizon. From the Hindu Kush, lower mountain ranges fan out in all direction, restricting agricultural activity to narrow valleys in between the mountain ranges. These valleys also provided the Buddhist communities, residing in these areas in the first centuries of the Common Era, the environment for the performance of their religious duties with zeal and enthusiasm.

In this period, when one crossed the political borders of Greater Gandhara into Central Asia, there was a remarkable continuity in the cultural environment. Along the entire section of the highway from Kabul to ancient Kapisa (modern Begram) one comes across numerous Buddhist monuments, which are very similar in design to that south of the Hindu Kush and in the core regions of Greater Gandhara. Like the sculptures of Greater Gandhara, the material used in these sculptures was either schist or stucco.

About 22 kilometers east of Kabul, near the town of Khairabad in the Moissec Valley, there is the Guldara monastery. It is actually a small sangharama, which is constructed on a pattern of sangharamas in Greater Gandhara. On one side there is the courtyard of the vihara, which was no doubt surrounded by monastic cells. Adjacent to that is the stupa yard with a number of stupas dating to the period 4th or 5th century CE. [123]

At a distance of about 100 kilometers from Kabul on the road to Bamiyan is the beautiful monastery complex of Fondukistan. The complex is located on a hill in the Ghorband Valley, about 5 kilometers south of Siahgird. The walls of the courtyard are provided with niches with elaborate decorations. The sculptures inside the niches are mostly made with clay and there are some frescoes around them. Among the better sculptures found from this site are seated statues of Buddha and Bodhisattvas, which date to the period around 7th century.

The famous medieval city of Kapisa was located near the junction of the Ghorband and Panjshir Valleys at a distance of about 60 kilometers from Kabul. The modern capital of Parwan Province, Charikar, is the nearest city to the medieval site. Kapisa was an important town when Menander was serving as a General in the Bactrian Greek army. Later in the first century CE, Kapisa acquired further importance due to its strategic location on the Silk Route. Archaeological excavations have revealed a magnificent palatial building nearby, which may have been used by Kanishka-I during his military engagements in this region. The artifacts found from the Palace site are mostly of western origin and articles of luxury.

Charikar is located in the foothills of the Hindu Kush, surrounded by lush green fertile valleys with hills in the background. An important cluster of Gandhara culture sites was located in the mountainous region around Charikar. Among the most famous these were Shotorak, Paitava, and Tapa Sardar.

Hsiuen Tsang, who visited the region in 630 CE, mentions that there were more than 100 sangharamas in the region, with more than 6000 monks who practiced the Mahayana religion. He mentions that "The stupas and

---

123 Fussman and Le Berra. *Monuments boudiques de la region de Caboul*, MDFA Paris, 1976.

sangharamas are of an imposing height, and are built on high level spots, from which they can be seen on every side, shining in their grandeur."[124]

Buddhism apparently started to gain converts in the Charikar region soon after Asoka launched his missionary campaigns in third century BCE. However, it was after the Kushans had extended their vast empire north of the Hindu Kush beyond the Amu Darya that major stupa complexes and sangharamas began to appear. Begram was the center around which a large number of Buddhist monasteries were constructed.

An important Buddhist site is located at Shotorak, about 4 kilometers from Begram. The site, which is also known as Kuh-i-Pahlavan, is located on the southern bank of Panjshir River, near the ancient fort of Kuh-i-Pahla-van. It is a relatively small sangharama with a monastery and a stupa yard comprising of seven or eight stupas. The sculptures and relief panels at the site were carved in schist. The most famous statue recovered from the site was that of Dipankara Buddha, which disappeared from the Kabul Museum recently.

Another site which yielded a number of sculptures executed in the Gandhara style was located at Paitava, 15 kilometers from Begram. The sculptures recovered from the remains of a stupa and monastery court belong to the Kushan Period, 1st to 3rd century. Among the better art pieces recovered from the site is a statue of Maitreya Bodhisattva and a sculpture depicting the Miracle of Sravasti, both made from schist and with gilded surface.[125]

At Tapa Sardar, also in the vicinity of Begram, the Buddhist monastery complex included a large stupa and several smaller ones. A 15-meter long statue of Reclining Buddha was also recovered from this site.[126] The site belongs to period 5th to 8th century, when Kushan rule in Gandhara had come to an end, but Kushan influence in Central Afghanistan continued to prevail. The foundations of Gandharan culture laid in this region during Kushan rule were strong enough to generate a lot of activity among the Buddhist communities, which had sprung up in this area.

Towards the west, located in a long valley about 150 kilometers northwest of Kabul, was Bamiyan, one of the most important cultural centers in this region. The site remained active for five centuries, between 200 CE and

---

124 Samuel Beal. *Xuanzong's Record of the Western Regions*, Book I, 1884.
125 Joseph Hackin, DAFA, 1924.
126 Taddei and Verardi. *Tapa Sardar: Second Preliminary Report*, 1978.

700 CE, Bamiyan was situated at the intersection of two important routes, one coming from China to Iran through the Yarkhand River Valley and across the Pamir and the Hindu Kush mountain ranges, and the other route running from Gandhara to Bactra (Balkh). It therefore served as a gateway for transmission of ideas and arts from Gandhara to entire Central Asia, and dissemination of Western, Central Asian and Chinese ideas to Gandhara. Under the influence of Gandhara, Buddhism spread rapidly in the entire Bamiyan Valley and important monastic complexes emerged at Bamiyan itself and at nearby sites of Fondukistan and Kakrak.

Because of Bamiyan's location in a mountainous region, the religious architecture has some affinity with that in the mountainous regions of Swat and northern areas of Pakistan. Bamiyan is famous for its three colossal statues of Buddha carved on the face of cliffs. The largest statue, that of Vairocana, the cosmic Buddha, was built in the fourth century CE and was 55 meters high; the other big statue is that of Buddha Sakyamuni. It was 38 meters high and was separated the Vairocana statue by a distance of about one kilometer. In between the two big statues was a smaller statue, about 6.5 meters in height, belonging to an earlier period, sometime in 3rd century CE. After the Buddha statues were carved into the cliffs, the statues were covered with clay and the final decoration such as the folds of Buddha's robe were finished in stucco. The standing posture and the folds are typical of the style developed in Gandhara and the basic idea of carving Buddha statues on rocks and cliffs came from Swat, where such carvings were common. During the 5th century CE, a syncretic style of sculpture emerged in the huge monastery complex at Bamiyan, in which Gandharan, Chinese and some Persian elements were incorporated.

Hsiuen Tsang who visited the site in 630 CE, describes the two large Buddha Statues. He observed that "golden hues sparkle on every side and its precious ornaments dazzle the eyes with their brightness." Hsiuen Tsang also mentions that the region produces wheat, fruits and flowers and provides rich pasture for sheep, cattle and horses.[127]

Four kilometers from Bamiyan, in the valley of the Fuladi River there are about fifty caves, which were decorated with paintings, which show some similarities with cave sites in Chinese Xinjiang region. These Buddhist decorations belong to a period later than those at Bamiyan.

---

127 Samuel Beal. *Buddhist Records of the Western World.* Book I, 1884.

Bactria: Amu Darya Valley

Bactria and Gandhara shared a long common history which went back to the days when both these regions were prominent satrapies in the Achaemenid Empire. As independent states with common Hellenistic influences, they were destined to enter into a cultural union, which they did when both states became a part of the Kushan Empire.

Bactria comprised of that part of Afghanistan and Uzbekistan which lies north of the Hindu Kush and south of the Guissar Mountain ranges. Culturally the most active part of Bactria was the region along the southern and northern banks of the Amu Darya. In northern Afghanistan, on the southern bank of the Amu Darya, there were three important Buddhist sites, namely Bactra, Kunduz and Taloquan. In Southern Uzbekistan, on the northern bank of the Amu Darya, the important Buddhist sites were Termez, Fayaz Tepe and Kara Tepe. All these sites came under strong cultural influence of Gandhara.

Balkh (Bactra) became an important center of Buddhism. It played an important part in bringing different regions in Central Asia and China under the cultural influence of the Buddhist civilization of Gandhara. The Buddhist temples at Bactra were mostly constructed in the Gandharan style by Hellenistic artisans. Among the important Buddhist monuments in this region was a 61-meter high stupa located at Tepe-i-Rustam, which was said to contain the relics of Buddha. At another mound in the vicinity, known as Takht-i-Rustam, there was a cave monastery. Hsiuen Tsang mentions that there were 100 monasteries in the vicinity of Balkh (Po Ho), where 3000 monks reside.[128]

Kunduz was located about 300 kilometers west of Bactra in the mountainous Afghan province of Badakshan. The Kunduz River flows near the site of a third century Buddhist monastery, and debouches into the Amu Darya. The site was visited by Hsiuen Tsang in 630 CE. He states that at this site there were many relics said to be those of Buddha, including his tooth relic.

Gandharan Sites in South Uzbekistan

South Uzbekistan was closely linked culturally with the Buddhist Region in Northern Afghanistan. Termez, located on the northern bank of the

---

128 Ibid

Amu Darya, in Surkhondarya Province of Southern Uzbekistan became one of the most important centers of Buddhism in Central Asia in the first and second centuries CE. In this period, there was regular trade and movement of pilgrims between Gandhara and Greater Bactria, of which Termez was a part. In and around Termez the Buddhists built a large number of stupas and monasteries.

Figure 12.2: Buddhas in Dharmachakra, Termez Museum.

In Old Termez (Termita), there was a 16-meter high stupa built of mud and burnt bricks, which is described by the Chinese pilgrim, Hsiuen Tsang. Hsiuen Tsang, who visited the city in 630 CE, also mentions that the city had 5 kilometer long walls and twelve monasteries were located in its vicinity, which were served by 1000 Buddhist monks.

All around Termez there are a number of important Buddhist sites. In the suburbs of Termez, towards the northwest there are two important sites about one kilometer apart, Fayaz Tepe and Kara Tepe.

Fayaz Tepe is famous for its monastery, refectory, Buddhist temple and a number of stupas. The complex, 34 meters by 113 meters, comprises of three adjacent courts. The outer courts had monastic cells all round its periphery. The walls of the large chamber in the central part were covered with clay and stucco sculptures, Buddhas and reliefs. Inside the shrine there were two natural sized standing Buddha statues constructed in the Gandhara style. Among the many donative inscriptions on pottery pieces found from inside the refectory, there were about 35 in the Kharoshthi script. Also a large number of coins belonging to various Kushan rulers from Vima Kadphises to Vasudeva-I, were found from the site.

At Kara Tepe there was a cave monastery. One of the biggest monasteries in the Termez area, it was spread over an area of about 7 hectares. At the entrance to the underground part of the monastery, at ground level, there was a square stupa court with colonnades, a stupa and a water tank pedestal, which were decorated with sculptures. The site remained occupied from first century till fourth century, with peak period around the 3rd century CE.

In the eastern part of Termez is the site of Zurmala Tower, which belongs to 1st century BCE. A Kharoshthi inscription was found here along with some Buddhist sculptures.

Another important Gandharan site in the region was at Airtam, about 18 kilometers north-west of Termez. The site was spread over an area of 90 hectares. Initially a Bactrian Greek settlement existed at the site, belonging to the period around 2nd century BCE. It converted into an important Buddhist center in the Kushan era. Among the Buddhist monuments spread over a distance of 3 kilometers, there was a monastery complex, a Buddhist shrine and other religious buildings decorated with Buddhist sculptures and architectural decors made with marble-like limestone. Among the better type of friezes, was one in limestone, depicting heavily adorned male and female musicians with a number of musical instruments, including a drum, a lute and a harp.

Yet another large Buddhist center was located at Dal'versin (Dalverzin), at the border of the Suchan and Hissar Valleys, about seven kilometers from the town of Scurchi.

At the meeting point of the Kafirzingan and Amu Darya Rivers there was the monastery of Ustur-Millo. The stupa at the monastery was covered with stone slabs, which were covered with reliefs and paintings.

A number of Gandhara style panels with Buddha, painted statues of Bodhisattvas and donors, and other sculptures from these sites are on display in the museums of Tashkent. Among these, the outstanding piece is a typically Gandharan limestone relief of Buddha Sakyamuni seated in Dhyana-mudra, between two Corinthian columns.

GANDHARAN SITES IN TURKMENISTAN

Gandhara type stupas have been found at Merv and Ashkabad in Turkmenistan. Also Buddhist caves were located on the outskirts of Ashkabad.

At Gyaur Kala, one of the suburbs of Merv, there was a 4th century Buddhist sangharama, built in the typical Gandhara style. Along the four walls of the rectangular vihara were thirty-two cells, which served as chapels as well as resting places for the monks. Separated from the cells by walkways was an inner quadrangle.

In the stupa complex there was a typical Gandhara style statue of Buddha in Dharmachakra mudra seated on a lotus pedestal. On the base of the main panel is another statue of Buddha, this time in Dhyana mudra. Buddha is accompanied by a number of other worshippers. The statue, dating to the 3rd century CE, is executed in schist, the preferred material of the Gandhara sculptors in the early period.[129]

The artifacts and monuments at Merv represent the westernmost Gandhara influenced Buddhist sculptures and architecture belonging to the 1st–7th century CE.

GANDHARAN SITES IN KYRGYZSTAN

In ancient times, the present republic of Kyrgyzstan formed a common cultural region with Eastern Turkistan. Buddhism took roots in this region as far back as the 2nd century BCE.

A number of Buddhist monuments were discovered in Kyrgyzstan by A.N. Bernshtam. He found Gandhara type architecture, sculpture, and paintings at a number of sites in the Chui Valley, including Ak-Beshim, Krasnaya Rechka, Karadjygach, Novopavlovka and Sokuluk.

Among the important Gandhara style Buddhist monuments found on the territory of Kyrgyzstan were four temples in Ak-Beshim, which had square bases on which the domes were constructed.

GANDHARAN SITES IN TAJIKISTAN

An important Gandharan site was located south of the Tajik capital Dushanbe, on a hill known as Ajina Tepe. A typical Gandhara type stupa courtyard and an adjacent monastery courtyard were located at this site, which contained a 14-meter long statue of reclining Buddha (now on display at Tajikistan Museum of National Antiquities in Dushanbe).[130]

Other Gandharan monuments near Ajina (Adzhina) Tepe were the monasteries located at Khist Tepe, Kalan Kafirnigan and Kafir Kala.

---

129 G.M. Pugachenkova and Z. Usmanova. "Buddhist Monuments in Merv," in the *Land of the Gryphons*. Papers in Central Asian Archeology and Antiquity. Florence 1995.

130 B.A. Livinsky. *Adzhina Tepe Architecture, Paintings and Sculptures,* 1971

Chapter 13: Gandhara and Chinese Buddhism

Buddhism was introduced in the Tarim Basin, now known as Xinjiang Uyghur Autonomous Region, from Gandhara through the passes in the Karakoram Mountain ranges. In the 3rd century BCE, Asoka's missionaries traveled through the passes in the Karakorams to preach in the region around the Tarim Basin; one of Asoka's edicts is inscribed on a rock near the town of Mansehra, on the modern Karakoram Highway, which links the Indus Valley with the Khunjerab Pass.

Tibetan and Chinese legends state that Khotan, a town in Chinese Xinjiang famous for its Buddhist monuments, was populated by the Mauryan noblemen banished by Asoka after they gouged out the eyes of his son, Kunala. (A sangharama at Kunala, near Buddha's regional capital of Taxila, marks the site where this heinous act is said to have been committed.) Buddhist documents recovered by Aurel Stein early in the 20th century from the region around Kashgar indicate that during the third century BCE a large number of Kushans (Gandharans) from Gandhara Region traveled to Xinjiang. The Gandharan immigrants from Taxila colonized Tarim Basin and founded a kingdom there.[131]

---

131 M. Aurel Stein: *Serindia* 1904.

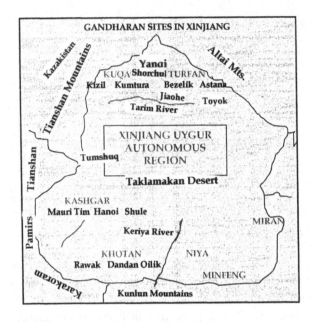

Figure 13.1: Buddhist sites in Tarim Basin

These immigrants who occupied the Tarim Basin brought with them the Kharoshthi script, Buddhist beliefs, and entrepreneurial skills. Thereafter Mahayana Buddhism or "Great Vehicle" spread from Gandhara to China via the trade route. In 68 CE the Han emperor, Ming, sent a minister named Cai Yin (Zhao Qian) to Gandhara to learn more about the Buddhist religion. Yin returned with large quantity of Buddhist sculptures, scriptures, and two Buddhist monks to teach their faith to the Chinese. *Han Shu* (Han Chronicles) indicates that impressed with the accounts of Ca Yin, Emperor Ming had a Buddhist temple constructed in Luoyang, which is commonly known as the Temple of the White Horse.

In first century CE, the great Kushan emperor Kanishka conquered the Tarim Basin, and this region became a part of the Kushan Empire. This conquest provided increased stimulus to missionaries and traders from Gandhara to fortify their contacts with this region and some of these missionaries and traders probably settled permanently in the Tarim Basin. Tarim Basin regained independence during the rule of Kanishka's successor, Huvishka, in the 3rd century CE, but the special relations developed between Gandhara and Tarim Basin during Kanishka's rule, continued to be maintained, and even strengthened in the centuries to come.

Thus Xinjiang became a region where the Buddhist religion and art traditions of Gandhara flourished. Buddhist religious texts compiled in the scriptoriums of Greater Gandhara began to pour into Xinjiang in large numbers, and Gandharan concepts of beautifully decorated sangharamas, began to be adapted in Xinjiang to suit the local physical environment and cultural traditions. Buddhist Rock cut temples and shrines began to emerge everywhere and the beautiful paintings and murals, statues of Buddha and Bodhisattvas, and reliefs showing episodes from the life of Buddha caught the imagination of the common folks, warmed their hearts and generated considerable enthusiasm in the practice of the new religion. As in Greater Gandhara, richly decorated Buddhist monuments contributed immensely to the culture and growth of these oases towns. The huge statues of Buddha, images of the compassionate Bodhisattvas and paintings and reliefs depicting scenes from the life of Buddha and the Jatakas made these places the focal point of a large number of travelers and immigrants and contributed immensely to the popularity of the Buddhist religion in this region.

From Tarim Basin the religion, art and culture of Greater Gandhara traveled eastwards. In a short period of time, large Buddhist complexes began to appear also in the Chinese provinces of Gansu and Shaanxi and Henan. With the help of Gandharan Buddhist monks, translation bureaus were set up in the monasteries of Dunhuang and Changan, where great enthusiasm was witnessed in the translation of Buddhist texts from Gandhari-Kharoshthi into local languages. Buddhism was well on its way to making a major impact in the entire region of China, as well as in Japan and Korea.

Buddhism made its greatest impact in China during the Northern Wei Dynasty in the 4th–5th century CE. During this time, the Chinese Empire witnessed a boom in the construction of Buddhist monasteries, stupas and grottos (cave sanctuaries). Grottos carved into soft sandstone cliffs were especially abundant on the edge of the Taklamakan Desert. By 514 CE, at least two million people in China were practicing the religion.

In the 6th century CE, with the decline of the Gandhara Civilization, Buddhism also entered into a steady decline; there was a marked decrease in the number of Buddhist monuments being constructed in Gandhara. But in China, Buddhism continued to increase in popularity. All through the rule of the Tang Dynasty, Buddhism received favorable treatment and Buddhist institutions were considerably strengthened.

The huge treasure of Buddhists artifacts resulting from the 1000-year long impact of the Buddhist civilization of Gandhara in China began to generate considerable interest among Western scholars in the closing years of the 19ᵗʰ century. Archaeological missions were launched and archaeological explorations carried out at several Buddhist sites, particularly in Xinjiang. Among the scholars who spent long periods of time in exploring these areas and revealing these hidden treasures were Aurel Stein from Great Britain, Albert Gruenwedel and Albert von le Coq from Germany, Paul Pelliot from France and Count Otani from Japan.

Ancient Khotan: Detailed Report on Archaeological Explorations in Chinese Turkistan, by Aurel Stein, provides comprehensive information on his explorations. His excavations at various sites in Xinjiang and Gansu yielded large number of clay and stucco sculptures, mural fragments, decorative reliefs, pieces of paintings on various materials including silk and paper, wood carvings and Buddhist manuscripts. A large number of these artifacts reveal considerable influence of the Buddhist Civilization of Gandhara on the culture of this region.

KASHGAR-TUMSHUQ REGION

The Tarim Basin, where Kashgar-Tumshuq region was located, constitutes the major part of Chinese westernmost and largest Province of Xinjiang. The Tarim Basin covers an area of around 1.6 million square kilometers. It is surrounded on all sides by the mountains; on the north by the Tianshan, the Celestial mountain, on the south by the Kunlun, on the east by the Nanshan, in the north-west the continuation of Tianshan Mountains, and in the southwest by the Pamirs. While about 50% area in the central portion of the Tarim Basin comprises of the dry and inhospitable Taklamakan Desert, in the remaining portion all round the desert there were a number of oases towns, which became highly prosperous and important cultural and trade centers on the Northern and Southern Silk Routes.

Kashgar is strategically located in the western-most region of Xinjiang. It has a long history of interactions with the Greater Gandhara region, dating back to prehistoric times. These interactions took place through the Khunjerab and other passes in the Karakoram Mountains.

In prehistoric times traders and fortune seekers used the passes in the Karakoram Mountains to cross into each others territory just after the snows had begun to melt, and throughout summer this activity was maintained. In more recent times the refugees, who migrated into Xinjiang when they faced persecution in third century BCE during the rule of the Mauryans in Gandhara, took this route. In fourth century BCE, the famous Gandharan-Chinese monk, Kumarajiva, used these passes to travel between Kashgar and Kashmir, and in the period when Silk Road became active, a substantial portion of Gandhara's trade with the Silk Route countries was conducted via Taxila and Kashgar.

Kashgar was one of the three major feudatories of the Han empire conquered by Kanishka early in second century CE, the other two being Yarkhand and Khotan. These kingdoms remained a part of the Kushan Empire all through Kanishka's reign but reverted to their previous status in the Han Empire after the death of Kanishka.

Because of its strategic location on ancient trade routes, Kashgar developed into a thriving metropolis and an important commercial and cultural center in the Han period. This status of Kashgar was utilized by the missionaries from Gandhara to establish their strong presence in this region.

Thus, Kashgar became one of the earliest centers of Buddhist religion in Xinjiang. A number of Buddhist sites also emerged within a radius of 30 kilometers from Kashgar. Notable among these are the Hanoi, Mauri-Tim, Kurghan Tim and the caves of Sanxiandong.

Hanoi is located about 30 kilometers to the east of Kashgar. Here Stein found a number of stupas, the oldest of which dates to first century CE. On the other side of Kashgar, towards the northwest, is the 25-meter high Kurghan-Tim stupa, which is similar in design to the stupas built in the Uddhyana region of Greater Gandhara. It also has a square base which became a prominent feature of all stupas constructed in Gandhara after first century CE. Towards the north of Kashgar is the Mauri-Tim stupa, typical of the stupas constructed on raised ground in Xinjiang in somewhat later period—around the 5th century CE.

About 20 kilometers west of Kashgar are the 'Three Immortal Caves' of Sanxiandong, which housed statues of Buddha. In the middle cave a headless statue of seated Buddha was found. The construction at the site belongs to the 2nd or 3rd century CE. Perhaps it was at Sanxiandong that the tradition began in China of constructing Buddhist shrines in caves cut in cliffs.

A large number of people related to the Buddhist movement in China visited the monasteries at Kashgar and spent some time there. Among them was Hui Chao, a famous Korean monk who spent time in the monasteries at Kashgar, probably on his way to Gandhara;[132] Kumarajiva studied Mahayana Buddhism in Kashgar in the fourth century CE; and Hsiuen Tsang spent some time in Kashgar in 644 CE on his return journey from Gandhara. Hsiuen Tsang informs us that there were more than 100 monasteries in the Kashgar Region and about 1000 monks residing there.

According to the Chinese journal Weishu, during the reign of Wenching Di (452–466 CE), the King of Kashgar presented a relic of Buddha to the Wei emperor.

NORTHERN SILK ROUTE

A large number of Buddhist sites are located al along the Northern Silk route between Tumshuq in the east and Turfan in the west. Major clusters on this route were located around the towns of Kucha and Turfan.

Extensive archaeological explorations were carried out at the sites along the Northern Silk Route by the German and French teams. During the five expeditions organized by the German between 1902 and 1909, sites were investigated by teams under Albert Gruenwedel and Albert von Le Coq. They recovered a large number of artifacts from these sites which were removed to Berlin Museum in Germany.

Paul Pelliot was extensively engaged in explorations at Tumshuq, Tun-Huang and other sites in this region. The artifacts from the sites explored by the French missions are presently available at the Guimet Museum in Paris.

Tumshuq, known in the early period as Toqqum Sarai, is the most important Buddhist site between Kashgar and Aksu. It is located 300 kilometers east of Kashgar. A large number of wooden figures, painted clay statues and fragments of murals were found from the site.

Among the better wooden artifacts found by Albert von le Coq from the vicinity of the Great Temple at Tumshuq is an 8-centimeter-high, 3rd century figure of seated Buddha with prominent folds in the drapery, and five small Buddha statues which were placed on a table in the front hall of a cave. Coq also found a large number of painted clay statues of Devas, Devis and Bodhisattvas with East Asian features but otherwise sculptured typically in the Gandhara style, from the caves at Tumshuq.[133]

---

132 Kashgar Prefecture, 2005
133 A. von Le Coq. *Die Buddhistische Spaitenantike in Mittelasien.* Volume I. Dietrich Reimer Verlag, Berlin.

Among the sculptures recovered by Pelliot are three beautiful 5th century reliefs, with clay figures depicting scenes from the life of Buddha.

Aksu-Kucha Region

Aksu was an important oasis town east of Kashgar on the Northern Silk Route at the crossing point of the Tarim River with the Northern Highway. To the east of Aksu is the important Buddhist city of Kucha. Hsiuen Tsang stopped at Kucha on his way to Gandhara in the 7th century. He mentions that there were about one hundred sangharamas in this region, with about 5000 disciples (monks).[134]

Kucha retained its importance as a center of Buddhist culture for seven centuries from 2nd century CE till the 9th century CE. A huge cluster of important Buddhist sites was located around Kucha. These include Kizil, Kumtura, Subashi and the monastic complex at Duldin Aqur.

The Kizil grottoes consist of about 250 cave temples cut into the hills, about 70 kilometers northwest of Kucha. Each cave consists of two chambers. The lavishly decorated Hall of Worship was located in front, while the rather austere looking monks' quarters were located behind it. The statue of Buddha was placed in a niche in the Hall of Worship and the side walls of the hall were painted with murals. The monks' quarters were usually undecorated. A number of 5th century pedestals of images of Buddha and murals depicting Preaching Buddha, Bodhisattvas and scenes from the Jatakas, were discovered by Le Coq in these caves.[135] Gruenwedel found a large number of beautiful stucco heads and torsos, of Bodhisattvas, Devas and godly figures from the caves in and around Kizil.[136] The heads were between 24 and 38 centimeter in height and were painted. Most of the artifacts show affinity with the late Gandhara style.

Another cave complex comprising of more than hundred rock-cut temples and shrines was located at Kumtura, about 28 kilometers northwest of Kucha. The temples, carved into cliffs, are located near the bank of Muzart River. They are similar in layout to the ones at Kizil, but the paintings differ appreciably in design from those at Kizil. The paintings mostly belong to a later period, around the 8th century CE. Gandharan as well as Chinese influ-

---

134 Samuel Beal. *Buddhist Records of the Western World*, Book I. Trubner & Co., London, 1884

135 A. Von le Coq. *Auf Helles Spuren in Ostturkestan* (Buried Treasures of Chinese Turkestan), Leipzig, Germany 1926.

136 A. Gruenwedel. *Alt Kutcha*, Volume I, Berlin 1920.

ences are apparent in the paintings at this site. A stucco mould for making heads of Devis and a stone core of a Buddha Statue were found from the first temple at Kumtura.

The monasteries of Subashi and Duldur Agur were located north and west of Kucha respectively. Two Bodhisattva Heads were found from the monastery at Duldur Agur. They are made from clay and then painted, and are Gandharan in appearance.

Kucha is associated with the famous Buddhist scholar, Kumarajiva (343–413 CE). Kumarajiva's father was from Gandhara. In the 3rd century, after visiting a number of places in Xinjiang, he finally settled down at Kucha, where he married a Kuchean princess. Kumarajiva was born in Kucha. When he came of age he went on a tour of several places, spending time in different monasteries, studying Buddhism. He later settled in Changan, where he translated a large number of Mahayana Sutras. Some of his manuscripts, including the Lotus Sutra, were also recovered in the first decade of the 20th century by the Otani Expedition from Turfan.

Karashahr-Turfan Region

Karashahr is the old name for Yanqi. It is located near of the largest lakes in Xinjiang, Lake Bosten. About 65 kilometers south of Karashahr is, Shorchuk, another important Buddhist site. Extensive archaeological explorations at Karashahr and Shorchuk were carried out by A. Gruenwedel and Albert von le Coq in the period 1902–07.

At Shorchuk Gruenwedel found stucco heads, half figures and statues of Buddha, Bodhisattvas and Devas and wooden statues.[137] Among the artifacts found by A. von le Coq from Shorchuk was a statue of Standing Buddha executed in the Gandhara style.[138]

Turfan, the largest oasis in Xinjiang, is located 300 kilometers east of Karashahr, about 150 meters below sea level. It was an important Buddhist center. Among other important Buddhist sites located near Turfan are Bezezlik, Jiaohe, and Toyuk. The stupas located in this region show striking similarity to the style developed in Jaulian, near Taxila, in the 4th century CE.

The Otani Mission from Japan carried out archaeological investigations at Turfan from 1902–14. Among many other artifacts excavated from

---

137 Ibid.
138 A. von Le Coq. *Die Buddhistische Spaetenantike in Mittelasien*, Volume I, Berlin.

the site, were a number of Mahayana Manuscripts including Kumarajiva's translation of the Lotus Sutra.

Eight kilometers west of Turfan, at Jiaohe, there was a large stupa complex executed in a style very similar to that of Jaulian, near Taxila. Like Jaulian, the main stupa and almost hundred smaller stupas surrounding it have stucco-plastered surfaces. There were several tiers of decorations consisting of seated Buddhas in stucco placed inside niches.

A similar three-tiered stupa with statues of Buddhas in niches was also located at Gaochang, 45 kilometers southeast of Turfan.

KASHGAR-KHOTAN-NIYA REGION

Khotan, located on the banks of the Khotan River, was the center of a large oasis on the southern edge of the Taklamakan Desert. It became the most important Buddhist center on the Southern Silk route. Some of the most important Gandhara-influenced Buddhist sites were located in this region.

According to Fa-Hsien, who visited Khotan in the year 400 CE Khotan was "a pleasant and prosperous kingdom, with a numerous and flourishing population. The inhabitants all profess our Law, . . . The monks amount to several myriads, most of whom are students of the Mahayana." He further mentions that the monastery where he stayed "contained 3000 monks of the Mahayana school."[139]

Chinese and Tibeten legends link the founding of Khotan with the settlement of Buddhist nobles from the Taxila Region, who were banished by Asoka in the 3rd century BCE after the eyes of his son Kunala were gouged out by some nobles working under him. Following this incident Asoka banished the nobles "to a sandy desert to the northeast of the snowy mountains."[140]

Important Buddhist sites located around Khotan, which show affinity with Gandhara, include Dandan-Uilik, Rawak and Niya. Artifacts recovered from various shrines in Dandan-Uilik include small figures of Buddhas standing in Abhayamudra pose, measuring 6.5 inches above the lotus pedestal, small, 5 inches high clay Buddhas and Bodhisattvas from reliefs, with draping reflecting the folds of robes found in Gandhara statues of Buddha

139 Fa-Hsien. *A Record of Buddhist Kingdoms.* Translated by James Legge.
140 Samuel Beal. *Buddhist Records of the Western World,* 1884. Hsieun Tsang describes a legend he had heard in Taxila, which forms the basis of this story.

and Bodhisattvas and images of Yaksha kings, particularly Kubera or Vais-rana. Some stucco images of Buddhas and Gandharvas discovered by Stein at Dandan Uilik were also similar in style to those of Jaulian. These images were fixed on the walls of a number of shrines located in the area. "There can be little doubt," says Aurel Stein, "that just as in the case of its sculpture, the original models of pictorial art in Old Khotan were derived from Gand-hara and other adjoining regions."[141]

At the Jumbe-Kum site of Rawak there was a large stupa with masonry of sun-dried bricks. The square base of the stupa rose in form of stepped terraces to a height of 22.5 feet above the court. Above the top platform of the base there was a 3 feet high circular drum, which served as the plinth for another drum forming a part of a 32-foot diameter dome. The surviving masonry, which does not include the top part of the dome, rises to a height of 31 feet above the level of the court. Excavations carried out by Stein and the Japanese and German archaeologists at the site of the Rawak stupa re-vealed stupa walls, well decorated with reliefs of large-size painted stucco images of standing Buddhas, Bodhisattvas and other figures. These reliefs and statues are contemporary to the ones in Jaulian monastery near Taxila and were executed in the same style.

"The affinity," Aurel Stein says, "which the Rawak reliefs show in style, and most [Rawak] sculptures to the Greco-Buddhist sculptures of Gand-hara, is far closer to those elsewhere."[142]

Niya, located on the other side of the Keriya River, east of Khotan, was a favorite spot for travelers from Gandhara. A 3rd century mud-brick stupa with cylindrical dome and square base discovered at this site by Stein is very similar in architectural style to those in Gandhara.

A large number of inscribed wooden tablets in Kharoshthi and other side languages were found from the sites around Khotan. The wooden piec-es on which these legends were described were either wedge shaped or rect-angular. The tablets belonging to the period around 3rd century were mostly inscribed in Kharoshthi-Gandhari, while those belonging to the period around 8th century CE used an 'East Iranian' language with Brahmi script. Most of these inscriptions are of a secular character. The famous Gandhari Dharmapada manuscript on birch bark, was also purchased by Dutreuil de

---

141 Aurel Stein. *Ancient Khotan*, 1907.
142 Ibid.

Rhins in 1891–92 from the Niya area. It is generally accepted that the birch bark manuscript was brought here by monks from Gandhara.

DUNHUANG-LOULAN REGION

The oasis town of Dunhuang (Tun-huang) is situated at the edge of the Gobi desert, in the west of the present-day Chinese province of Gansu. Buddhist monks from Gandhara began to travel to the Dunhuang region after the conquest of Tarim basin by the Chinese emperor Han Wudi around 140 BCE. Among the more prominent Buddhist monks from Gandhara, who established their presence in Dunhuang, was Dharmaraksa.

Dunhuang soon became an important station on the trade route linking the prosperous trade and cultural centers around the Tarim basin with Changan (Xian). The Buddhist monks, who settled in this region, dug grottoes to carve out a place suitable for worship, meditation and accommodation for themselves and for travelers. The first grottoes at Dunhuang date from the middle of the 4th century and the statues belonging to this early period show Buddha in an ascetic mode as in the statues produced in Gandhara. The Buddha sitting in a niche, is shown in the meditating or teaching posture, and is usually accompanied by two disciples or Bodhisattvas. In the sculptures at Dunhuang belonging to the later period, the more glamorously attired Bodhisattvas replaced the Gandharan ascetic style of images.

The paintings and sculptures at the Dunhuang (Mogao) belonging to the period until end of the 4th century CE or early 5th century CE show influences from Gandhara. From the 5th century onwards Chinese Art figures more prominently in the paintings and sculptures of Dunhuang. Chinese Art at Dunhuang achieved its peak in the Tang period, from the 7th to 10th century CE.

The Caves of the Thousand Buddhas were carved on cliffs in a valley southeast of the Dunhuang Oasis. The detailed description of the Buddhist paintings and images of Buddha and Bodhisattvas provided by Aurel Stein indicate that the main subjects covered in the paintings inside the caves of Dunhuang are Amitabha's Western Paradise, single figures of Avalokitesvara and other Bodhisattvas, scenes from Gautama's life and stories of Buddha's previous lives (Jatakas).[143]

---

143 Aurel Stein. *One Thousand Buddhas*, Oxford University Press 1921.

The treasures from Dunhuang appear on various formats including clay and stucco images of Buddha and Bodhisattvas, murals painted on walls and embroideries and paintings on silk.

Several thousand manuscripts were recovered from the caves at Dunhuang, mostly from cave 17. A few of these manuscripts or prints are translations of original Gandhari-Kharoshthi Buddhist texts; some are Buddhist related records of statements made by devotees and monks, others are purely Chinese texts falling in the category of narrative ballads, historical records and legal documents.

The manuscripts from Dunhuang Caves were acquired in large numbers by various European and Japanese archaeological missions and are preserved in their national institutions. Paul Pelliot of the French Archaeological Mission purchased 6,000 manuscripts which are preserved in Bibliothèque Nationale de France and the Guimet Museum in Paris. Aurel Stein acquired more than 10,000 manuscripts from the period from the Han to the Tang Dynasties. Most of these manuscripts are now in the British Library. About 600 scrolls were also acquired by Sergei Oldenburg for St. Petersburg Institute of Oriental Studies.

Yungang Caves: Shanxi Province

Figure 13.2: Seated Buddha from Yungang

The rock cut Yungang Caves are located about 15 kilometers west of Datong in Shanxi Province. They date from the period after 460 CE. Experienced artisans from Dunhuang (Tun-Huang) initiated the Buddhist sculptural art at Yungang. As a result the Buddha images of Yungang indicate strong influence from Gandhara. The most popular deities portrayed in the early period rule were the historical Buddha Sakyamuni and the Bodhisattva Maitreya. As in the Buddha images in Gandhara, the Yungang Buddhas have wavy hairstyles culminating in a topknot. The flaming nimbus around the Buddha, which became quite common in the images produced in northern

Gandhara regions and parts of Central Asia, also features in the images at this site.

The stone images of Buddha at the Yugang Caves show similarities with images from the Uddhyana region of Greater Gandhara and Bamiyan, in central Afghanistan. The decorations at the caves also include a number of bas reliefs of Buddha Sakyamuni.

Longmen Caves: Henan Province

Like the Yungang caves, the Longmen Caves are also cut in rocks. They are located about 15 kilometers south of Luoyang. There are about 2500 caves in this region belonging to the period from 500 CE to 900 CE. Some of the most beautiful sculptures in the Longmen Caves come from the Fengxian Monastery. They indicate some influence of the late Gandhara styles.

GANDHARAN MISSIONARIES IN CHINA

A number of monks and missionaries from Gandhara made valuable contributions towards establishment of strong roots of Mahayana Buddhism in China. These include Lokaksema, An Stigao, An Quan, Dharmaraksa and Kumarajiva. Lokaksema reached Luoyang, the capital of the Han Dynasty around 150 CE. He set up a translation bureau there and was actively involved in these translations from 178 to 189 CE. His student Zhi Yao was also involved in these translations. Among the works translated by Lokaksema was Pratyupanna Sutra, which is the first Sutra in which Amitabha and his Pure Land are mentioned.

An Stigao also went to the Han Dynasty capital of Luoyang. He was a monk belonging to the Sarvastivada sect of Buddhism, which ultimately made way for emergence of Mahayana Buddhism in Gandhara. He is said to have arrived in China around 148 CE and is referred to in early Chinese records as a Bodhisattva. He is reported to have translated Mahayana scriptures related to meditation and Abhidharma.

Dharmaraksa's family migrated from Gandhara in third century CE and settled in Dunhuang, where Dharmaraksa was born in 230 CE. In Dunhuang, Dharmaraksa worked with the Chinese monk Zhu Gaozhin. Later he traveled widely in the Western regions of China in connection with his missionary work. Among the places where he spent some time were Luoyang and Xian. He is credited with the translation of a number of Mahayana Sutras.

Kumarajiva was born of Gandharan and Kuchean parentage in 343 CE. He received training as a Buddhist monk and initially arrived in Kucha in Western China on a missionary assignment. In 401 CE he moved to Changan (Xian), where with the help of the Imperial court he set up a translating bureau. He is credited with translating more than 300 Mahayana Buddhist texts from Gandhari into Chinese.

The earliest official contacts between Chinese emperors and Buddhist Gandhara were probably established in the first century CE. Chinese traditions speak of envoys sent by Han emperor Mingdi to Gandhara in the first century CE. On their way back these envoys were accompanied by Gandharan monks who brought loads of Buddhist texts with them. These texts were later placed in the White Horse Temple in Louyang.

The contacts established by the missionaries from Gandhara with the Chinese religious institutions and the tremendous progress made by Buddhism in China during the rule of Northern Wei Dynasty (4th–5th century CE) led to a regular flow of Chinese Buddhist scholars and pilgrims from China to Gandhara. They collected texts of Buddhist scriptures from scriptoriums and monasteries in Taxila, Purushapura, Takht-i-Bahi, Butkara and other parts of Gandhara, and visited places of pilgrimages in the land of Buddha's birth in north-eastern India.

The first of the well-known Chinese scholars to visit Gandhara was Fa-Hsien. After a long and hazardous journey across deserts and high mountain regions, Fa-Hsien ultimately arrived in Swat in 403 CE. His published accounts indicate that he was highly impressed with the functioning of the Buddhist institutions in Gandhara at that time.[144] Obviously the foundations of the Gandhara Civilization laid during the rule of Kanishka and Huvishka were strong enough to withstand the disruptions caused by the Sassanian invasions. The Kidara Kushan rulers had once again put Gandhara on the path of progress. Peace was restored, there was economic prosperity all around and institutions of learning were sprouting up all over the Greater Gandhara region.

---

144 Samuel Beal. *Buddhist Records of the Western World*, 1884. Beal's Book originally contained accounts of travel of Hiuen Tsang. Later accounts of other Chinese pilgrims were also included in his book.

Fa-Hsien observes that the pilgrims, devotees and lay Buddhists thronged to the numerous sangharamas in the region. He provides first hand account of more than 500 monasteries in Swat and thousands of Buddhist monks wandering around from place to place. Fa-Hsien also provides useful information on the Patracaitya near Peshawar, where more than 700 monks carried out their religious duties. He describes the Great stupa built by the great Kushan emperor, Kanishka, at Shahji-ki-Dheri near Peshawar and the stupa of the Eye Gift at Pushkalavati.

The next famous Chinese pilgrim was Sung-Yuen, who took a different route to Gandhara. He crossed the Pamir Plateau to the valley of the Amu Darya before making his way to Swat via Kafiristan in 519 CE. He provides enthusiastic description of a country with a congenial climate, fertile, and rich in growth of fruits and flowers.

Sung-Yuen provides detailed account of the large-scale destruction carried out by the Ye-tha (White Huns) in the fifth century CE. However, inspite of the destruction carried out by these wild tribes from Central Asia in the period around 465 CE, it seems that a lot had still survived when Sung-Yuen visited this region. Mihiragula carried out destruction on a much larger scale in the period following Sung-Yuen's visit.

During his stay of more than six months in the Swat Region, Sung-Yuen gathered a lot of information on Buddhist legends relating to the charities and gift of the limbs by the Buddha to the needy, during his visits to this region as Bodhisattva in his previous lives. He writes about the King strictly living his life according to the Buddhist Dharma and about the air being filled at midnight by the chimes of bells from the numerous monasteries. He also visited Gandhara proper for a further period of over a year. Among his candid observations is a vivid description of the gold and polychrome embellished dazzling images of the Bodhisattvas at Po-lu-sha (Shahbaz-Garhi).

About a hundred years after the visit of Sung-Yuen, came the visit of another famous Chinese pilgrim and a Buddhist sage, Hsiuen-Tsang. What Hsiuen Tsang saw was quite different what Sung-Yuen had seen a century earlier. He found about 1600 deserted sangharamas in the Gandhara Region in total ruins. Mihiragula had carried out large-scale slaughter of the inhabitants of the region in less than a decade before Hsiuen Tsang arrived in Gandhara.

Mihiragula died in 628 CE; Hsiuen Tsang arrived in the Peshawar Valley from Kabul in 629 CE. He was therefore almost an eyewitness to the destruction wrought by Mihiragula. He found that most of the 1400 sang-haramas on the banks of the Su-po-su-tu (Swat River) were in total ruins and out of more than 18000 monks, who resided in these sangharamas at one time, only a few remained.

Hsiuen Tsang spent almost 16 years in Greater Gandhara. During the next 19 years, which he spent in his home country, before his death in 664 CE, Hsiuen Tsang wrote the most detailed account of the conditions in Gandhara. He has a lot to say on a number of topics; he writes about the pleasant climate and fertility of the land, of numerous streams and high mountains. He had built up an idealized picture of the Holy Land on the basis of information recorded by earlier Chinese pilgrims. In this he was somewhat disappointed; over the years the high moral standards of the so-ciety had declined after the havoc wreaked by the White Huns. Although Buddhism was still the religion of the majority of the people in Gandhara, he found that the monks "fond of reading [holy Buddhist] texts but incapable of penetrating their meaning, cultivating instead the service of the magic formulas."

The period during which Hsiuen Tsang visited Gandhara is noticeable for a gradual decline in the orthodox Buddhist view of the religion. The Ma-hayana School of Buddhism, with which the Buddhists of Gandhara were associated, had always attached a great deal of importance to the differ-ent Buddhas and Bodhisattvas, each with their own special attributes. Dif-ferent monasteries were devoted to the Bodhisattva or celestial Buddha of their choice, much in the way the Greeks constructed temples in different cities in honour of the particular deity to which they were particularly de-voted. Thus, some monasteries were constructed in Swat and other regions of Greater Gandhara, which were devoted to Avalokitesvara, the dispenser of mercy and help. Others similarly singled out a particular Buddha or Bo-dhisattva from the Buddha Pantheon, for example Buddha Amitabha, for devotion or worship. The enlarged Buddha Pantheon had already appeared in the revered Buddhist texts as early as in the third century BCE; however, in the art and sculpture of Gandhara, the enlarged Buddha Pantheon seems to have received more attention only in the later phases.

The last of the important Chinese pilgrims and chroniclers, who left valuable written record of the conditions prevailing in Gandhara dur-ing the heydays of Buddhism in this region, was Wu-Kung. A political emissary from the court of the Chinese emperor to the Turkish ruler of

Kabul, Wu-Kung arrived in Gandhara in 751 CE after completion of his political Mission, to pay pilgrimage to the Buddhist holy places in Gandhara, Hazara, Swat and Kashmir. He became a Buddhist monk during his visit to Gandhara and spent some time in this capacity in a monastery in Swat. On return to China sometime after 784, he described the state of the monasteries, other religious institutions, the social conditions and the geography of the areas where he spent almost 30 years. His accounts reveal that after the large-scale destruction carried out by Mihiragula, a lot of reconstruction work was carried out in the Buddhist monasteries in Gandhara and Swat and Buddhism was still a living religion in these areas in the eighth century CE.

DHYANA SCHOOL IN CHINA

The roots of Dhyana go back to early days of evolution of Mahayana philosophy in Gandhara. Buddhists in Gandhara were inspired by the fact that Siddhartha Gautama achieved enlightenment through deep meditation. Accordingly Dhyana or meditation was incorporated as the fifth perfection in Mahayana scriptures and thus became an essential part of Mahayana worship.

Dhyana School, which focuses on contemplation and meditation (mind to mind transmission) was introduced in China by a Gandharan monk named Bodhidharma in 520 CE. Bodhidharma spent several years in a monastery near Luoyang, where his teachings generated a lot of interest. The Chan School, as the Dhyana School came to be known in China, soon won a large number of adherents in China.

The development of Chan School in Southern China in its present form is credited to Hui-neng, who is regarded by the Chan Buddhists as the sixth Patriarch of Chan Buddhism. His doctrine proclaimed that Buddha-nature is present in all beings and it can be recovered through detached meditation, which leads to instant enlightenment.

PURE LAND SCHOOL IN CHINA

The basic teachings of the Pure Land School are provided in Sukhavativyuha Sutra, which was compiled during the first century in Gandhara. The Gandharan monks An Shi Kao and Lokaksema brought the texts of the Pure Land Sutras to China in the second century. The basic doctrine of these Sutras was incorporated in the teachings of the Pure Land School, which was founded in China by Chinese monk Hui Yuan in the 3rd century CE.

According to the Mahayana doctrine of Trikaya, the Body of Bliss occupies the heavens in the form of ruling and governing god of the universe. The form of the Body of Bliss in our world is said to be Amitabha, who rules in a paradise in the western heavens called Sukhavati or the Land of Pure Bliss. The devotees belonging to the Pure Land School believe that by chanting the name of Amitabha in faith they would be reborn in the Pure Land.

Chapter 14: Gandhara & Japanese Buddhism

Historic records indicate that a group of Buddhist monks from Gandhara took the first steps of introducing Buddhism in Japan.

The Chinese historic treatise *Liang Shu* mentions that in the second year of *Da Ming* of Song Dynasty (467 CE), five monks from Gandhara (*Kipin*) traveled by ship to the country of the Fusang—"the country of the extreme east beyond the sea" The location of Fusang is mentioned as 20,000 li (1500 kilometers) east of the State of *Du Han* in modern Kyushu. The journal goes on to mention that in Fusang the Gandharan monks "propagated the Buddhist doctrine, circulated scriptures and drawings and advised the people to relinquish worldly attachment. As a result the customs of Fusang changed."

From 500 CE onwards, translations of texts on Mahayana Buddhism imported into China from Gandhara through Gandharan missionaries and Chinese pilgrims were freely available in various monasteries and centers of Buddhist excellence all over China. It was now the turn of Chinese and Korean Buddhists to convey these Mahayana texts to Japan.

Historic sources also indicate that in 538 CE a delegation of Buddhist missionaries arrived in Japan from Korea. They brought statues of Buddha, Buddhist literature and other religious gifts for the emperor. In *Nihon Shoki* it is indicated that monks from Korea were sent to Nara in Japan in 552 CE to propagate the teachings of Buddha.

Thereafter there was a regular traffic of Buddhist monks between Japan and China. This led to the introduction of six Mahayana-based Chinese schools in Japan. The existence of large Buddhist temples such as Todai-ji and Hokkai-ji in the Japanese capital, Nara, indicates that Nara became the first major center of Buddhism in Japan and in the 6th century the Buddhist religion enjoyed substantial support from the Japanese Imperial Court. Prince Shotoku perhaps stands out among the Japanese royalty as a major supporter of Buddhism in Japan. He made Buddhism the State religion in 594 CE and ordered the construction of Buddhist temples all over Japan. The construction of the Todai-ji Temple at Nara around 600 CE marks the establishment of Buddhism as state religion.

In the Heian period after the capital of Japan shifted to Kyoto great dynamism was witnessed in the Buddhist establishment. This resulted in several new schools of Buddhism, of which the Tendai School became particularly popular. The Tendai School was founded by the Japanese monk Saicho, who constructed the Buddhist temple at Mount Hiei near Kyoto. The Tendai Doctrine is based on the Mahayana Saddharmapundarika Sutra (Lotus Sutra), and embodies the heart of Mahayana Buddhism, making Nirvana within the reach of all.

Among the Mahayana sects which achieved great popularity in Japan and which have the largest following in modern Japan, are Nichiren, Zen and Pure Land. They derive their inspiration and strength from different Sutras incorporated in the Buddhavacana texts developed by the Gandharan scholars during the formative period of Mahayana Buddhism. In the 3rd century Gandharan monks like Dharmaraksa brought the texts of major Mahayana Sutras to China from where they reached Japan. Japanese Mahayana Buddhist monks carried out the process of rationalization and specialization further and based on the Sutra of their choice, developed their own set of rituals and practices, which touched the souls of the worshippers more effectively.

The emergence of various Mahayana schools in Japan like the Nichiren, Zen and Pure Land should be seen as a phase in the continuous process of refinement, rationalization and specialization in the area of worship and practice of Mahayana Buddhism. The theoretical process, which led to the crystallization of Mahayana philosophy, gained momentum in Gandhara around 100 BCE during the Saka-Parthian rule, reached maturity in first and second century CE during the rule of Kanishka-I, when Mahayana Buddhism received official recognition in the Fourth Buddhist Council meetings and final shape was given to the Buddhavacana texts, which form the base of Mahayana philosophy. Thereafter, while the sanctity of various Bud-dhavacana texts including the Lotus Sutra, continued to be maintained, a process of refinement, and rationalization in the area of worship and prac-tice started, which saw the growth of various Mahayana Schools, particu-larly in China and Japan.

The Nichiren sect, founded by a Buddhist monk of that name in the 13th century, proclaims the overall dominance of the Saddharma-pundarika Sutra (Lotus of True Law) or the Myoto Renge Kyo or Myo Ho Ren Ge Kyo, as the Japanese call it, in Buddhist religion. Among the early Mahayana scholars in ancient Gandhara, Saddharmapundarika also occupied a central place, perhaps the most important place among all the Buddhavacana texts. The difference in Nichiren's teachings and the teachings of early Gandharan Buddhist scholars lies in the fact the Nichiren denounces all other texts, while the Gandharan scholars believed that other Buddhavacana texts also make a substantial contribution towards the understanding and practice of the Revelation of Buddha.

In the Lotus Sutra, which Mahayana Buddhists regard as the last dis-course delivered by Buddha, Buddha, through an articulate use of allegory and parables, vividly illustrated the path to be followed to achieve full Bud-dhahood. The rendering of the Lotus Sutra in this manner makes it easy to understand for people with very different social backgrounds and intellec-tual capabilities. The Lotus Sutra explains the role of the Buddhas vis-à-vis the common man:

> The Buddhas, the world Honored Ones, wish to open the door of Buddha Wisdom to all living beings to allow them to attain purity.... They wish to cause the living beings to awaken to the Buddha Wis-dom, and therefore appear in this world."

The Sutra makes it clear that the common people and lay Buddhists are as much within reach of Nirvana as the laity. The Nichiren sect in Japan, which believes in the exclusivity of Lotus Sutra in providing salvation, was successful in establishing several lay societies of worshippers and was therefore able to attract a large number of devotees.

In substance, the Lotus Sutra projects the popular concept of 'skilful means' ('hoben' in Japan)—the seventh paramita of perfection of the Bodhi-sattva, and the eternal nature of Buddha. Both these concepts are built into the Homage of the Lotus Sutra, which all Nichiren sect followers recite as a means to achieving Nirvana. To a Nichiren devotee regular practice and recital of chapters from the Lotus Sutra are the essence of religion. Particular importance is given to Chapter 2 (Hoben-pon), which proclaims that everyone is able to become a Buddha, and Chapter 16 (Nyorai Juryo-hon), which proclaims that Buddha's life is eternal. These two chapters of the Lotus Sutra are usually recited in Nichiren temple services.

The roots of Zen Buddhism, the second most popular Buddhist sect in Japan, also go back to early days of evolution of Mahayana philosophy in Gandhara. Early Buddhist schools in Gandhara drew inspiration from the belief that deep meditation was the medium through which Siddhartha achieved bodhi (enlightenment). Dhyana or meditation was incorporated as the fifth perfection or paramita in Mahayana scriptures and thus became an essential part of worship by both Buddhist laymen as well as the laity in ancient Gandhara.

Both the early protagonists of Dhyana in Gandhara and the practitioners of Zen Buddhism in Japan trace their origin of Meditative philosophy to the Flower Sermon delivered by Buddha to his disciples during his lifetime. Traditions refer to an incident when disciples had gathered around Sakyamuni Gautama to listen to the Dharma, and Sakyamuni Gautama did not utter a word but instead took out a white lotus and presented it to the Sangha. Nobody understood the significance of this gesture except Mahakasyapa (Maha kosha in Japanese). Buddha noticed the smile in Mahakasyapa's face, which conveyed Sakyamuni Gautama recognition of what he had tried to convey.

The direct transmission of prajna (wisdom) by Buddha to his disciple emphasized the purity of direct wordless communication which lies at the root of Zen Buddhism in Japan. In Zen Buddhism meditation became the exclusive medium for achieving enlightenment, discounting reading of scriptures and other religious rites, which Zen Buddhists believe act as impediments on the path of enlightenment.

The existence of the Dhyana School in Gandhara is indicated by the fact that Bodhidharma, a Buddhist monk from Gandhara, brought this concept into China in the 6th century CE and ultimately established the roots of Chan Buddhism in China. Japanese monks who studied Chan Buddhism in China introduced this philosophy in Japan, where further refinements on the practice of Dhyana took place particularly during the 12th and 13th centuries. This led to the emergence of Rinzai Zen and Soto Zen Schools in Japan in this period.

Figure 14.1: Sculpture from Gandhara portraying Sukhavati, Pure Land Paradise.

As a development of the traditional Meditation philosophy of the Dhyana School of Gandhara, Eisai, the founder of the Rinzai Buddhist sect in Japan emphasized the doctrine of sudden enlightenment. Eisai proclaimed that sudden enlightenment can be achieved through riddles, zaon or meditation problems and zozen or meditation.

Pure Land is the third most important Mahayana sect in Japan, where it is known by the names of Shin Buddhism and Amidism. Buddhist sources in China and common traditions indicate two monks from Gandhara, An Shi Kao and Lokaksema brought the texts of the Pure Land Sutras to China in the second century and were instrumental in the translation of these Sutras from Gandhari into Chinese. Pure Land Sutras centering on Amitabha (Amida in Japanese) and his Pure Land Paradise, known as Sukhavati, gained considerable popularity in China, which led to the emergence of Pure Land School of Buddhism in the 3rd century CE in China. The Pure Land Buddhism was then brought from China to Japan and it continued to attract a lot of followers all over Japan.

In the 12th century Honen Shonen, a Tendai monk, converted to Pure Land Buddhism and then established a separate Pure Land sect, known as Jodo Shu. Jodo sect followers believe that Nirvana is impossible to attain in this world. However by repeating Namu Amida Butsu, a mantra of devotion to Amitabha, one can gain admission to Pure Land Paradise on death. Another Pure Land sect in Japan is the Shin or Jodo Shinshu, which is basically a lay movement which preaches absolute devotion to Amida. Jodo Shinsu is also based on the Mahayana text Sukhavativyusha Sutra, which describes the Buddha Land of Bliss. The Sutra provides details about Dharmakara, who lived ages ago. He started as a Bodhisattva, and by chanting "nemu amida butsu," received enlightenment and was reborn as Amitabha Buddha in the Western Paradise of Sukhavati.

Three basic doctrines of Mahayana Buddhism, namely Saddharma-pundarika Sutra, Sukhavativyusha Sutra and Dhyana, continue to play an important part in Japanese culture. They provide different paths for the achievement of Nirvana. The medium may be different, but original source of inspiration and the ultimate destination remains the same.

Chapter 15: Gandhara & Korean Buddhism

Gandhara played both a direct as well as an indirect role in the development of Buddhist Culture in Korea.

In the early Kushan period the Mahayana Buddhist missionaries began to fan out in a big way to lands in Fareast. The active trade on the Silk Route facilitated the movement of the Gandharan monks. They latched on to trade caravans and were able to traverse long distances with relative ease.

Thus Mahayana Buddhist texts in Gandhari traveled in a receptive environment to important trade centers in China, some of which developed into regional bases for transmission of Buddha's thought.

At important centers such as Luoyang and Dunhuang in China, scholarly Buddhist monks from Gandhara armed with Gandhari texts of important Mahayana Sutras worked with Chinese monks and set up translation bureaus where these texts were translated into Chinese. In due course a base for Mahayana Buddhism had been firmly established in China, from where Buddhist monks from China began to penetrate into Korea.

Historical records indicate that the first contacts of Buddhist monks with practitioners of various religions in Korea took place around 372 CE At that time the Korean Peninsula was divided into the three Kingdoms of Kagaryo, Paekje and Silla, and Shamanism (nature worship), based on the three spirits was widely practiced in all the three kingdoms. In this period Buddhist faith preached by monks from Qin China developed slowly and

Buddhism absorbed the three spirits of Shamanism and a special form of Korean Buddhism evolved.

Subsequently monks from Gandhara also established direct contacts with monasteries in Korea. The *Samguk Yusa* records the arrival of the first Buddhist missionaries from Gandhara in South Korea in late fourth century. Maranata is the name given in these records of the Buddhist monk from Gandhara, who initially brought the Dharma to Korea.

Following the visits of Gandharan missionaries there was renewed interest in Maitreya in Korea. A Maitreya cult developed in which Maitreya began be projected as the god of fertility.

The interest generated by Buddhism in Korea led to visits of a number of Korean Buddhist monks to Gandhara in the 6th and 7th centuries. They collected manuscripts of Buddhist scriptures from the monasteries in Gandhara and then visited the land of birth of Gautama Buddha in the northeastern regions of South Asia for pilgrimage to sacred places. Among these early Korean monks who visited Gandhara, was Banya (562–613 CE), who brought large number of Buddhist texts into Korea.

The direct contacts between Gandhara and Korea and indirect contacts between Gandhara and Korea via China during the 5th and 6th centuries resulted in availability in Korea of a large number of Mahayana Buddhist texts. As a result Mahayana Buddhism made major strides in Korea during this period and great interest was generated in Sutras such as the Lotus Sutra, Perfection of Wisdom Sutra, Amitabha Sutra, Avatamsaka Sutra and Contemplation Sutra, which are the basic texts of Mahayana Buddhism.

By the 6th century, Korea had become a sort of a launching pad for Buddhism to Japan. In *Nihon Shoki* we find mention of Buddhist monks, who traveled from Korea to Nara in Japan in 522 CE to preach Buddhism.

Among the early Korean Buddhist monks, who played an important part in the spread of Buddhism in Korea was Jajing, who lived in the period 590–650 CE.

During the course of early development of Buddhism in Korea, varying influences from Buddhist schools in China and elsewhere began impinge on the thinking of the early converts to Buddhism in Korea.

Among the schools, which achieved prominence during the early period, were Samnon (Middle Path), Gyeyul (Vinaya) and Yeolson (Nirvana). These schools focused on Madhyamika doctrine, moral discipline and Mahaparinirvana Sutra respectively.

In the 7th century Hwaom sect (Hua-yen in Chinese, Kegon in Japan) gained popularity in Korea. Considerable interest was generated in Buddhist communities in the Hwaom doctrines of interdependence of all things and the presence of Buddha nature in all human beings.

In the Three Kingdoms period the basic foundations of Mahayana Buddhism were firmly established in all the three kingdoms of Korea. Buddhism needed a favorable political environment to make further progress. This came in the shape of a unified Silla State, which emerged in 668 CE. The Silla Period from 668 to 935 CE was the golden age of Buddhism in Korea. The rise of Buddhism and political stability were mutually supportive; Buddhism emerged as a strong unifying force of the Silla State, which comprised of the entire Korean Peninsula.

In the early Silla Period the two Mahayana Sutras, the Avatamsaka Sutra and the Lotus Sutra achieved great popularity and the majority of Korean Buddhists worshipped Amitabha the 'Buddha of Infinite Light' and Avalokiteshvara, the Bodhisattva in the Mahayana tradition, who represents the ultimate Compassion. But in the later Silla Period the growing interactions between Korea, Japan and China on the political, cultural and religious fronts led to development of similar religious schools. The growing popularity of Chan Buddhism in China began to influence Buddhist practices in Korea and Japan also. Meditation and direct experience began to be viewed as the sole medium for achieving Nirvana and reading or chanting of religious texts began to be regarded as a useless exercise. The Son or Soen Buddhism in Korea, as the Dhyana School was called in Korea, grew from strength to strength and meditation was universally practiced all over Korea. Nine schools of Soen Buddhism emerged in Korea, which came to be known as the Nine Mountains of Son.

The Silla kings procured a large number of Buddhist manuscripts from various sources and it became a tradition for the Silla emperors to be buried with Buddhist manuscripts. The manuscripts found from the tombs of Silla emperors, serve as important documents for building up the history of transmission of Buddhism to East Asia.

In the following historical period, from 935 to 1392 CE, when the Korya Dynasty was established in the Korean Peninsula, Buddhism continued to be the national religion and was patronized by all the kings of the dynasty. The unification of Korea and stability generated extra enthusiasm within the Buddhist community in Korea. The kings constructed beautiful shrines and temples all over the Korean Peninsula.

The exclusivity of Soen Schools in Korea could not be maintained after the end of the Silla Period. During the rule of the Korya Dynasty the Pure Land School caught the imagination of the Buddhist devotees. The Pure Land Sutra brought to China by the Gandharan monk Lokaksema and translated into Chinese in the second century CE now found its way into Korea and was translated into the Korean language. The Jeongtuzong, as the Pure Land School was known in Korea, restored the practice of chanting of Buddhist scriptures, in this case the chanting of the verses from the Pure Land Sutra describing Amitabha, the Buddha of Infinite Light, and his Land of Ultimate Bliss.

Pure Land and Soen doctrines derived from the early Mahayana doctrines of Sukhavativyusha and Dhyana, continue play an important part in the lives of a sizeable population of modern Koreas.

CHAPTER 16: TRADE AND COMMERCE

Trading activities between Greater Gandhara and the surrounding regions have been going on since prehistoric times.

A survey carried out in the upper Indus Valley and other regions in North-east Pakistan by Heidelberg Academy of Humanities and Sciences (Germany) in cooperation with Department of Archaeology and Museums, Karachi, in the last two decades of 20th century, revealed inscriptions and rock carvings made by nomads and traders from Central Asia, which date back to the third millennium BCE.

Out of tens of thousands of engravings, which came to light during these investigations, about five percent date back to the prehistoric period, mostly between 8th century BCE and 5th century BCE, the rest to the period after the Achaemenid conquest of Eastern and Western Gandhara. A very large percentage of engravings belonging to the period after 1st century CE are of Buddhist stupas and the Kharoshthi inscriptions above these engravings indicate that these inscriptions were sponsored by devotees, who considered this an act of piety. The concentration of Buddhist engravings around the strategically located town of Chilas, between Gilgit and Besham, indicates that Chilas probably served as an important regional marketplace. Buddhist travelers came to Chilas to sell textiles and spices against payment made with precious stones and gold.[145]

---

145 Ditte Bandini-Koenig, Martin Bemmann and Harald Hauptmann. *Rock Art in the Upper Indus Valley*, Islamabad 1997.

These engravings provide ample evidence of trade being conducted between Gandhara and Central Asia through nomads and settled traders since prehistoric times and continuity of this trade till well after the demise of the Gandhara Civilization.

During the period of the Indus Civilization, in the third millennium BCE trading posts were established at Shortughai at the confluence of the Amu Darya and Marghab Rivers in northern Afghanistan to tap the mineral resources of Central Asia and to market industrial goods manufactured at various settlements all along the Indus Valley. [146]

In second millennium BCE, after the demise of the Indus and Mesopotamian Civilizations, the regions released from the domination of these two great civilizations began to develop their own local cultures. Local cultures emerged in the valleys of the Swat and Kabul Rivers and in the Tepe Hissar, Tureng and other settlements in the Gorgan Plains. The culture developed in the Swat and Kabul River valleys in the period from 1600 BCE till 600 BCE came to be known as Gandhara Grave Culture, because of the large number of local and imported artifacts found in a large number of graves found in this region. Trading activity on a fairly large scale between Gandhara and north-eastern Iran, South Turkmenistan and North Afghanistan is also indicated by the large number artifacts found in all these regions.[147]

Then in the 6th century BCE a new phase of trading relationships began between Gandhara and the regions in Iran and Central Asia after these regions became a part of the vast Achaemenid Empire.

Trade and commerce (the volume of trade and the revenues generated from it) during various phases of the Gandhara Civilization closely followed the profile of the Gandhara Civilization itself. The trading activities gradually increased all through the embryonic and transient phases of the Gandhara Civilization. They achieved their peak in first and second centuries CE, which corresponds to the mature phase of the Gandhara Civilization. Then they registered a decline during the next seven centuries.

TRADE ROUTES

Although the entire northern boundary of Greater Gandhara was covered by high mountains, the Hindu Kush in the west and the Karakorams in the east, effective use was made of the passes in these mountains to carry on

---

146 H.-P. Francfort. *Excavations at Shortughai*, Ph D dissertation 1989 as reported by Gerard Fussman in his article *Southern Bactria and Northern India.*

147 A.H. Dani. *Recent Archaeological discoveries in Pakistan*, Center for East Asian Cultural Studies, Japan, 1988.

trade and commerce during all phases of Gandhara Civilization. In the west, the path taken by the Kabul River formed a natural trade route, while in the east the high mountain passes in the Karakorams connected to the Indus River near the point where this river enters the relatively easily accessible valleys of Gilgit and Skardu.

Western Trade Routes

Channels for formal trading activities between Western and Eastern territories of Greater Gandhara and the regions in Central and West Asia were established after the Achaemenids conquered Gandhara and established two satrapies in this region, one at Pushkalavati and the other at Takshasila in the 6th and early 5th centuries BCE. The Achaemenids operated from three power centers or capitals in Persia—Ectabana in the north, Persepolis in the south and Susa in the west. Takshasila and Pushkalavati were connected to each of these power centers in Persia and to other satrapies in the vast Achaemenid Empire through an extensive network of roads.

The northern route connected Takshasila and Puskalavati with Bactria. Through Bactria, Gandhara became connected to Sogdiana in the north and through Parthia with the three Achaemenid capitals in Persia.

The Southern route connected Takshasila and Pushkalavati through the Khyber Pass with Hadda (Jalalabad) and Kabul. From Kabul the southern route extended along the Helmand Valley, via Arachosia and Drangina to Persepolis, Ectabana and Susa.

Susa was connected by the Imperial Highway to Ephesus in Asia Minor. So indirectly Gandhara became connected with Asia Minor.

The Western Gandhara satrapy of the Achaemenid Empire was rich in timber, livestock and emeralds. The forests in Dir and Swat were rich sources for wood used in construction of buildings; the mines near Mingora in Swat were an important source of green emeralds, and livestock was surplus in the Charsadda-Mardan region.

The Eastern Region of Gandhara was rich in rubies, gold dust and ivory. Ruby mines were located in the Upper Neelum Valley; gold was available in the upper reaches of the Indus River and was panned in the valleys of the Indus and its tributaries in the North-eastern regions of Greater Gandhara. Ivory was available in the region around Taxila.

There is evidence in the form of Royal Inscriptions on Rocks at various sites in Persia and at the sites of royal residences, that yaka wood for the construction of Royal palaces in Susa and Persepolis, and ivory and gold dust were supplied to Achaemenid Heartland from Greater Gandhara.

The vast network of roads established by the Achaemenids continued to be used by the Greeks for Gandhara's trade with Central and West Asia after Alexander's invasion of Gandhara. After Alexander's death Seleucus established the Seleucid Empire, which included West Asia (Mesopotamia, Syria and Iran) as well as Parthia and Bactria. Later Parthia and Bactria seceded from the Seleucid Empire, but the Hellenistic regimes established there continued to interact with Greater Gandhara. With Hellenistic regimes ruling Bactria, Parthia and Greater Mesopotamia, Gandhara's trade and cultural contacts with Europe, North Africa and West Asia began to be established on firmer lines.

In the third century BCE the Mauryans drove out Alexander's satraps and established Gandhara as a Mauryan Province. Healthy trade relations developed between the Mauryan and the Seleucid Empires, which benefited Gandhara. Mauryan capital was located at Pataliputra in the north-east of South Asian sub-continent and the Mauryans conducted most their trading operations with the Seleucids and with Central Asia through Gandhara. Thus the status of Takshasila and Pushkalavati as commercial hubs and cultural centers were further enhanced.

The Indus Greeks, who conquered Gandhara early in 2nd century BCE, continued to interact with their fellow Bactrians north of the Hindu Kush. This strengthened the trade link between Gandhara and Central Asia. As long as their kinsmen were ruling Bactria, trade and cultural ties between Gandhara and the Bactrian capital, Bactra, continued to be maintained on a healthy footing. Through the Khyber Pass and Bactra, the region to the north of Amu Darya also became accessible to the Gandharan traders. Active trade with the Central Region around Begram and Bamiyan and with towns located on either side of Amu Darya is indicated by large number of coins belonging to the Indo-Scythians, Indo-Parthians and Kushans found from these sites.

Eastern Trade Routes

The 4703-meter high Khunjerab Pass in the Karakoram's has since ancient times provided relatively easy access to key regions of Gandhara Civilization. On the southern end of the pass there was a somewhat difficult stretch of about 150 kilometers but after crossing the Batura Glacier and entering Hunza's populated areas around present day town of Karimabad, the passage towards the Plains of the Indus did not cause any major problems for traders with mules laden with trade goods, or to missionaries and pilgrims.

Xinjiang and Gandhara remained connected with each other through nomadic camel caravans in the prehistoric period. Every summer, nomads from Xinjiang crossed the Khunjerab Pass into Gandhara bringing with them precious and semi-precious stones, wool and dried skins. Their caravans returned to Xinjiang before the advent of winter loaded with foodstuffs, cotton goods and jewelry.

The practability of using the passes in the north-eastern sector of Gandhara is demonstrated by two major invasions, which took place into Gandhara in the early historic period. In 327 BCE Alexander used the eastern passes to enter Gandhara, while in first century BCE Maues, the Scythian Chief, also took the eastern route.

In the third century BCE, during Mauryan Rule in Gandhara, the eastern trading channels were also activated. Taxila was connected via Abbotabad, Gilgit and Hunza and the passes in the Karakoram Mountains (e.g. Khunjerab Pass) with Tashkurgan in the Tarim Basin and from there with Kashgar in the north and Khotan in the southern part of the Tarim Basin.

Thus a qualitative change began to take place in the nature of traffic between Xinjiang and Gandhara, when Buddhist missionaries tagged themselves with the traders, establishing religious links which continued to be strengthened over the next eight centuries. The religious links between Xinjiang and Gandhara simultaneously strengthened trade relations between the two regions.

Travelers from Xinjiang could take two routes to enter Uddhyana (Swat). The first route, the more difficult of the two, ran westwards from Gilgit along the Gilgit River and then provided entry into Swat Kohistan. From Swat Kohistan, the route continued along the Swat River towards the Lower Swat Valley. The second route ran southwards from Gilgit along the Indus River and then entered the Lower Swat Region from Besham Qila. Both these routes provided access to the western regions of Greater Gandhara, the Swat Valley and then south of Malakand Pass to the Peshawar Valley. The famous Chinese pilgrim, Fa-Hsien, took the first of these routes in 403 CE to enter Swat Kohistan. To enter Taxila and the Eastern Region of Greater Gandhara, one just continued southwards along the Indus River till Ghazi and then entered Taxila through Ghazi-Haripur link. Both these channels were used to an increasing extent in the Transient and Mature Phases of the Gandhara Civilization.

Silk Route Trade

Major developments were taking place in West and East Asia in the 2nd and 1st century BCE.

Rome, after conquering Greece in 146 BCE, moved swiftly into Asia and established its control over the Hellenistic regimes west of the Euphrates. East of Euphrates the Parthian Empire grew from strength to strength and in China the Han Empire was at its peak.

The emergence of three powerful and prosperous regimes in Asia in first century BCE led to increased trade between these major powers. The so called Silk Road was fully activated. The Silk Route connected three mighty Empires—the Roman Empire west of the Euphrates, the Parthian Empire between the Euphrates and the Indus, and Han Empire in China (which included Xinjiang). Thus the Chinese capital, Xian was linked in trade with Europe, through Bactria, Sogdiana, and Greco-Roman colonies in West Asia.

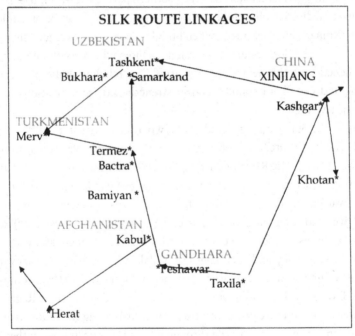

Figure 16.1: Trade Routes

With the great Chinese, Parthian and Roman Empires engaging in a healthy trade in silk in a variety of luxury items, all other countries in the region were also drawn towards healthy trading activities with other countries located on the Silk Route.

The conquest of Gandhara by the philhellenic Saka-Parthians in the first century BCE coincided with the activation of the Silk Route. With the establishment of Saka-Parthian rule in Gandhara, this region virtually became a part of the vast Parthian Empire which stretched from the Euphrates in the West to the Indus in the East and from Bactria in the north to the Arabian Sea and the Indian Ocean in the South.

Parthian presence in Bactria, Persia and Eastern Mesopotamia and Han presence in Xinjiang provided Gandhara access to the Silk Road through two important trading posts on this route—Bactra in Central Asia (through the Khyber Pass) and Kashgar in Xinjiang (through the Khunjerab Pass).

The active participation of Gandhara in the Silk Route Trade brought a great deal of prosperity to Gandhara during the rule of the Saka-Parthians. This is apparent from the large number of artifacts belonging to this period found various sites in Gandhara. In particular the artifacts recovered from the Saka-Parthian capital city, Takshasila-Sirkap, reveal the amount of wealth, which began to flow into Gandhara in this period. Among the large number of foreign artifacts recovered from Takshasila-Sirkap are gold bracelets, armlets, ear pendants, a Greco-Roman bronze statue of Harpocles, an incense burner with winge-lion-shaped handles, a copper model of Parthian chariot and silver goblets and perfume flasks.

However, it was during the reign of the Kushan emperors that Gandhara began to derive the maximum benefits from the Silk Route trade. The Kushans conquered Gandhara in 60 CE and having established themselves firmly in this region, launched attack in other neighboring regions. In early second century CE, during Kanishka's reign, the Kushan Empire was extended to regions beyond the Amu Darya in the north and as far east as Chinese Turkistan. As a result of these conquests, the Kushans became the facilitators, controllers and brokers in the Silk Route Trade between the Roman and the Han Empires. Because of this position Gandhara became much more actively engaged in trade with Central Asia and Western China.

Because of the dominating position of the Kushans in the region, Gandhara, Bactria and parts of Central Asia began to be referred to as the land of the Kushans and very often the businessmen and monks who engaged in trade and missionary work in Central Asia and Chinese Turkistan began to be referred to as Kushans irrespective of their ethnic backgrounds.

Gandharan trade with countries on the Silk Route was conducted in a variety of ways.

Gandhara had for centuries maintained close ties with Bactria. The Purushapura-Bactra Highway provided a convenient link to the traders in the two regions. The Buddhist monuments in the Greater Bactrian region and the large number of coins of all the Kushan emperors from Vima Kadphises to Vasudeva-I found from various sites in Greater Bactria, indicate that conventional trade was carried out between Gandhara and Greater Bactria on a fairly large scale. Initially, Gandharan traders followed the missionaries to regions in Central Asia and gained access to the local markets. Later some Gandharan traders may have established permanent residence or trading posts in places such as Bactra. At the same time a large number of Buddhists from Central Asia and Xinjiang began to visit Gandhara on pilgrimage and during these visits engaged in trading activity.

In the Xinjiang Region Kashgar and Khotan had been interacting with Gandhara at least since third century BCE. Khotan, in particular maintained very close links with Gandhara both during the period when it was a part of the Kushan Empire as well as for centuries afterwards. The extensive use of Kharoshthi in this region and other evidence of cultural influence, indicates that trade between Gandhara and Khotan was a regular activity.

There is also evidence in the form of large number of Roman coins found in Gandhara to indicate that Gandhara was actively engaged in trade with Rome from the time Julius Caesar conquered Alexandria.

During the first two centuries of the Common Era, when there was plenty of activity on the Silk Route, the trade between Gandhara and the Roman Empire was probably carried out through Exchange Stations on the Silk Route, mainly Bactra. Regular camel caravans carrying various types of goods came from Gandhara to Exchange Stations where they exchanged good brought by camel caravans from the western colonies of Rome.

The above arrangement worked smoothly till the first half of third century CE. However, around 226 CE the Sassanians came to power in Persia. After coming to power, the Sassanids made it their mission to drive out the Romans from all those territories, which once formed a part of the Achaemenid Empire. This caused a major interruption in the lucrative trade in silk between China and Rome.

Maritime Route

In the Achaemenid period and during Alexander's invasion, exploratory work had been done for utilizing the maritime route through the navigable Indus River and the Arabian Sea for trade of the landlocked countries of Central Asia with West Asia and Europe. This route was activated during the Kushan Period.

The Sassanian blockade of the land routes turned out to be a blessing in disguise for Gandhara. Because of the Sassanian blockade, trade between Rome and China was sustained by routing the trade goods through Gandhara and the Arabian Sea ports on the mouths of the Indus.

Thus the sea routes for trade between China/Central-Asia/Gandhara and Europe/West-Asia/Egypt were activated. Goods from Central Asia and China were brought to Gandhara by the normal land routes (Bactra-Purushapura/Pushkalavati and Kashgar-Taxila) and through navigational link provided by the Indus River, they were transported by Sea to destinations in Egypt, West Asia and Europe and vice versa.

Early accounts of Gandhara being used for Transit trade appear in 'Periplus of the Erythraein Sea' a Greek trade journal dating to the period when the Parthians were ruling Gandhara (47 CE). The Periplus indicates that the ports Barbaricum and Barygaza were used to link up with Gandhara. Barbaricum was the only major navigable port on the mouths of the Indus and is identified with modern Karachi. Barygaza was located on the Gulf of Besaca (Cutch) and is identified as Broach. Topographical studies indicate that in ancient times a branch of the Indus taking off from the area around Sukkur, flowed into the Gulf of Cutch.

The Periplus mentions that plain clothing, flowered cottons, yellow stone, topaz, coral, frankincense, glass vessels, silver plates and wine were imported through the port of Barbarican, and the exports through this port included costus (a spice), bdellium (an aromatic substance), emeralds and green stones, sapphires, furs from China, silk, thread and indigo.

In Barygaza the items traded were wheat, rice, sesame oil, cotton and cloth.

Several writers have commented on the mention made in the Periplus with regard to use of Barbaricum port for trade with the northern regions of South Asia. This is what the translator of the Periplus of the Erythraein Sea, William H. Schoff, has to say about the mention in the Periplus of Barbaricum being used as the port for Roman trade with Proclais (Pushkalavati) and other regions in the north:

> The trade-route briefly referred to in the mention of Gandhara and Pushkalavati was that leading to Bactria, whence it branched westward to the Caspian and the Euphrates, and eastward through Turkistan to China.[148]

Confirmation of routing of Chinese trade through Gandhara is also provided by the account appearing in the Chinese annals.

The flooding of Gandhara by goods produced in Roman colonies is specifically mentioned in the Chinese historical chronicles pertaining to first and second centuries CE. These chronicles indicate that a large variety of Roman goods were found in Gandhara, ranging from luxury items to fine cloth and carpets to eatables and spices. This is further confirmed by the large number of luxury goods of Roman and Chinese origin found from the palace premises in Begram, the summer capital of the Kushan rulers.

A number of scholars have commented on the thriving trade between the Roman Empire and Gandhara. These trading relations commenced soon after Augustus extended the boundaries of the Roman Empire as far East as the Euphrates. However, the peak period of trade between Rome and Gandhara was the 1st and 2nd centuries CE, during the rule of Parthians and the Kushan in Gandhara.[149]

V.A. Smith comments on the huge quantity of Roman gold flowing into Gandhara in the Kushan period:

> Roman arts and ideas traveled with the stream of Roman gold, which flowed into the treasuries of the Rajas in payment for the silks, gems and spices of the Orient. During the Kushan Period influence on India was at its height, and it is impossible to understand or tell aright the history of Kanishka without reference to that of Hadrian and his predecessors.[150]

The diversion of Silk Route trade through Gandhara also resulted in inflow of large number of Roman coins into Gandhara. About a hundred Roman coins have been found from various regions in Gandhara. These include a number of gold coins.[151] A number of scholars believe that the actual

---

148 William H. Schoff. *Periplus of the Erythraein Sea*, Translation and Commentary, 1914.

149 H.G. Rawlinson. *Intercourse between India and the Western World*, New York, 1971.

150 V.A. Smith. *The Kushan Period of History*, Journal Royal Asiatic Society of Great Britain and Ireland, London, 1903.

151 *Numismatic Chronicle*, London. Also C.J. Rogers, *Catalogue of Coins*, Part 3.

number of Roman gold Dinars must have been fairly large, much more than what has been indicated by the finds. They believe that the gold used by Kushan emperors in the coins issued by them during the period 80 CE till late third century CE was obtained by melting Roman gold coins:

> The implication is that all Roman gold, which could be recovered, was absorbed by the Kushan Empire and thus regulated and reminted.[152]

Similar views have been expressed by Rosenfeld also.[153]

The revenues generated through this East–West trade gave rise to a number of trading houses in Gandhara, and honed up the existing institutions related to trade, commerce and taxation. For the smooth passage of trade goods, considerable improvement took place in the physical infrastructure; road and transport sectors were completely overhauled and communications between different regions of Gandhara were improved. These improvements had a beneficial effect on all sectors of the economy.

---

152 Wheeler Mortimer. *Rome beyond the Imperial Frontiers.*
153 Rosenfeld. *Dynastic Art of the Kushans,* Los Angeles. 1968.

Chapter 17: Afterword

The fifteen centuries from the 6th century BCE till the 10th century CE, during which the Gandhara Civilization evolved, thrived and went into a prolonged decline, is but a short period in Gandhara's long and turbulent history. Stone tools discovered at a nearby site of Rewat (about 35 kilometers from Taxila and 8 kilometers from Pakistan's capital of Islamabad) indicate that hominids were roaming the region in search of food and shelter as early as 3 million years earlier. In and around the Sanghao Caves, near Mardan, in the heart of ancient Gandhara, stone spearheads, arrow-heads and scrapers were being employed 35,000 years ago. Similar tools dating to the Middle Stone Age have also been discovered in Nawagai in the Bajaur Agency and other sites along the border of Pakistan with Afghanistan.

The next important phase in Gandhara's history was when this region served as the peripheral area of the great Indus Civilization, which thrived in the Lower Indus Valley between 2500 BCE and 1600 BCE. In this period Gandhara provided Indus traders access to the resource areas in northern Pakistan and Afghanistan.

The dominance of the Indus and Mesopotamian civilizations in the Western, Central and South Asian regions in the period 2500–1600 BCE had stifled growth of regional cultures in regions such as Gandhara. This period came to an end in 1600 BC.

The demise of the Indus and Mesopotamian Civilizations around 1600 BCE released Gandhara from their all-pervasive influence. This led to the emergence of a regional culture in Gandhara for the next thousand years, from 1600 till 600 BCE. This culture came to be known as Gandhara Grave Culture, as most of the evidence of this culture comes from graves all along the banks of the Kabul, Swat, and Panjkora Rivers in Peshawar, Swat, Dir and Chitral Valleys.

The globe-shaped pottery, beads, ornaments and articles made of copper, bronze and iron found from the graves bear striking resemblance to the artifacts from this period found from cultural sites in South Caspian region of northeastern Iran and in the Murghabo–Bactrian Region of Central Asia. The construction of the graves and the associated burial practices in the three regions also show a great deal of similarity. This indicates that a fair amount of interaction was taking place between Gandhara and the southern Caspian region of northeastern Iran and Murghabo–Bactrian region in Central Asia in the period 1600–600 BC. These interactions were, however, mainly at the level of small traders and nomads.

In the period 535 BCE till 380 CE a series of high profile invasions took the Gandhara region by storm. Most invaders entered the Peshawar Valley through the Khyber Pass, a 53-kilometer long passage in the Safed Koh Mountains, an extension of the Hindu Kush range. The ancient caravan route through the Khyber Pass ran along the Kabul River, which linked the Afghan towns of Kabul and Jalalabad with the Peshawar Valley.

The Khyber Pass, which has a maximum elevation of 1070 meters at Landikotal, about 8 kilometers inside Pakistan territory, seemed to be the automatic choice for invaders coming from the Kabul–Jalalabad region. However, some invaders, including Alexander the Great, found it more convenient to enter Gandhara through the eastern section of the Hindu Kush and Karakoram Mountains, even though the elevation of the passes in this region is around 5000 meters. The entry through the eastern passes provides entry to the mountainous regions of Bajaur, Dir and Swat, which probably provided some tactical advantage to these invaders.

During the period 535 BCE and 380 C.E intense activity was witnessed in the Gandhara Region, which led to evolution of the Gandhara Civilization.

After reaching its peak in the opening centuries of the Common Era, Gandhara Civilization began to buckle under the pressures which were developing along its northern borders. The Ephthalites and the Sassanians released their destructive power on the peaceful Gandharans in the late fifth and early sixth centuries. After that the region slowly drifted towards chaos and inactivity.

The last Buddhist rulers of Gandhara were the Turk Shahis, who initially ruled Gandhara from Kabul but later shifted their capital to Hund in the Peshawar Valley, about 18 kilometers from the modern Attock Bridge on the Indus River.

The official end of Gandhara as a Buddhist entity came in 879 CE, when the Hindu Shahis dislodged the Turk Shahis and established the Hindu Shahi kingdom with Hund as its capital. This signaled the end of the era.

While the Hindu Shahis were still ruling large parts of Gandhara, including the Kabul Valley, important developments were taking place in eastern Iran. In 977 CE, the Samanid Governor of Ghazni established an independent kingdom in western Afghanistan with Ghazni as his capital. Thereafter, Ghazni, about 120 kilometers west of Kabul, became a new area of political turbulence. When the Ghaznavids started expanding their empire eastwards, they came into conflict with the Hindu Shahi regime in the Kabul Valley. This prompted the Hindu Shahi ruler of Gandhara to form an alliance with the Rajput rulers of Punjab and other neighboring territories. This move had far-reaching consequences for Gandhara.

After the emergence of Hindu Shahi rule in Gandhara in 879 CE, even though the Buddhist civilization in Gandhara had come to an end, Gandhara continued to maintain some degree of political identity. After the formation of alliance with the Rajput rulers in the neighboring kingdoms, this political identity of Gandhara was also eroded.

The increasing conflicts between the Ghaznavids and the Hindu Shahis in the Kabul Valley in due course led to the invasions of Mahmud Ghaznavi across the Khyber Pass to the Hindu Shahi capital of Hund, and beyond.

In 1003 CE, Mahmud Ghaznavi defeated the last Hindu Shahi ruler, Jaipal, and extended his conquests to Punjab, Sindh and the Jumna-Ganges Basin around Delhi, Mathura, Kanauj and Lucknow. The semi-independent political status of Gandhara in the South Asian region thus came to an end.

Mahmud Ghaznavi's numerous invasions between 1002 CE and 1026 CE established Muslim dominance in northern regions of South Asia. In 1173 the Ghauris, from the town of Ghaur (Ghor) near Ghazni, displaced the Ghaznavids in Ghazni. A new series of invasions of South Asia under the Muslim rulers of the Ghauri Dynasty commenced immediately afterwards. In 1202, Qutub-ud-Din Aibak, a general in the army of Shahab-ud-

Din Ghauri established the first Muslim Sultanate in Delhi. Gandhara now began to be ruled from Delhi.

This was the beginning of a new era. Conditions in Gandhara (and the rest of the northern regions of South Asia) had remained fluid from 879 CE to 1202 CE. After 1202, Gandhara became part and parcel of the political world of Northern India.

SHORT BIBLIOGRAPHY

Beal, Samuel: *Buddhist Records of the Western World*. 1884

Boucher, Daniel: "Gandhari and the early Chinese Buddhist translations reconsidered: the case of Saddharmapundarikasutra." *Journal of the American Oriental Society*, October 1998.

Coq, Albert von Le: *Die Buddhistische Spaetenantike in Mittelasien* (Post-ancient Buddhist Culture in Central Asia), Dietrich Reimer Verlag, Berlin.

——:*Auf Helles Spuren in Ostturkestan* (Buried Treasures in Chinese Turkistan), Leipzig, Germany, 1926.

Dani, A.H.: "Environs of Chakdara," *Ancient Pakistan* Vol. IV, 1968-69.

——: *Recent Archaeological Discoveries in Pakistan*, Japan, 1988.

Dar, Dr. Saifur Rahman: *Taxila and the Western World*, Lahore 1988.

Foucher, A.: *Notes on Ancient Geography of Gandhara*, Calcutta, 1915.

Frifelt, Karen & Sorenson, Per: *South Asian Archaeology*, Curzon Press, The Riverdale Company, 1985.

Fussman, Gerard: "Southern Bactria and Northern India before Islam." *The Journal of the American Oriental Society*, Ann Arbor, April 1, 1996.

Gruenwedel, Albert: *Alt Kutcha* (Ancient Kucha), Volume I, 1923

Hauptmann, Harald, Bemman Martin, Bandini Koenig: "Rock Art in the Upper Indus Valley," in *The Indus Cradle and Crossroads of Civilizations*, Islamabad 1997.

Herodotus: *The Histories*: Aubrey de Selincourt's translation, 1972.

Jettmar, K.: *Rock Carvings and Inscriptions in the Northern Areas of Pakistan*. Islamabad, 1982.

Khan, Ahmed Nabi: *Gandhara Illustrated Guide*, Department of Archaeology and Museums, Karachi, Pakistan, 1994.

Mahmud, S.F.: *A Concise History of Indo-Pakistan*, OUP Karachi 1988

Marshall, Sir John: *The Buddhist Art of Gandhara*, Cambridge University Press, 1960.

——: *A Guide to Taxila*, University Press, Cambridge, 1960.

——: *An Illustrated Account of Archaeological Excavations Carried out at Taxila*, Vols. 1-3, Cambridge, 1951.

M'Crindle, J.W.: *The Invasion of India by Alexander the Great*, Indus Publications, Karachi.

Murthy, K. Krishnan: *The Gandhara Sculptures*, Ajanta Publications, Delhi, 1977.

Narain, A.K.: *The Indo-Greeks*, Oxford University Press, Great Britain, 1962.

Saloman, Richard: A preliminary survey of some early Buddhist manuscripts recently acquired by the British Library (University of Washington).

Samad, Rafi U.: *The Greeks in Ancient Pakistan*, Indus Publications, Karachi, 2002.

Soon Teoh Eng: *The Lotus in Buddhist Art of India*, Singapore, 2002.

Spooner, D.B.: *Handbook of Sculptures in Peshawar Museum*, 1909–10.

Stein, Aurel: *Ancient Khotan: Detailed Report on Archaeological Explorations in Chinese Turkistan*, 1907

——: *On Alexander's Track to the Indus*, Indus Publications, Karachi, 1995.

——: *One Thousand Caves—Buddhist Paintings from the Cave Temples of Tung-Huang, Western Frontiers of China*. Published by Bernard Quartch Ltd. in 1921.

——: *On The Silk Road*. Serindia Publications.

Tucker, Jonathan: *The Silk Road, Art and History*. Philip Wilson Publishers, London, 2003.

Whitehead, R.B.: *Catalogue of Coins in Punjab Museum*, Lahore. Oxford University Press, 1914.

Acknowledgements

The material for this book has been obtained from the books and articles published by various research scholars, archaeologists and other specialists. A list of the most important of those is included in the Short Bibliography.

Efforts have been made to specify the original sources of photographs and diagrams used in this book. These photographs have been reproduced through the courtesy of Paramount Archives, Karachi, the Department of Archaeology and Museums, Pakistan, the Tourist Bureau, Government of Pakistan and other agencies, as specified. I apologise for any omissions.

My special thanks are due to the Exploration Branch of the Department of Archaeology and Museums for allowing me to peruse through the Reports of Archaeological Excavations at various Gandharan sites maintained in their Library at the Shahrah Faisal Branch, Karachi.

I am also grateful to the Curator, National Museum of Pakistan, Karachi, for allowing me to use the National Museum Library.

Finally, I would like to express my appreciation for the help and guidance provided during my visits to various archaeological sites around Taxila, Peshawar, Mardan and Swat, by the officers and staff of the Archaeology Department, Government of Pakistan.

INDEX